Public
Speaking

Public Speaking

☐ **Frank E. X. Dance**
University of Denver

☐ **Carol C. Zak-Dance**
University of Denver, Weekend College

1817

HARPER & ROW, PUBLISHERS, New York
Cambridge, Philadelphia, San Francisco
London, Mexico City, São Paulo, Singapore, Sydney

Sponsoring Editor: Louise Waller
Project Coordination, Cover and Text Design, and Text Art: Caliber Design
    Planning, Inc.
Photo Research: Cheryl Mannes
Compositor: Waldman Graphics, Inc.
Printer and Binder: R. R. Donnelley & Sons Company

Photo Credits

Chapter One: UPI/Bettmann Newsphotos / Chapter Two: Hilda Bijur, Monkmeyer Press
Photo Service / Chapter Three: © Kip Brundage 1985, Woodfin Camp & Associates /
Chapter Four: © Ellis Herwig, Stock, Boston / Chapter Five: NASA / Chapter Six: ©
Erich Hartmann, Magnum / Chapter Seven: © Bill Bachman 1982, Photo Researchers,
Inc. / Chapter Eight: Van Bucher, Photo Researchers, Inc. / Chapter Nine: AP
LASERPHOTO / Chapter Ten: UPI/Bettmann Newsphotos / Chapter Eleven: George
Bellerose, Stock, Boston

Library of Congress Cataloging-in-Publication Data

Dance, Frank E.
  Public speaking.

  Includes bibliographies and index.
  1. Public speaking. I. Zak-Dance, Carol C.
II. Title.
PN4121.D334 1986   808.5′1   85-24886
ISBN 0-06-041482-0

85 86 87 88 9 8 7 6 5 4 3 2 1

Dedicated to
Clifton L. and Catherine M. Dance
Joseph T. and Alice M. Zak
Zachary, Gabriel, and Caleb Dance

Contents

# Preface

Public Speaking is intended as a short introductory textbook on the subject of public speaking. It is a new primer, a handbook for beginning speakers. The authors have made it new by including fresh theory (for example, work on inner speech and on decentering), new ideas for the practical use of theory (such as a solid rationale for rehearsal out loud), new approaches to traditional theory (the interrelationship of ethos and ethics), and a renewed enthusiasm for the importance of the spoken word in both private and public life. In almost all instances we have tested theoretical materials against our own experience and the experience of others who give public presentations.

Together we have spent over 40 years testing public speaking theory in actual practice and believe that there is a place for a text that presents the results of that testing process. We believe that there is a need for and room for a new primer blending contemporary and current theory with experiences in actual platform speaking.

After 2500 public speeches delivered before audiences of speech communication professionals, business executives, marketing representatives, manufacturing managers, nurses, state and federal government employees, military scientists, computer programmers, chaplains, pilots, Rotarians, members of unions, and on and on, we have decided that there is some theory which may be good theory but not always practicable for the beginning speaker. There is as well some very practical advice for which the theory has not always been presented. Problems of the theory/practice relationship are addressed in this book. Theory, reflection, and practice are all included. Our goal is to present the beginning public speaker with a theoretically grounded yet practical guide to the acquisition of good and rewarding public speaking skills.

This textbook is organized along a time line, the progressive sequence that we have found most people follow in putting together and then presenting a public speech.

Although this book is written primarily for a student working under the guidance of a skilled teacher, we have tried to write so that a person who is without the assistance of a teacher can also benefit from the materials presented. The guidance of a knowledgeable and skilled teacher should, however, make this process easier.

Since we have both taught in community college settings as well as in university settings, we have written with both student audiences in mind. Even without the benefit of the immediacy of the spoken word, we hope that the reader can sense and share our enthusiasm for the act and art of public speaking.

Since we are theoreticians as well as practicing public speakers, we are most interested in how this new primer works, or does not work, for the speaker and the teacher. If you have comments or questions, please send them to us in care of the publisher, Harper & Row, Publishers, Inc., College Department, 10 East 53d Street, New York, N.Y. 10022.

Frank E. X. Dance
Carol C. Zak-Dance

Public
Speaking

Public Speaking and Personal Power

Chapter One

". . . the power of speech, to stir men's blood:"
W. Shakespeare, *Julius Caesar*, III, ii, 225

Power has been defined as the ability to influence the behavior of others. In a very real sense we must have power over ourselves, we must be able to influence our own behavior or control ourselves, before we can hope to exert power over anybody else. Power is rooted in our ability to consciously influence our own behavior. Power begins at home. If we cannot influence or control ourselves, how can we hope to influence others? In infancy we are continually developing and practicing the ability of self-control. From infancy on we are also trying to influence the behavior of others. Infants cry and smile and influence their parents' attention and other parental behaviors. As infants grow into childhood, the infant's formerly unconscious efforts to influence her or his parents become increasingly conscious. All life is, to some degree, a quest to increase our influence over ourselves and over others, a search for power. During our lives we try to control what is happening to us or what may happen to us, we try to exert some power over our destiny. Humans join together to increase their ability to exert power or control over their lives and over their environment. Societies exemplify the organized search for power by groups of human beings.

Most of us have very mixed feelings about power. We are simultaneously attracted to power and repelled by power. We find ourselves wishing for more power for ourselves while complaining about the power others have over us. Especially in our society in the United States the concept of power raises suspicions of manipulation and abuse. Americans distrust a politician with too much power. Yet, power is not automatically evil. Power is neither good nor evil. But power may be *used* for either good or evil. For example, electricity provides power to move machinery and to run equipment of various kinds. The power of electricity can be harnessed to build cities or it can be used in weapons systems aimed at the destruction of cities. A person can use power to help other people (like Martin Luther King) or to hurt other people (like Adolf Hitler).

Sometimes make-believe or fictional characters can help us examine the uses of power and to reflect on how we feel about the uses of power. The heroes and heroines of early comic books provided readers with glamorous simplifications and dramatizations of human desires and dreams. We can easily find in those comic book figures reflections of the human search for power. *Superman, Wonder Woman,*

5

The Power of the Spoken Word (DC Comics Inc. © 1982)

Batman and *Robin* all showed how power could be used for good. Their adversaries demonstrated the use of power for evil.

In the opening segment of the *Captain Marvel* comic strip little Billy Batson, a teen-age newsboy, acquires the power of (and is actually transformed into) Captain Marvel by uttering the word "SHAZAM." SHAZAM is an acronym. An acronym is a word composed of the first letters of a series of other words. An example of an acronym is the name used for a popular computer language—BASIC. BASIC is an acronym for *b*eginners *a*ll-purpose *s*ymbolic *i*nstruction *c*ode.

SHAZAM is an acronym composed of the first letters of names of a combination of mythical and historical characters—*S*olomon, *H*ercules, *A*tlas, *Z*eus, *A*chilles, and *M*ercury. By uttering "SHAZAM," little Billy Batson magically acquired the outstanding characteristics of each of the acronymically enshrined characters (the wisdom of Solomon, the strength of Hercules, etc.). SHAZAM was the spoken word that gave little Billy the power to do good used by Captain Marvel.

☐ Communication as Power

Communication is the process of interacting with and acting upon information. In the process of acting upon information the information often is exchanged or shared among the creatures engaged in communication. Communication is a form of power. Communication allows creatures to reduce their uncertainty, to organize their perceptions and their actions. This process of organization is a form of power, a means by which the creature exerts some influence over its surroundings. General communication capacities are present in many creatures: dogs, fish, chimpanzees, porpoises, and humans all share general communicative skills. Even organisms as tiny as microbes and as primitive as molds use touch, and sometimes a form of smell, to organize (to exert influence over or power over) their environment.

☐ Spoken Language as Power

In addition to the general communicative capacities and skills we share with other creatures, humans have the specific and unique capacity of using spoken language. *Spoken language* is the result of the joining together of the human being's inborn capacity for speaking with the human being's socially acquired language. All normal human babies speak. The particular language (English, Spanish, Vietnamese) that a human baby learns to speak depends on where and how and with whom the baby is raised. Humans use spoken language as a uniquely human means of communication. This uniquely human ability to use spoken language to communicate gives humans additional and unusual power over themselves (you can tell yourself what to do), over each other (you can use spoken language to persuade someone to do something for you), over other creatures (you can use spoken words to train other animals), and over your own environment (you can use spoken language to coordinate your energy and to work with others in building a system for controlling the energy created by a waterfall). The power given us by spoken language is so strong that the power also creates for us ethical considerations (e.g., do we have the right to treat nature in certain ways?) which we need to take into account.

People in general respect those who have great speaking skills. Oftentimes unusual speaking skills bring so much power to the speaker that the speaker finds people following her or his advice without as much reflective thought as is desirable. In such situations the gifted speaker, the powerful speaker, has special ethical obligations.

Spoken language, and the words used in it, is often considered the greatest human tool for the acquisition of uniquely human power. It is through words that humans rise to positions of political eminence in a democratic society, and it is often through words that these positions are maintained. As children we speak, then we learn to speak a language, and then in school we learn to transpose our spoken words into writing. Words are originally spoken and secondarily written. Communication in general and communication through spoken language in particular is used by humans to talk to themselves, to establish relationships with other people, and even to establish almost human relationships with animals and with inanimate objects such as automobiles (next time you are driving along the highway take note of vanity license plates and of the names that people give their cars) and computers.

Humans use spoken language to anticipate events (when talking about a football game that is to be played next week, we sometimes find ourselves getting as excited about the game as if it were already in progress). Humans also use spoken language to relive pleasant moments (almost all of us fantasize, recall fun times we have had in the past, great meals we have enjoyed). Our human ability, through spoken language, to free ourselves from the confines of the present moment, enlarges our power to control our own destiny by making plans for the future based upon our past successes or failures, based upon our wishes and upon our dreams.

☐ Human Communication and Its Components

Human communication is the unique way in which humans act upon information so as to communicate through spoken language and its derivatives such as writing, symbolic gestures, and gesture systems. Communication in general is an attribute we share with other creatures. Uniquely human communication is carried on through spoken language and builds upon the skills of communication in general. In other words human beings possess the ability to use the communicative skills present in all creatures (although the range of these communicative skills vary among species, e.g., dogs can hear sounds that are generally outside of the human's hearing range) plus the communicative skill of spoken language which seems to be unique to humans. Humans communicate through touch (as do other creatures), through odor (as do other creatures), through other channels shared with other creatures, and in addition through the use of spoken language. As mentioned earlier, one of the most obvious uses of communication in general is sharing, or exchanging information between or among creatures, including human creatures (Dance and Larson, 1976).

Human communication usually involves a sender of a message, the message itself, and a receiver of the message (see Figure 1.1). There are additional components which affect this communicative act. One such additional component is noise. *Noise* is anything which varies the message in a manner unintended and usually undesired by the sender. An example of noise would be background sound so loud as to drown out the message. Not all noise is acoustic. Visual interference such as the sun shining in your eyes when you are trying to read, or emotional interference such as anger so intense that you are unable to concentrate on the conversation in progress, are also examples of noise. Feedback is an additional component which is useful in the human communicative act. *Feedback* involves testing the received message in terms of its variance with the message intended by the sender. When we observe the successess or failures of our past behavior and use them to correct present or future behavior, we are using feedback. When we ask the person with whom we are speaking what she or he thinks we meant to say, and then measure the person's response against what we actually intended to communicate, we are using feedback.

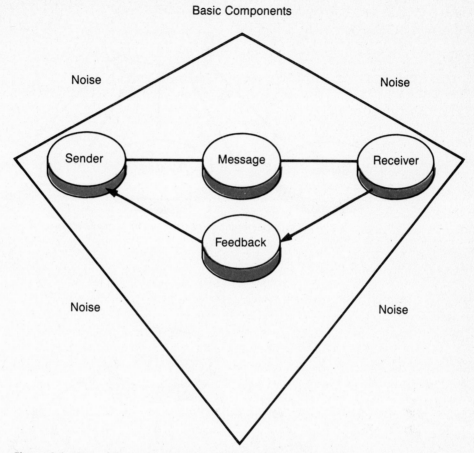

Figure 1.1 List of Basic Components of Human Communication

Human communication also exists in time; there is a sense of progression in human communication. Try to imagine a geometrical representation of the human communication act, a representation such as a line (Figure 1.2). Do you start to speak and then just go on and on without ever coming back to your earlier comments—is the flow of human communication linear? Or at the end of a statement do you find yourself back exactly where you started from—is the pattern circular (Figure 1.3)?

It has been suggested that the geometrical pattern closest to communicative reality is the helix. A helix is like the thread on a wood screw. A tornado often takes a helical form. A helix starts from a finite point and then winds upward (or, if you are looking at it lying on its side—forward) in graceful turnings. Each revolution brings the motion back upon itself while simultaneously moving ahead. A helical model of the process of human communication (Figure 1.4) involves learning from the past, involves taking the best of past experience and building

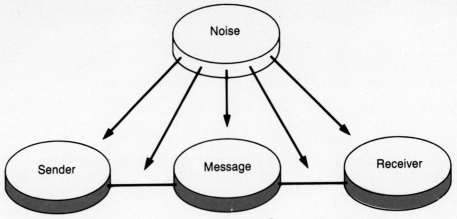

Figure 1.2 Linear Representation of the Human Communication Process

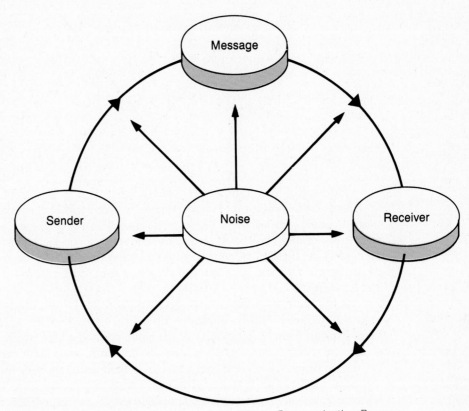

Figure 1.3 Circular Representation of the Human Communication Process

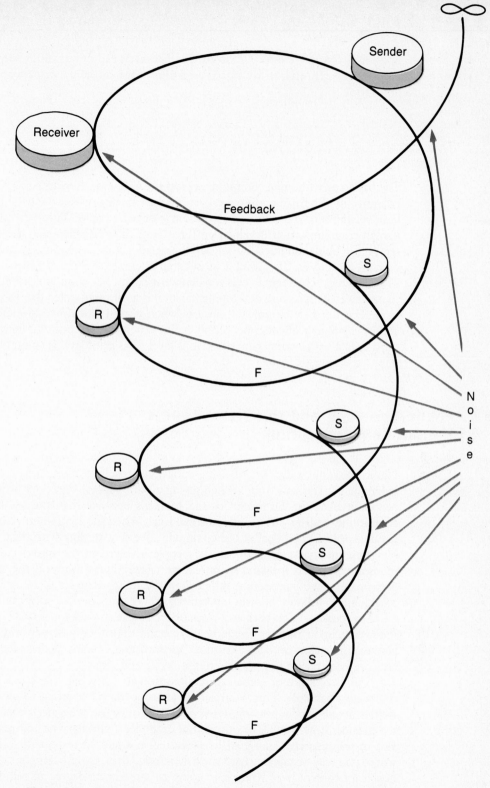

Figure 1.4 Helical Representation of the Human Communication Process

upon it as you move into the future. The helical thread of human experience may never completely end, so we placed an infinity mark at the upper part of the helix illustration.

☐ The Three Levels of Human Communication

The basic unit of human communication is the individual human being. The basic relationship of human communication involves at least two of the basic units, the basic relationship is dyadic and involves at least two people. Within the individual, human communication develops on three levels. Developmentally, the first level is our use of communication to develop relationships with others, such as our parents, around us. This level is most often referred to as the interpersonal level. The second developmental level is when we use symbolic communication to "talk" to ourselves. This second developmental level is most often called the intrapersonal level. The third developmental level is when we use human communication to address a number of other people all at the same time. In technical literature this third level is called the person to persons level. This third level is commonly called public speaking.

☐ Public Speaking and the Three Levels of Human Communication

Public speaking is the act of using spoken words to communicate with many individuals at the same time. When giving a public speech there are usually more people involved in the receipt of the speaker's message than the speaker could comfortably address on the interpersonal level. When speaking interpersonally, we usually spend a good deal of our communicative time dealing with the differences of viewpoint that exist between the people involved in the interpersonal communication. When speaking in public we usually focus more on the things the participants have in common rather than the things that set them apart. Public speaking also follows the helical progression. We start learning to speak in public, we try a speech, we go back and work over our speech with the goal of constantly improving upon our early speeches, we build upon our past performances, we eliminate mistakes, we strive to move forward and upward as in graceful helical arcs, we keep trying to improve, to get better and better.

All three levels of human communication are interrelated in our actual communicative behavior. This interrelationship of levels is important to remember as we talk about public speaking. How we talk to ourselves is a crucial concern when we consider how we talk to others. For example, if you have no self-respect, this lack of self-respect is going to be projected in a lack of respect for others with whom you may be talking. Earlier we mentioned that power begins at home. Your degree of control over yourself is going to affect your degree of influence over anybody else. When considering how to say something to a large group of individuals, it is often worthwhile to consider exactly how we would express the thought aloud to ourselves or to a single other individual. This dynamic movement among the levels of human communication from intrapersonal to interpersonal to person to persons can be most useful in preparing or revising a public speech.

☐ Public Speaking and Power

Public speaking allows us to attempt the exercise of power over ourselves while simultaneously attempting the exercise of influence over a group of other human beings. When preparing and delivering a public speech, we are trying to organize our materials and our behaviors so as to affect the thoughts and behaviors of our listeners. The group of others being addressed may be quite small or may number into the thousands. In fact, electronic means of mass communication now enable a single person to address millions of other human beings, all at the same time. Obviously the potential for exercising influence or power is tremendous. Public speaking is both a powerful skill and a skill of power.

Power and manipulation are not the same thing. An individual can be powerful without being manipulative. Manipulativeness suggests the use of others for achieving one's own goals even if this use hurts the others involved. History tells that there have been many public speakers who used their skills for manipulative ends, but manipulation is not a worthy goal for an ethical public speaker. Nor do your authors believe fame to be the most desirable goal for a public speaker, or the most desirable end of public speaking as an activity. Fame is a by-product of great public speaking. There have been effective public speakers who acquired fame but who seemed personally to be quite shy. Shy or not, these individuals (such as Gandhi) were driven by their convictions, by their beliefs, to share their thoughts with others.

☐ Public Speaking and Thought

If public speaking does not have as its goal manipulation or fame, what may be the most desirable goals of public speaking? (1) Public speaking is important if we wish to share our thoughts with many others. (2) Public speaking is important if we wish to introduce our personal ideas or beliefs into the forum of public opinion where these ideas or beliefs will be subjected to public examination, discussion, and possible acceptance. (3) Public speaking is important for gathering the support of large numbers of people on behalf of causes in which we believe.

"Thoughts," "ideas," "beliefs" provide the real currency spent by the public speaker. Whereas renown, wealth, and political power may all follow from success, as a public speaker the real goals, the most desirable ends, of public speaking are to ethically expand the conceptual horizons of the speaker, of the audience, and

The Past Speaks Eloquently in the Present (David Burnett, Contract Press Images, Inc.)

hopefully of society in general. It is through spoken language that humans know, know more, and try to know better. The primary goal of spoken language is thought, or mentation. Public speaking is a means of thinking—out loud. Public speaking is a means of thinking in public so as to expand thought as well as to share thought. There will likely be times when you are giving a public speech and find yourself amazed at how the words you are uttering assist you in clarifying the thoughts you are trying to convey. Aristotle states:

> Nature, as we often say, makes nothing in vain, and Man is the only animal whom she has endowed with the gift of speech. And whereas mere voice is but an indication of pleasure and pain, and therefore found in other animals (for their nature attains to the perception of pleasure and pain and the intimation of them to one another, and not further), the power of speech is intended to set forth the expedient and the inexpedient, and therefore likewise the just and the unjust. (Aristotle, *Politica*)

☐ Public Speaking and Personal Responsibility

In today's world it is essential that each of us accepts the responsibility of thinking and then of speaking his or her mind. "She really speaks her mind"—that's an interesting old expression, isn't it? It reinforces our theme that public speaking is the human means of expressing, of announcing, human reason and human intellect. Rationality, mentation, mind, and spoken language are tightly intertwined. "The ability of speech then is closely related to the rational principle, which Aristotle also attributed only to humans and added that it prevented them from following habit blindly as do animals" (O'Neill, 1980, p. 38).

Each individual in a democracy is important since the public voice is composed of millions of individual voices. These millions of individual voices are sometimes joined and find expression in the words of a single human being, as in the case of Abraham Lincoln. Since we cannot always depend on finding a universal spokesperson such as Lincoln, individual speakers must find the courage and the resources to be heard individually if their being heard together as if with a single voice is ever to make a difference. It is sometimes difficult for us to see the part we play in the overall scheme of things. Even if you have a problem in seeing how your individual voice plays a part in the shaping of society in general, you should be aware that your individual public speaking will probably play an important part in your own personal success.

☐ Public Speaking and Personal Success

Successful men and women are almost always marked by skill in public speaking. The polished public speaker, whether in business or in the professions, is often destined for success in his or her chosen field. Blaise Pascal once observed "Man is like a rabbit, you catch him by the ears." Even though Pascal's observation smacks of manipulating other people, a suggestion uncongenial to your authors, he is correct in drawing our attention to the fact that although we have eyelids and can voluntarily close our eyes and thus avoid looking at something, we lack "earlids" so that it is virtually impossible to physically close our ears to avoid hearing something being uttered.

If observation indicates that people at the top almost always do fairly well at public speaking, then the probability of rising to the top would seem to be greater if we are able to give a good public speech. There seems to be an observable correlation between public speaking ability and personal success; thus learning to speak in public seems to be a worthwhile goal.

☐ Learning to Speak in Public

Public speaking has been successfully taught and successfully learned longer than we have had a written alphabet. Babies are born crying, not writing. Even today there are many people who go through life without knowing how to read or write.

There are very few people who go through life not knowing how to talk. Speaking, from which writing and reading are derived, is essential to the humanness of our species even though it is important to note that writing and reading have greatly expanded the options of the human race.

People recognized the power of the spoken word long before the advent of literacy (of reading and writing). In times and in lands where there was almost no reading or writing much attention was still paid to the spoken word and to public speaking. Eric Havelock suggests that the unique force of the classical Greek mind and intellect may be traced to the fact that the ancient Greeks, prior to Plato, lived in a predominantly oral culture. According to Havelock, the oral culture of the Greeks resulted in certain ways of thinking which differ from the thought patterns encouraged by the world of writing and print. For example, an oral culture encourages a more immediate thought pattern than does a written culture since writing allows for thoughts to be written down and held aside in time (Havelock, 1967). These observations highlight the earlier mentioned relationship between thought and speech.

All normal people of average intelligence can learn to give an acceptable public speech. Cicero, a great Roman, was also a great public speaker, an orator. Cicero said "Orator fit, non nascitur!" "Orators are made, not born!" Literally hundreds of thousands of people have learned to speak in public. Public speaking *can* be learned. The history and theory of public speaking can be learned without ever giving a speech. The skill of public speaking can be learned only through using public speaking theory in the practical process of preparing and delivering public speeches. The personal power that flows from public speaking does not flow from knowledge about speaking in public; it flows from the act of giving speeches in public.

The destination that all of us (you, your teacher, we the authors) are striving toward together is your ability to prepare and deliver an ethical, effective public speech. The road that leads to this destination is long, sometimes hilly, but generally well marked. Your teacher and this new primer will point out the road signs, indicate shortcuts, and will tell you of places along the journey where some have smoothed the way and others have slipped, tripped, or fallen. However it is essential that you remember that even with the help of this book and your teacher, only *you* can actually travel the road. It is also worth mentioning that the walking of the road should be, in itself, an enjoyable experience. Walking the road, and accurately following the signposts, is made much easier through the guidance of a teacher who has made the same journey earlier. Make good, and constant, use of your teacher. Ask questions, request feedback. Try things out that you read about in this text or that you hear in class lectures or in discussions with your fellow students or by observing professional public speakers. Your teacher wants very much to help you reach your public speaking destination.

When this course and book are completed, you should be able to put together and present a public speech which helps you successfully achieve your desired goals. Reaching your desired public speaking goals is our mutual destination.

☐ Public Speaking Theory and Public Speaking Practice

One of the problems some people have when starting to study public speaking is the idea that since they have been speaking almost all their lives they probably know all there is to know about speaking. This is a fundamentally false idea. There is a real and important difference between "knowing" and "knowing about." There are those who can play the piano without ever having had a formal lesson, perhaps without being able even to read musical notation. Those people "know" how to play the piano, but they don't "know about" playing the piano. In a real sense we all know life simply by living it and sharing it. There are few of us who claim to know about life all that we wish or all that there is to know about life.

So what? If you know something, is there any good reason you should also want to know about it?

We think so.

Knowing is good!

Knowing about is also good!

Knowing *and* knowing about is the best!

The basketball player who plays well and also knows what he is doing in terms of performance and strategy both knows and knows about. The speaker who speaks well and also knows what she is doing that makes her speaking successful can then plan future successful speeches. Personal power is enhanced when we combine knowing with knowing about. We can further our talents for successful public speaking through a combination of experiences that help us develop our individual skills (or knowing) in public speaking while at the same time developing our understanding of (or knowing about) the principles of successful public speaking.

"But," you might be saying, "all of this may be well and good, but it sure sounds too theoretical to me." You go on to ask, "Isn't it true that something can be true in theory but false in practice?"

No! Something cannot be at one and the same time true in theory and false in practice. If the theory is accurate, then the practice which flows from the theory should conform to predicted theoretical results. If the practical outcomes differ from the theoretically predicted outcomes, you have every reason to question whether or not the theory could have been considered to be accurate in the first place.

Although something that has a sound theoretical base should work out in practice, it is certainly possible that we might misapply the theory. We might apply the wrong theory in a particular case (the principles for winning at chess don't work when playing bridge), or we might apply a theory incorrectly in an appropriate case (we make a mistake in entering the data when programming a computer).

Theory should help us explain, predict, and sometimes control the behaviors with which the theory deals. Public speaking theory comes from a number of sources. Since people have been speaking, and speaking to other people, ever since the earliest civilizations, much public speaking theory comes from the study of how people have spoken to others throughout history. Who were considered successful public speakers? What did those who were considered to be successful public speakers do that made others judge them to be successful? Aside from random observations made in the past, public speaking has been an academic subject matter since at least the fourth or fifth century B.C., and teachers and students of public speaking have gathered thousands upon thousands of examples of successful and unsuccessful public speaking, analyzed them, and drawn from the analysis theoretical propositions and advice. This historical technique is still used. We listen for instances of good (effective, successful) public speaking. We gather a number of such successful instances and then examine the collected sample to see if any general theoretical observation or rule can reasonably be inferred from the practical cases collected. Next we test any inferred rule or theory in our own practice. In this way we can move from observation, to theory, to testing the theory in practice.

With some theory to draw upon, we can then consider a practical situation in which we will try to test the theory. For example, theoretically we are told that when giving information in a public speech, it is often helpful to involve more than a single sensory modality. Rather than using sound (the spoken word) alone, we are encouraged to reinforce the sound with sight, with a visual aid. So we speak, but we support our spoken message with some type of visual aid—a slide, movie, handout, chalk graph, etc. Thus we have used a theoretical observation (use multiple sensory modalities when giving information) in a practical manner, and the results provide us with a means of judging the practicality of the theory.

If you try to apply some theory recommended either by your teacher or by this book or by other resources and the application fails, then you must examine both the theory and your application of the theory. Perhaps the theory is wrong. Perhaps you applied the theory incorrectly. Perhaps you used the wrong theory for the purpose. Perhaps you do not fully understand the theory. When you test the theory against your own practical experience, you join actively in the adventure of building public speaking theory.

□ Learning Public Speaking from Models

Speakers, other speakers, and ourselves when we speak in public may be considered as models, as examples from whom we may learn. Models are a rich source of information and example. Not just successful models, but unsuccessful models as well. We can learn a lot about what seems to work and what seems not to work just by carefully watching and listening to the public speakers around us. Our public speaking teacher, teachers of other subjects, fellow students, religious leaders, sales personnel, politicians—all these individuals are examples, models, of public speaking in action. Do you consider your minister, priest, rabbi, congresswoman, senator effective or ineffective when speaking? If effective—why? If ineffective—why? When judging speaking models, be as specific as possible. General, or global, judgments such as "Boy, was that a great speech!" are never as helpful as more specific observations such as:

"She spoke loud enough so that she could be heard easily by everyone."

"He spoke at just the right rate, not too fast, not too slow."

"His argument was really convincing, it made sense and there was a lot of logical support."

"Her speech was funny, but the jokes didn't fit into the overall topic, so her humor hurt rather than helped."

Examime each of these specific judgments and you will find some hints as to how you can be more successful in your own public speaking.

Earlier we defined feedback as the observation of past successes or failures used as a means of correcting present and future behavior. Model speakers give us a type of feedback. You can also be your own model. Look in the mirror. Are you dressed in such a manner as to impress the audience with your concern for making a good appearance, or do your clothes suggest that you couldn't care less about what this audience thinks of you or of your speech? We are not talking about high style or expensive clothing as much as we are considering appropriateness, cleanliness, and neatness. How you look and the judgment you make about how you think your clothing is going to affect the reception of your speech is an example of how you can serve as a model for yourself.

Always be alert for good feedback—"good" meaning specific and accurate, not necessarily complimentary. Seek feedback wherever and whenever you can get it. Try out your ideas in conversation with your friends and then ask them what they think of the ideas and of your manner of presenting them. Ask your teacher for feedback. Always give yourself feedback. Since you can always be extra nice to yourself at some other time, you can afford to be pretty hard with your own self-criticism.

☐ Public Speaking and Personal Ethics

It is through the spoken word that we seek truth. It is also through the spoken word that we express truthfulness. The commitment to being truthful is seen by some as part and parcel of this unique gift of spoken language. We will consider this argument in more detail in Chapter Ten on ethics. Audiences generally expect a speaker's words to be the speaker's own, to be original with the speaker. When we borrow someone else's words, ideas, or line of argument and utter them as if they were our own—without giving credit to the person who first originated them—we are guilty of misrepresentation of the source of our message. In classroom usage this kind of misrepresentation is called plagiarism, and plagiarism is considered absolutely unacceptable. Plagiarism is also a form of manipulation, and manipulation must be consciously avoided both in the preparation and the presentation of a public speech. Be sure to do your own work and to give credit when you borrow the work of others.

☐ Public Speaking and Personal Power

In this chapter we've discussed some of the elements involved in gaining non-manipulative power first over yourself and then over others through the study and practice of public speaking. Set your ambition to become a master of the skill of speaking in public. Enjoy your efforts as you would enjoy playing a challenging game. Hermann Hesse was a Nobel prize-winning German novelist. One of his most delightful stories bears two titles, *The Glass Bead Game* and *Magister Ludi.* The second title translates to "Game Master." Hesse's story makes many important points in an entertaining manner and deals with an individual who is in charge of conducting competition surrounding a game of the intellect known as the glass bead game. Hesse tells us that the glass bead game is extraordinarily complex because it involves interrelationships among many different aspects of thought, science, and art. Here is how Hesse talks about the game early in his book:

> The Glass Bead Game is thus a mode of playing with the total contents of our culture: . . . all the insights, noble thoughts, and works of art that the human race has produced in its creative eras, all that subsequent periods of scholarly study have reduced to concepts and converted into intellectual property—on all this immense body of intellectual values the Glass Bead Game player plays like the organist on the organ. (Hesse, 1969, p. 15)

We ask you to view language as the organ and to use your speech to play upon that organ. Use public speaking as your way of playing the glass bead game. This new primer is intended to be a relatively small, introductory book on the subject of public speaking. Public speaking is a uniquely human game which we invite you to play for enjoyment, for essential mental development, and for the acquisition of nonmanipulative personal power.

☐ Summary

Power, the ability to influence others, is a valuable personal attribute that begins with self-control, power over one's own self. Communication, the process of acting upon information, is a generalized ability common to humans and other creatures. Spoken language, which results from joining the inborn capacity for utterance, for speech, with a particular learned language (such as English or Spanish) seems to be unique to humans. Spoken language enables humans to develop specifically human power over themselves, their surroundings, and other human beings. Human communication usually involves a sender, a message, and a receiver. Human communication is often affected by noise and feedback. The process of human communication, which may be described as helical, involves the individual as the basic unit and the dyad (two individuals) as the basic relationship. Human communication may be thought of as occurring on three levels; intrapersonal, interpersonal, and person to persons. The third level, person to persons, is commonly called public speaking. All three levels of human communication are interrelated in actual communicative behavior. Power and manipulation are not the same thing. Public speaking allows us simultaneously to attempt the exercise of power over self and over others. The basic goals of public speaking are the expansion and the sharing of thought. Mentation, rationality, should define the product of thoughtful public expression. In the working world there often seems to be a direct correlation between personal success and public speaking ability. Public speakers are made, not born. Successful public speaking, as demonstrated throughout history, can be learned. Public speaking theory and practice are mutually reinforcing. In learning to speak in public you should use yourself and others as models of public speaking practice. You should actively seek and make use of feedback. Personal ethics for public speaking make clear that the public speaker should make a commitment to truthfulness and should always acknowledge when he or she makes substantial use of the words or work of others.

Exercises ■

1 List three public present-day figures you consider powerful. What behaviors do these individuals exhibit that cause you to consider them powerful? What are the public speaking abilities of these public figures?

2 In this chapter we mention the components of human communication. There are many different ways in which these components have been arranged. There are those who suggest additional components. Prepare a short speech setting forth two additional models of human communication.

3 After you complete your first class speech, prepare a short paper in which you discuss how the three levels of human communication seemed to interrelate in the preparation and delivery of your speech.

4 Prepare a short speech setting forth whom you believe to have been the most powerful person in the history of the human race and a description of the public speaking practices of that person.

5 Discuss the interrelationship between power over self and power over others.

Bibliographic References ■

Aristotle: *Politica*. B. Jowett (trans.), Oxford University Press, Oxford, England, 1921.

Dance, Frank E. X., and C. E. Larson: *The Functions of Human Communication: A Theoretical Approach*. Holt, Rinehart and Winston, New York, 1976. Especially Appendix A, "Some definitions of communication," pp. 171–192.

Havelock, Eric A.: *Preface To Plato*. Grosset and Dunlap, New York, 1967.

Hesse, Herman: *The Glass Bead Game,* Holt, Rinehart and Winston, New York, 1969.

O'Neill, Ynez V.: *Speech and Speech Disorders in Western Thought before 1600.* Greenwood Press, Westport, Conn., 1980.

Recommended Readings ■

Cherry, Colin: *On Human Communication: A Review, a Survey, and a Criticism,* 3d ed., MIT Press, Cambridge, Mass., 1978. A great deal of historical information about the study and understanding of human communication. Not always easy reading but worthwhile.

Dance, Frank E. X. (ed.): *Human Communication Theory: Comparative Essays,* Harper & Row, New York, 1982. Chapters by contemporary speech communication theorists which can give you some idea of the current state of theory in the field.

Sebeok, Thomas A., and R. Rosenthal (eds.): *The Clever Hans Phenomenon: Communication with Horses, Whales, Apes, and People,* New York Academy of Sciences, New York, 1981. A volume which gives lots of information on the current studies of animal communication and how those studies relate to human communication.

Appendix to Chapter One

Your First Speech

"One ought, every day at least, to hear a little song, read a good poem, see a fine picture, and, if it were possible, to speak a few reasonable words."
Goethe, *Wilhelm Meisters Apprenticeship,* V, 1

This whole book is about how to give a public speech. But we know that most likely you won't be able to finish studying the whole book before you are called upon to give your first public speech. That's why we've prepared this appendix—to help you give your first public speech, and to enjoy that experience, even before you've been able to finish the whole book or the entire course.

☐ The Use of GOTO

Throughout this appendix you will find notations that say [GOTO]. These notations refer to places in the text where you can find more fully developed information about the immediate subject being discussed. However, we don't expect you to stop each time you meet a GOTO and read other parts of the text. We just wanted you to know where you could find additional information if you wanted it. This appendix is self-contained for your first speech and you needn't go to a GOTO unless you really want to do so.

Remember, in getting ready for this first assigned speech, that you have been speaking since you were about 1½ years old. That means you have many years of speaking experience upon which to draw in getting ready for this first speech. Every speech you have ever given, this speech you are preparing to give, and every speech you will ever give all share certain common qualities. Each speech shapes your abilities for all future speeches—this first speech is not a trivial or "throwaway" exercise, it deserves your attention and work. This first speech should be an enjoyable experience. As anyone who has played a sport knows, there is nothing incompatible between strenuous effort and enjoyment or having fun. There are those who consider public speaking a type of intellectual sporting event and find much enjoyment in the activity. All the class members are in exactly the same boat as you and all of them will be rooting for you—as they expect you to be rooting for them when their turn to speak comes. You can, and we truly hope you will, enjoy this speech and this course and profit from both.

Speaking and thinking are very closely intertwined. Your goal is to use spoken language to make your thoughts public. [**GOTO Chapter One.**] Some nervousness is absolutely natural and virtually universal. Don't let the nervousness control you; you can control it. Think, prepare, rehearse, and when you get up to speak, think about what you are saying. [**GOTO Chapter Three.**] If you have any special questions or problems, consult your teacher.

☐ Ten Steps to Your First Public Speech

Now, here are 10 steps to follow to make your first public speech successful.

1. Your topic for this first speech may be assigned by your teacher (in which case the question of topic selection need not bother you) or may be left up to your own choice. If the topic is of your own choosing, pick something that interests you since what really interests you will probably hold some interest for others as well. [**GOTO Chapter Three.**]
2. On the opposite page is a sample outline for a 3-minute speech on the subject "Why I am taking this public speaking course." Following this outline and a few steps dealing with organization and outlining we present a formatted but unfinished outline for you to complete for your first speech. Do it! Since your instructor might collect these outlines after your speech, write or type neatly. [**GOTO Chapter Five.**]
3. When organizing your thoughts and the public remarks flowing from those thoughts:
   a. Reflect on how your past experience bears upon the speech topic. [**GOTO Chapter Two.**]
   b. Consider what your audience already knows about the topic and what you can tell them about the topic that might interest them. [**GOTO Chapters Three and Four.**]
   c. Give special attention to how you are going to start your speech (the introduction) and how you are going to finish your speech (the conclusion). In your introduction you want to capture the voluntary attention of your audience, maybe tell them what you are going to tell them, perhaps use an opening quotation from some authority. Among the ways in which you can conclude would be with a summary statement, a quotation, or a challenge. It is neither necessary nor recommended that you conclude by saying "Thank you." [**GOTO Chapter Five.**]
   d. In the main part of your outline (the body) include the major points you wish to make and appropriate supporting statements for the major points. [**GOTO Chapters Five and Nine.**]
      Here is a sample of an unfinished, but formatted, outline. Either use this one or make a copy of it and complete it by filling in the material for your first speech.

N. E. Wun
Your name

1/8/88
Date of the Speech

Intro. Pub. Spk.
Course

Specific Purpose: To develop within the class an understanding of the main reasons for my studying public speaking.
Time: 3 minutes.

Introduction

   I. Throughout history public speaking has played an important part in the development of civilization.
      A. The Greek and Roman orators were excellent public speakers.
      B. Religious leaders such as Christ spoke eloquently in public.

Body

  II. Public speaking is important in our time.
      A. Through their public speaking Hitler, Churchill, and Roosevelt shaped the modern world.
      B. Contemporary political leaders continue to use public speaking as a means of influence and control.
 III. The main reason for public speaking's importance is that it allows people to develop their thoughts and then to share these thoughts with each other.

Conclusion

 IV. I believe that public speaking will continue to play an important role in the lives of individuals and of civilizations. Because of this belief I want to know about public speaking as well as how to speak in public. As the novelist Thomas Mann reminded us: "Speech is civilization itself. The word, even the most contradictory word, preserves contact—it is silence which isolates."

_____

_____
Your name

_____
Date of the speech

_____
Course

Topic: May be assigned by teacher or chosen by you. Check with your teacher. [**GOTO Chapter Three.**]

Specific Purpose: Here write down, in one sentence, _exactly_ what you would like to accomplish in this speech, with this audience, at this time. [**GOTO Chapter Five.**]

Time: How long is this speech supposed to last? [**GOTO Chapters Six and Seven.**]

Introduction
   I.
      A.
      B.
         1.
         2.

Body
   II.
      A.
      B.
         1.
         2.

Conclusion
III.
      A.
      B.
         1.
         2.

_____

4. Rehearse your speech *aloud!* Use a tape recorder, or preferably a VTR, in rehearsing your speech. If you don't have access to either a tape recorder or a VTR, try to get a friend to listen to your rehearsal. Rehearse until you feel comfortable with the general development of the speech and with meeting the time requirements of the speech. Always rehearse *aloud!* [**GOTO Chapter Six.**]

5. Don't worry about gestures—worry about making your idea or ideas clear to the audience. In the event that you are motivated to gesture, you should keep your hands free (not in your pockets or locked behind your back). [**GOTO Chapter Seven.**]

6. Look pleasant. Smile, if you can do so without forcing.

7. Speak loud enough so that everyone in the audience can easily hear you, but don't shout. If you are concerned about whether or not you will speak loudly enough, ask a friend to sit in the back of the audience and signal to you if you can't be easily heard.

8. Use your outline as notes. One page at most. Rehearse with the outline so that you aren't tied to it and can look at your audience.

9. Don't use profanity, swearing, or vulgar language unless you have a definite reason for doing so and are aware of the possible negative consequences.

10. Wear clothing that you think compliments your appearance but doesn't call attention to itself. [**GOTO Chapter Seven.**]

Now, when called to speak, take two or three deep breaths, make sure you have your notes, rise, walk confidently to the lectern, keep your opening remarks in mind, look at your audience, pleasantly, and "speak a few reasonable words," in this, your first public speech.

Remote Preparation

Chapter Two

"There's a magic in the distance."
Alfred Noyes, *Forty Singing Seamen*

In public speaking, as in all other aspects of our daily living, our past lives and experiences play an important role. *Remote preparation* includes all that we have learned in our past lives that we can apply to the present challenge of speaking in public.

No one is surprised when the president of a company is able to make a few intelligent, what seem to be off-the-cuff, remarks concerning the state of the business. No one is surprised when a practicing physician is able, with little immediate preparation, to deliver a 5-minute speech on the wisdom of good health practices. The company president and the practicing physician have simply drawn upon their own remote preparation to meet the public speaking challenge. Remote preparation is an essential element in intelligently meeting immediate needs.

Important happenings in our past may be distant in time, but fresh in our memory. Each new experience we encounter fits into the overall pattern of our past experiences. Each time we stand up it isn't as if it were the very first time we ever stood. A baby learning to walk gives his or her full attention to the correct execution of the act. But once that baby has learned to walk, he or she seldom gives the mechanics of walking a second thought. Our daily activities include numerous behaviors which take their form from our past maturation, learning, and experiences. Life would be terribly difficult if when we awoke each day we had lost all memory of how to perform those everyday behaviors we take for granted. We would begin each day like a newborn baby—we wouldn't get much new done since so much time would be used up just relearning the basic routines necessary for living. Some people do have such problems as a result of serious strokes or unusual psychological trauma. Fortunately most normal and healthy people are able to learn and to build new learning upon past learning. In this manner each of us acquires continually more sophisticated patterns of thinking and behaving. This "magic in the distance" of our past experiences was not the same magic as Alfred Noyes was thinking of in the words with which we prefaced this chapter, but our remote past—our personal distant experiences—do have a magic of their own upon which we depend in our present days.

The human ability to recall distant experiences and to build upon the past is important both for the human individual and the human race. Perhaps the most important tool available to us in building upon remote experiences is spoken language. Spoken language and the writing and reading based upon spoken language allow us to build today upon the knowledge and discoveries of past centuries of human endeavor. There is no need to reinvent the wheel since thousands of years of human experience have shown us how it may be used. The inventiveness which has allowed humans to improve farming techniques, to achieve medical breakthroughs, to build computers, and to travel in space is based upon records of past experiments, past successes and failures, which we can apply to the new challenges that we face.

In *The Tempest,* Shakespeare reminds us that "What's past is prologue." As individuals we must learn from our pasts. An important part of education is fittng us with a knowledge of the past so that we may use the experiences of the past to live better in the present and to improve the future for ourselves and for our descendants. The prehistorical (before written records) and historical past may seem quite remote, but we can recall the past through spoken language and written records, as well as through observation of buildings, art, roads, and other artifacts of earlier times. Symbols give us the power to travel through time. Through language and through learning we can bring the remote past to bear on our individual present. We can use language to reconstruct what we think the past may have been like. Such reconstructions take life once again in literature. We can use language to tell fables and fairy tales which have a message for present-day living. Aesop's fables tell us today that the qualities of life present in the past still have importance for us. Greed and selfishness brought sorrow centuries ago. Greed and selfishness still bring sorrow today.

> "For always roaming with a hungry heart
> Much have I seen and known; cities of men,
> And manners, climates, councils, governments, . . .
> I am part of all that I have met."
> Alfred Lord Tennyson, *Ulysses*

Tennyson's hero, Ulysses, testifies to the importance of past experience in making us what we are. Ulysses drew upon all his past experiences in meeting new challenges. For each of us our own past experience (which may seem quite remote) is an invaluable source of information and knowledge in meeting the challenge of daily living.

☐ I and Thou

One of the earliest milestones (and remotest personal experiences) in the development of each human being is the realization that oneself is a being separate from everything else. This *self-concept,* or *awareness of self as a separate being,* an "I," occurs so early in our lives as to be impossible to recall. In terms of the development of an individual, self-concept precedes self-esteem. *Self-esteem* refers to how we feel about the being we are. Knowing that I am demonstrates self-concept.

Liking who I am is an example of self-esteem. Both self-concept and self-esteem develop so early in our lives and become so intertwined that they are very difficult to separate in our later lives. The early formation of a self-concept is vitally important. Although the exact manner in which humans form a self-concept is unclear, research in the study of spoken language suggests that the infant's experience in uttering sound plays a central part in the infant's creation of a self-concept (Zak-Dance, 1979). The normal infant's experience in uttering sound and simultaneously hearing his or her own utterance (referred to as an oral/aural experience) may occasion the development of the infant's first conscious awareness of contrast (Dance, 1978). This contrast between internal experience and external input resulting from that internal experience (the child utters the sound and then hears his or her own utterance) may start the infant on the track of appreciating that there may be something outside of himself or herself.

At birth, and for a while thereafter, human infants perceive themselves as the center of all that happens in their environment and may be considered "egocentric." The contrast which the infant experiences as a result of oral/aural behavior may cause the infant to begin contrasting his or her own being with the being of others. Logically for there to be a self-concept, there must also be a concept of other than self. In order for there to be a self, there must be an other. In order for there to be an other, there must be a self. The infant progresses through stages of differentiation of self from all that surrounds self, using the contrast born of speech to develop a self-concept. With the self-concept there develops a concept of other, an "I" and a "you," or, more formally, an "I" and a "thou."

The child's development of a self-concept is accompanied by an increasing awareness, by the child, that he or she may not be the center of all that happens in the environment. The child is beginning the movement away from egocentrism, from seeing himself or herself as the center of all that is or happens. As the child moves away from complete egocentrism, he or she begins to acquire the capacity to decenter.

☐ Decentering

Decentering is the ability to take into consideration perceptual and conceptual points of view other than one's own (Piaget, 1955). Perception usually involves physical things or objects that are present. Conception involves thoughts, concepts, and abstractions. When we decenter, we shift from an egocentric view of the universe to a view in which varying perspectives are recognized and considered. In the process of decentering an individual shifts attention from the perceptually most dominant aspects of an object or situation so as to differentiate his or her own point of view from others and so as to shift his or her own mental perspective both in physical and social situations (J. R. Johnson, 1978, 1982; M. Friedeman, classroom remarks). An egocentric infant only perceives things from his or her own point of view. As the child begins to be able to decenter, he or she can begin to imagine how an object might appear to someone else, standing in another part

"Mountains of the Inner Eye"—A Visual Expression of Decentering (Eric Hilton, artist. Used with permission of Steuben Glass.)

of the room. An egocentric infant, as far as we can determine, conceives of things only in terms of himself or herself. As a child acquires the ability to decenter, he or she begins to be able to conceive of how someone else might have a different way of thinking about something. Decentering, like self-concept, is rooted in contrast. In its earliest developmental stages decentering is more perceptual than conceptual. The ability to decenter begins by developing the capacity to appreciate the difference in physical, or *perceptual*, viewpoints (a toy house able to be seen from one physical position or location may be hidden from view if the child changes position or location). Gradually the capacity to appreciate differences in *conceptual* viewpoints develops (the child appreciates that what might seem like a great idea to the child, such as having a couple of friends over for an overnight, may have entirely different implications for a parent).

As we grow older, as we move from infancy to childhood, to adolescence, to adulthood, our self-concept, self-esteem, egocentrism, and decentering all also change. We get better and better at decentering as we acquire more and different experiences with ourselves and with others. The more people we know and the more different kinds of people we know (different races, different religious persuasions, different educational levels), the greater our opportunity to learn how things look differently to different people and how different people may think differently about a wide variety of subjects. We grow sophisticated in our spoken language so that we are better able to put into words our own point of view and through words to contrast our own viewpoint with that of others. The emotional demands of adolescence are absorbed into a better balanced life picture, and as we move away from adolescence we usually find ourselves better able to voluntarily take the other person's perceptual or conceptual viewpoint. In other words, we usually find our capacity for spoken language (human communication) and de-centering growing side by side.

From our consideration of spoken language, self-concept, and decentering we would like to suggest three observations that seem to bear directly on the use of human communication in public speaking.

1. *Since there needs to be a self in order for there to be an other, it is important to know who you are if you intend to communicate effectively with others.* We believe this is an important concept in the study and practice of human communication. You must spend as much time as needed in becoming realistically comfortable with who you are (self-concept) and how you feel about yourself (self-esteem) if you wish to become as comfortable as possible in communicating with others. The "realistically" in the preceding sentence implies that your self-concept and self-esteem should have roots in reality rather than in fantasy or "wishing." This human communication rule is true for communicating with others whether the others be one, a few, or many.

2. *Since decentering helps in perceiving perceptual and conceptual differences in point of view of self as compared with other(s), it is important to continually develop our decentering ability.* Starting from a base of a realistic self-concept and self-esteem, we should try to acquire as many experiences as possible that will enable us to develop insight into how things may appear differently to different people and how ideas may hold different meanings and implications for others. The better we are at decentering, the better chance we have of communicating our ideas to others in a manner acceptable to them.

3. *Since contrast is at the root of self-concept and decentering, we may be able to use contrast as a technique to define our own self and to enhance our ability to decenter.* Contrast is a useful tool in developing our general communicative abilities and our public speaking ability in particular.

Let's consider each of these three observations in more detail.

☐ Self-Concept and Public Speaking

An important part of your remote preparation for public speaking is coming to terms with who you are before rising to speak to others. It is difficult to give a convincing speech on a topic if you are unsure of how you yourself feel about the topic. It is even more difficult to give a convincing speech if you are unsure of how you feel about yourself! We are not suggesting that public speakers must go through extensive psychoanalysis in order to know all the facets of the self. We are suggesting that from time to time, and especially before you've had much experience in speech making, you should reflect on your own identity as it affects how you communicate to others. Trying to answer the question "Who am I?" is a valuable exercise. The better able you are to answer this question, the tighter the grip you'll have on your own self-concept. This grip will allow you more freedom with the ideas you wish to communicate to others. Since you will know how you believe and feel about yourself, the fear of allowing your own convictions to be unwittingly changed will be allayed. How do you see yourself? As a student? As a family member? As a member of a profession? Do you see yourself as having both desirable and undesirable attributes? A person who doesn't like himself or herself finds it very difficult, if not impossible, to like someone else. This liking, or not liking, is subtly but almost always communicated to an audience. If I don't care about me, why should I care about you? Since we have mentioned in Chapter One that the goal of public speaking involves helping ourselves and others, a speaker who doesn't care about others may well have difficulty in convincing his or her audience otherwise.

All of us are composites of desirable and undesirable traits, of strengths and weaknesses. What most of us strive for is to keep the balance in favor of strength and desirability even though we probably cannot eliminate each and every weakness. Knowing our weaknesses can enable us to be alert for their appearance, to guard against them, and to compensate for them. When standing before an audience to speak, it is comforting to know that you already know your own weak points and that you have done your best to handle them wisely in your speech preparation and presentation. For example, in reflecting upon yourself, perhaps you recognize that you have a tendency to come on "too strong" for many people. This problem can be handled in your speech preparation and rehearsal by consciously toning down your remarks and your delivery. (Such compensatory treatment is not unethical as long as it is not done with the intention of deceiving your audience but rather with the intention of gaining a fair hearing for your speech as well as improving some personal habits.) Or perhaps you have reason to believe that you are usually too diffident or wishy-washy. To overcome this weakness, you might make certain that in preparing your remarks you make your point of view clear and strong. You should also practice delivering your remarks without hesitation and with appropriate vigor.

There is absolutely nothing wrong with trying to make the best of our strengths and trying to overcome or compensate for our weaknesses. Such compensation is not easy. It takes accurate self-diagnosis, appropriate humility, and great fortitude. The payoff is self-comfort. This self-comfort is obviously going to enhance your own self-esteem, which in turn will make you increasingly comfortable in your public presentation. Certainly, as you consider effective public speakers, you will note that most such individuals come across as being fairly comfortable with themselves. Note that we are not advocating a false bravado or an overwhelming ego in public speaking, just a realistic and fair appraisal of one's own self and an effort to make the best of one's own capabilities.

One of the unanticipated benefits of a course in public speaking is the opportunity given you to reflect upon your own self-concept as well as to participate in an activity which can enhance your own self-esteem. Reflecting on your past and your present so as to discern "who you are" is a fundamental resource in preparing and presenting an effective public speech.

☐ Decentering and Public Speaking

Your self-concept is your centering point, the anchor point from which you de-center. There is a danger of moving so far from your own centering point as to lose touch with yourself. You have probably met someone who seems to have no opinions of his or her own, who seems to take on the attitudes and opinions of whomever he or she is with at the moment. This kind of person seems to have abandoned his or her own center in favor of looking at everything through the eyes of others. With such people it is difficult to tell what they believe. The work you have already gone through in reflecting upon who you are will guard you from decentering too far.

Earlier we described the process some scholars believe individuals follow in acquiring their decentering ability—the process of recognizing, through contrast, that others are different from themselves and that those others may have points of view different from one's own. This awareness is essential to successful public communication since it enables us to understand the mental point of view of others. In decentering we are saying, "I understand how you *think* about this problem. I can move outside myself and see things from your point of view." A person who is egocentric—who is able to see things only from his or her own point of view—will find it difficult to communicate effectively with other humans. Why is this so? Why is decentering so important in human communication?

Although many people believe that when humans communicate they merely transfer facts, thoughts, ideas, and emotions to others, this is not in fact what is really happening. Human communication requires that we find ways of associating, or linking, our experiences and thoughts with the experiences and thoughts of the persons with whom we are trying to communicate. We must be able to find some commonality between their past experiences and ours. The egocentric person, according to Piaget, is in a state where there is a lack of differentiation between his or her own point of view and other possible ones (Piaget, 1955). Obviously, to the degree that one succumbs to egocentrism, it will be impossible to take the point of view of someone else and consequently find common experiences with that person.

As egocentrism maintains itself, or as voluntary selfishness is asserted, de-centering is suppressed. A public speaker who is only able to see things from his or her own point of view, who is blind to the viewpoints and needs of others, will find it almost impossible to locate and use spoken language associations most appropriate for successful communication with an audience.

Anything that heightens egocentrism is likely to detract from successful public speaking. For example, uncontrolled personal emotion suppresses decentering and usually interferes with successful public speaking. By uncontrolled personal emotion we mean a situation where the speaker becomes so personally emotional that he loses the capacity to decenter and as a result loses the ability to locate and apply the appropriate associations for successfully communicating with his audience. Most of us have had occasion to witness examples of how uncontrolled emotion can interfere with communication. Perhaps you know someone who has been terribly frightened by a near accident. Her fear may have been so dominant that she was unable to tell you what had almost happened. Once she gained control of herself, she was able to decenter again so as to help you understand what took place.

Excessive power is another factor which can suppress decentering. Usually the more powerful the speaker, the less the speaker tries to take the mental or emotional point of view of the audience (political speechwriters make a special effort to build audience concerns into their prepared speeches). For example, the boss may be so impressed with her own power and importance that she fails to notice the visible resentment of her employees when she tells them that the company won't be giving raises this year. A teacher may have a sense of self-importance that interferes with his ability to communicate the subject to his students. As one acquires power over others, one must make a sustained and conscious effort to decenter.

It is the ability to decenter which enables us to assess, appreciate, and through association, approximate the experiences of others. As decentering capacity and ability develops, egocentrism usually is increasingly controlled. The person who can decenter is able to associate his or her own experiences with experiences the listener(s) has already had so that the listener will be able to draw connections and understand the speaker's message. It is through association that we build understanding between human beings. The consciously planned use of association is central to public speaking success.

Consciously planned association is made possible through decentering. You are asked to speak to a group of accounting majors. What are important questions to accounting majors? How do accounting majors view value questions—the search for truth, beauty, goodness? Are accounting majors likely to view values differently from philosophy majors? Whatever your own major, decentering will help you look at things from the accounting major's point of view and choose illustrations, examples, and other speech aids that will assist the accounting major in associating his or her experiences with the experiences and thoughts you are presenting. If you were going to speak on the topic of final examinations, your speech might well contain different materials if your audience consisted of college freshmen rather than college professors. The differences of viewpoint on the speaker's subject held by these two audiences should affect the speaker's choice of approach and treatment. Decentering is essential to selecting those associations most conducive to the achievement of your public speaking goals. The public speaker will profit from enhancing his or her own decentering development.

What are some of the ways by which you might improve your ability to see things from another's viewpoint? How can you enhance your decentering?

Physical Decentering

To refine your sense of physical decentering, consider how a physical object might look from a perspective other than the one dictated by your physical position relative to the object. You are presently reading this book. Consider how it looks to you at this moment. How would the book appear to someone standing behind you? To someone looking through a window opposite where you are sitting? To

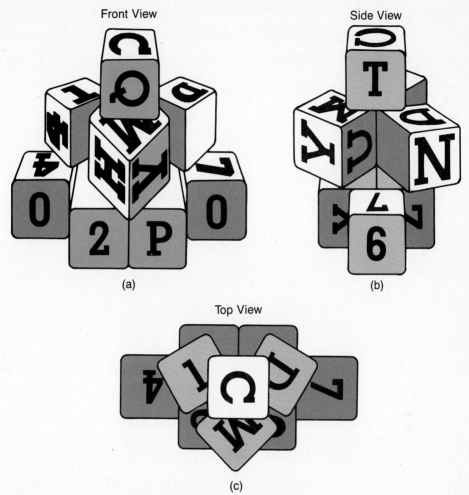

Figure 2.1 (a) Front View; (b) Side View; (c) Top View

a person able to look straight down upon it from the ceiling? Get some wooden blocks or egg cartons or shoes and pile them on top of each other. Position yourself in front of the pile but far enough away that you can't look down upon the pile or see its other side. Now draw a sketch of the pile from the point of view of all four compass points as well as from directly above. When you have finished, walk around the pile and check your sketches against the actual perspectives. How well did you do in this exercise in perceptual decentering? (See Figure 2.1.)

One of the most popular writers of novels about the old West, Louis L'Amour, often had his characters take special pains when riding a trail to look back at where they had been as well as to look forward to where they were going. Why? Because a trail looks quite different when being retraced than when being ridden along the first time. Skills in perceptual or physical decentering are useful in helping to accelerate the development of skills in mental or conceptual decentering.

Mental Decentering

To improve your ability to understand the mental, or conceptual, viewpoint of others, nothing can take the place of direct experience with many people from various walks of life. This is one reason why traveling has always been considered "broadening." For many of us, however, traveling is not a practical option. Whether we travel or not, we always can talk. Conversation and reading are almost always available. Talk to people, ask them how they think about certain topics, how they feel about certain happenings. Even if it is customary to discuss trivial topics (the weather, having a cold, the latest clothing styles), most people enjoy being asked their feelings and opinions about more serious matters (the economy, probable presidential candidates, the morality of war, the abuse of the environment). If you do not have anyone to talk with about worthwhile matters, then read. Read poetry, fiction, history, biography. Reading allows you to move through time as well as through space. If you are tired of reading, then watch TV or to go the movies or a stage play. But don't just be a passive viewer. Question the ideas presented in a show. View not just for entertainment but for understanding as well. Discuss what you've seen with your friends. What did they think about the program you liked so much—and why?

If you are tired of reading, and there are no good shows to watch, and no one's around to talk with, consider the radical idea of talking with yourself—aloud! Now don't immediately shy away from the idea of talking out loud to yourself. In a later chapter we will tell you about some fascinating research done on the subject of inner speech and how inner speech relates to thinking. Without covering the research here (skip to Chapter Six, page 142–143, if you want fuller coverage), believe us when we say that talking out loud to yourself can help develop sharper habits of thought and of expression. Pick a topic that interests you (the future maybe) and then talk to yourself about that subject. In your out-loud self-conversation examine the idea or subject from different perspectives. What do you think your future will be like? What would you really like your future to be like? Who would you like to share your future with? Given the possibility of nuclear war, do you think there will be a future? Take a positive point of view and then contrast that positive point of view with a negative viewpoint. Discuss the topic from the point of view of a city dweller and then from the point of view of someone from the country. Each time you change perspectives you exercise your capacity to conceptually, or mentally, decenter. Each time you put your internal change of perspective into out-loud conversation you practice your ability to use decentering to build associational linkages in human communication. Other things being equal, the more comfortable you become with mental decentering, the greater the likelihood that you will develop into an effective public speaker.

☐ Contrast and Public Speaking

As discussed earlier, self-concept and decentering both seem to flow from contrast. Contrast can be consciously used to our advantage in developing public speaking skills. What we are recommending is the *conscious* use of contrast in developing your public speaking skills. Perhaps you can appreciate the benefits of the conscious use of contrast by looking at some of the ideas given at the end of the last section where we suggested talking to yourself from differing points of view. Contrast was at work there when we contrasted a city dweller with a country dweller and when we contrasted a positive and a negative position. Contrast is an easy and readily available technique. Consider one of the important roles contrast plays in human life, that of providing stimulation and variety. In order to retain an active interest in our environment, each of us requires stimulation or novelty. The ordinary pattern of our day can become boring if endlessly repeated; it needs to be punctuated with a variety of stimuli—new events, new people, new ideas. These new stimuli provide a contrast with too similar a pattern and keep us interested in life. When everything is the same, we tend to become lethargic and lose interest. On the other hand, suppose we are bombarded by many different stimuli all at the same time. As we're working at our desk the phone starts ringing, someone is trying to talk to us, a piercing whistle is blowing, and we spill a cup of coffee all over the desk. So much is happening that we can't concentrate on any one thing. There is no contrast because everything is calling for our attention at once. In such a situation we may simply withdraw and block everything out. Indeed we need enough contrast to keep us stimulated, but not so much variety that we will be unable to focus on the things that really merit our attention. We need to be able to differentiate, to contrast one thing with another, but we must still maintain a comfortable relationship between too much variety and too much predictability. In Chapter Five we will suggest some ideas on how to maintain this comfortable relationship in public speaking as well as in other human communication settings.

Contrast is important in life in general and in public speaking in particular. Here are some examples of how the conscious use of contrast can help you in improving your public speaking. One situation in which the use of contrast helps is when you're presenting difficult concepts. When explaining something that is difficult to grasp, try telling your listeners what the subject under consideration contrasts with, what is its opposite. For many years one of us worked with the concept of "higher mental processes" and found that the concept was difficult to explain to others. This difficulty, however, was resolved by the simple practice of explaining what was meant by "lower mental processes" and then contrasting the "lower" with "higher" mental processes (Dance and Larson, 1972, 1976). Contrast can also be profitably used to enhance your public speaking performance skills. Some speakers find it difficult to establish a comfortable rate of delivery in giving a speech. They either speak too fast for the audience to comfortably keep up with them or they speak so slowly that they lose the audience's attention. Contrast offers a means of getting a sense of the most appropriate rate of delivery. Get a tape recorder and record this exercise. First, deliver a specific passage of a speech as fast as you possibly can. Then, deliver the same passage as slowly as you can. You are contrasting "too fast" with "too slow." Play the tape back and begin working toward a delivery rate comfortable for you as the speaker and acceptable to a first-time listener. We believe that you will be pleased with the results of consciously using contrast in the preparation and rehearsal of your speeches.

☐ The Functions and Purposes of Spoken Language

In this chapter we've been considering the part your past experience plays in preparing you to speak in public. You've had a lot of past experience in talking. Exactly what difference does the ability to talk, to use spoken language, make to us as human beings? If the ability to use spoken language does make any difference, how does that difference relate to public speaking?

There is some research that suggests that certain important behaviors of human beings are the result of the human capacity for spoken language (Dance, 1967; Dance and Larson, 1972, 1976). These behaviors have been called "functions" of spoken language. The functions of spoken language are (1) the linking of the individual in a uniquely human manner with other individuals and with the environment; (2) the development of the individual's higher mental processes or complex cognition; and (3) the regulation of the individual's behavior, first by others (such as parents), then by himself or herself, and finally the individual's regulation of the behavior of others. Although the study of the functions of spoken language is interesting and worthwhile in itself, we are only interested in functions here because of their relationship to the purposes of public speaking. Purposes flow from functions but are not the same as functions. Let's use contrast to try and clarify this function/purpose relationship. Functions are automatic and need not be intended by the individual. In contrast, purposes are always intentional. Perhaps the purpose of our public speech is to inform the audience about a new product. This purpose of informing is "intended" by you, the speaker. Perhaps we are giving a persuasive speech in which we "intend" to persuade someone to contribute to a charitable cause. We intend to convince someone of the correctness of our argument and this intention gives our speech a purpose. Purpose entails intent on the part of the public speaker. Intent to do what?

Recall that in Chapter One we commented on the long history of public speaking as an area of study and practice. Many scholars and public speaking practitioners have considered the purposes of public speaking. Traditionally public speaking is intended to serve the following general (sometimes called "rhetorical") purposes:

1. **To inform:** The speech to inform has as its goal the audience's enlightenment as to who, what, where, when, how, and/or why.
2. **To convince:** The speech to convince has as its goal the audience's acceptance of the speaker's argument.
3. **To persuade:** The speech to persuade has as its goal the audience's active support and pursuit of the speaker's recommendation(s).
4. **To entertain:** The speech to entertain has as its goal the audience's enjoyment of the presentation and of the occasion.

Each of the general purposes is defined by audience outcomes, by how the audience is supposed to respond to the speech rather than to the speaker's behavior. From the very beginning of speech preparation it is important for the speaker to try and hear things through the audience's ears, to plan with the audience response in mind. Each public speech usually contains elements of more than one of these general purposes, but one of the purposes is almost always dominant. A speaker must decide at the outset the primary purpose of the speech.

Preparing a public speech requires five general steps:

1. Choosing a topic and deciding how you will approach that topic for this particular audience on this particular occasion
2. Planning how you will arrange the material for the most effective presentation
3. Determining the language you will use in your presentation
4. Committing the general elements of your speech in outline form, and sometimes specific wording, to memory
5. Rehearsing and delivering the speech

The five steps just listed probably seem like just plain common sense (with the possible exception of memory). In a way they are. These five steps are among the oldest of the instructions given to aspiring public speakers. The book, *Rhetorica ad Herennium,* published around 86 B.C., listed the same five steps. Cicero, a great Roman politician and orator, possibly the book's author, listed five aspects, or parts, of rhetoric: (1) *inventio* (the discovery of topics and materials); (2) *dispositio* (the arrangement of the materials); (3) *elocutio* (style or the choice of language); (4) *memoria* (memory); and (5) *pronuntiatio* (the delivery of the speech) (Thonssen and Baird, 1948, pp. 77–80). The word "rhetoric" was used by Cicero to refer to what we now usually call public speaking. The five steps are known as the Ciceronian canon (or rule) of public speaking. We listed them here to help you recognize and appreciate the importance of the combination of common sense, scholarly reflection, history, public speaking practice, and contemporary theory available to you in your effort to become an effective public speaker.

☐ Summary

Remote preparation consists of all your life experiences up to the point where you begin to prepare a specific speech for a specific audience on a specific occasion. Remote preparation is an important resource for meeting immediate needs. There is some research which suggests that speech is central to the development and maintenance of an individual's self-concept and self-esteem. There is also research which states that it is through his or her oral/aural experiences that a human child develops the capacity for differentiation and the sense of contrast. Decentering is the process of shifting from an egocentric view of the universe to a view in which varying perspectives are recognized and considered. Decentering helps us to perceive perceptual and conceptual differences between our own point of view and the point of view of others. Decentering is the source of successful association, and association rather than transference is essential to effective human communication. Heightened emotion suppresses decentering.

Spoken language performs the functions of linking, mentation, and regulation; these form the base for the purposes of human communication in general and of public speaking in particular. The general purposes of public speaking are to inform, to convince, to persuade, and to entertain. The informative speech has as its goal the audience's enlightenment as to who, what, where, when, how, and why. The speech to convince has as its purpose the audience's acceptance of the speaker's argument. The persuasive speech has as its purpose the audience's active support and pursuit of the speaker's recommendations. The speech to entertain has as its goal the audience's enjoyment of the presentation and of the occasion. Present-day advice on the general steps of speech preparation is similar to that given in 86 B.C. by Cicero in what is known as the Ciceronian canon of rhetoric. The Ciceronian canon consists of five elements: invention, arrangement, style, memory, and delivery. History, tradition, past and present public speaking experience, and contemporary human communication theory all may be used in learning to be an effective public speaker. The organization of topics in this new primer follows what seems to be the natural order in which most public speakers put together their speeches. Your own past experience is the natural beginning from which you should start to plot out your speech plan. Your most fully stocked reserve is your own life experience—use it! The place to start in preparing a public speech is with your*self.* Make an inventory of what you already know, believe, and feel about the probable speech subject, the probable speech audience, and the probable speech occasion. Consciously decenter to the audience. This kind of inventory can be made while walking, driving, eating, or just sitting. Don't leave the inventory to chance—decide to do it, do it, and make notes of what you come up with during your remote preparation inventory. Keep these notes handy for further use in the immediate preparation of your speech. We started this chapter with a quote from a poem by Alfred Noyes. The quote says "There's a magic in the distance." We believe that there is a magic in remote preparation, a magic that will transform past experiences into material suitable for use in today's speeches.

Exercises ■

1 Throughout this chapter we've stressed the importance of understanding self before speaking with others. In order to help you in understanding yourself, prepare an essay on the topic *Who Am I?* Be as specific and concise as possible. There is no need or call for intimate self-disclosure in this essay; its purpose is to help you in centering on your personal point of view of reality.

2 Making notes on your results, interview three adolescents, three adults, and three people over 60 years of age. Ask each person the same question: *"Who are you?"* Try not to lead the respondent in any direction in giving his or her answer. When collecting this data dress neatly, behave professionally, and assure the respondent that the data is for a classroom assignment and will be treated confidentially.

What you are investigating is the degree to which individuals in different age groups identify with varying roles. Roles are a product of decentering and as such are often a measure of an individual's ability to use association in human communication. Do your respondents simply give you their names, their job titles, their professional identifications, or their family roles (i.e., grandmother, uncle), or are their answers more complicated, taking into consideration a number of roles played as well as other personal values?

Examine your data, make whatever generalizations you believe the data supports, prepare a simple outline, and present your material in an informative classroom speech 3 to 5 minutes long.

3 Pick a specific topic from the editorial page of a current newspaper. Using only your own past experiences (remote preparation), prepare an inventory of how your experiences affect how you would present a speech on this particular topic before your class. Use this remote preparation inventory as a model for such inventories directed to future public speeches.

4 Pick a specific point concerning a sport or hobby with which you have had personal experience (e.g., the platoon system, computer games) and give examples of how through the use of association you would try to communicate that specific point to two people with backgrounds substantially different from your own. Specify how the two people's backgrounds differ from yours (e.g., perhaps they are from a different culture, maybe even a different planet, or are much older). Use contrast in preparing this assignment. Check with your instructor on suggested speech length.

Bibliographic References ■

Dance, F. E. X.: "The Functions of Speech Communciation as an Integrative Concept in the Field of Communication," in *Proceedings of the XV International Congress of Communications*. The International Institute of Communications, Genoa, Italy, 1967.

————: "The Acoustic Trigger to Conceptualizaton," *Health Communication and Informatics,* vol. 5, no. 4, 1979, pp. 204–213.

———— and C. E. Larson: *Speech Communication: Concepts and Behaviors,* Holt, Rinehart and Winston, New York, 1972.

———— and ————: *The Functions of Human Communication: A Theoretical Approach,* Holt, Rinehart and Winston, New York, 1976.

Johnson, J. R.: "The Relationship Between Speech Communication Egocentrism and Reading Achievement," unpublished doctoral dissertation. University of Denver, 1978.

————: "Egocentric Spoken Language and Reading Achievement: An Examination of Relationship," *Communication Education,* vol. 31, no. 2, April 1982, pp. 115–123.

Piaget, J.: *The Language and Thought of the Child,* The World Publishing Co., Cleveland, 1955.

Thonssen, L., and A. C. Baird: *Speech Criticism.* Ronald Press, New York, 1948.

Zak-Dance, C. C.: "The Differential Effects of a Child's Primary Mode of Human Communication on the Child's Self-concept Development," unpublished doctoral dissertation, University of Denver, 1979.

Recommended Reading ■

Clavell, James: *Shogun: A Novel of Japan,* Atheneum, New York, 1979. In this entrancing novel the American reader is given an opportunity of trying to decenter to a completely distinct culture.

Immediate Preparation

Chapter Three

"And in today already walks tomorrow."
Samuel Taylor Coleridge

"My interest is in the future because I am going to spend the rest of my life there."
Charles F. Kettering

Whereas the past is the subject matter of your remote preparation, the future is the concern of your immediate preparation. You are going to give a speech. You know when you are expected to give the speech. Now you have to focus your energies and your intellect in preparing for that speech, which may indeed be in the future—but a future that will all too soon be now. Knowing that you are scheduled to give a public speech not only reminds you of the need to prepare but often induces a state of anxiety and apprehension. In this chapter we tell you how to transform unpleasant feelings of anxiety into enthusiasm, how to choose an appropriate topic, how to use decentering to analyze your audience, and how to gauge and use expectations in immediate preparation. We also discuss the different modes of presenting a public speech, the role of memory in public speaking, the putting together of a preliminary specific purpose for your speech, and the importance of keeping good notes of the whole process of speech preparation.

☐ Stage Fright

Almost from the first moment you learn that you are really expected to get up and speak in public, certain bodily and mental reactions begin to show up and seem to become more and more noticeable the closer you get to the actual time of presenting your speech.

Your heart begins to beat faster.
Your mouth seems to "dry up."
You begin perspiring more.
Your stomach feels a little "queasy."
Your arms and legs begin to tremble slightly.
Your hands shake.
Your voice quavers.
You seem incapable of fine motor control.
You have a difficult time keeping your mind off the upcoming public speaking situation.

Your usually adroit and flexible intellect seems fixated on the most ordinary and concrete matters, such as your hands, or the color of the ink you are writing with, or the slowness with which time passes.

You can't imagine how an audience could possibly be interested in anything you might have to say to them.

These reactions are reactions to stress, and it is these reactions or responses to stress to which people are referring when they use the term "stage fright." If you look the list over, you will recognize that very few of the behaviors are confined to speech making but are symptoms of concern and stress associated with almost any new, untried, and challenging situation.

Remember when you started a new job, or the first time you drove a car by yourself, or tried skiing? In any of these novel situations you probably had some of the same feelings of nervousness and uncertainty that are associated with early experiences in giving public speeches. Why? Because as we suggested in Chapter Two, most of us draw upon our past experience to deal with new situations and in some new situations the organization of experience which had served us well for years and years seems inadequate to the challenge of so very many new, small, but demanding physical behaviors. There are just too many new things calling for our conscious attention all at the same time, and this seemingly excessive demand on our abilities calls forth the stress responses. In skiing you are up on top of a mountain looking down a very slick slope and trying to remember to keep your knees bent, your poles off the ground, your skis parallel, and so forth. In horseback riding you are instructed to keep your heels down, your chin up, your knees tight, your hands close together. When driving a car alone for the first time you have to watch the road, make certain the car is in the correct gear, keep alert to the actions of other drivers, let up slowly on the clutch while simultaneously and slowly giving the car some gas with the other foot, and so forth. Once you've had practical experience on your job, or driving the car, or skiing, excessive feelings of nervousness tend to disappear. One reason for this is that with practice you begin to integrate those numerous activities which seemed novel into overall and predictable bodily responses. In driving the car you get control of shifting smoothly, of checking the rearview mirror, of using the brake, clutch, and gas pedals in synchrony; eventually you give almost no attention at all to these separate actions and you simply "drive" your car.

We've never seen or heard a public speaking student who had all the previously listed symptoms at the same time. In fact a few people may have only one or two of them. All of us have experienced stage fright at some time. Because the public speaking situation changes with each audience, occasion, and speech, there is always enough novelty in it that many of us experience some degree of stage fright every time we give a public speech. We use the word "experienced," rather than "suffered" because the constellation of feelings and bodily responses labeled stage fright is a normal experience that has many positive attributes. It is an experience that can make us more effective public speakers. The presence of some degree of nervous concern actually is beneficial since such heightened nervous activity adds some sparkle to the eye, heightens the color of the cheeks, makes you so conscious of things like posture and breathing that it enhances general bodily tone—as a matter of fact, some degree of speech anxiety makes most speakers a little more physically attractive than usual. We don't want to eliminate any and all concerns, but we want to maintain controlled concern. The total absence of public speaking anxiety may signal more serious problems than signaled by its presence, problems such as total insensitivity to the importance of the speaker's responsibility to the audience or of a general lack of appropriate responses to social situations.

As with all stressful situations, the more elements of the public speaking situation you can successfully integrate and control, the better you will be able to cope with the challenges of the public speaking experience. As you become more comfortable with the various demands of the speaking situation, you simultaneously raise your "coping quotient," and as you raise your coping quotient you automatically lower your anxiety level.

☐ The Coping Quotient

The *coping quotient* is our label for the degree to which a speaker is able to cope with the variety of responses called for by the public speaking situation. Beginning public speakers have to work at raising their coping quotient. Even accomplished public speakers will encounter new speaking situations which challenge their ability to cope. The novice speaker might be greatly distressed by having a breeze blow the speech outline off the lectern. The veteran speaker might handle the same incident calmly, even humorously, but might be disconcerted by heckling from the audience (an unusual happening, but one that does occur!).

Raising Your Coping Quotient

We just said, a couple of paragraphs ago, that your coping quotient is raised as you become more comfortable with the various demands of the public speaking situation, and that as you raise your coping quotient your anxiety level is automatically lowered. Now we recommend four simple techniques you can use to actually raise your coping quotient. To help you remember them, we have coined the term "PIER." PIER is an acronym composed of the first letters of the words *prepare, idea, experience,* and *relax.* Just as the function of a pier is to support some type of structure (such as a bridge or a highway overpass), the four concepts we'll describe can help provide a foundation enabling you to cope successfully as a public speaker.

Prepare

In public speaking, as in most other challenging activities, preparation is essential. The better we are prepared, the less fearful, anxious, or nervous we will be since we will not be confronted by the totally unexpected and we will have considered during our preparation the variety of challenges we will be facing when actually delivering the speech. It has been suggested that the first three, and most important, watchwords for successful public speaking are (1) prepare, (2) prepare, and (3) prepare. With sufficient preparation there will be relatively few things that will be able to throw us off our stride, while with inadequate preparation the least little unexpected event might totally unnerve us. One of the things that causes public speakers to freeze is knowing that they are unprepared—obviously, preparation takes care of this concern.

Idea

Concentrate on the ideas you are trying to communicate to your audience, rather than on yourself, and you will find your coping quotient rising nicely. If you are really involved in the material you are trying to tell your audience about, you will have correspondingly less concern about how you look or sound. When we are neglecting to concentrate on our ideas and are instead concentrating on whether the audience likes our clothes, or our tone of voice, or our gestures, we tend to become frazzled. During Christmas season, have you ever come upon street musicians playing carols and collecting money for a charitable cause? Many of those players are not professional musicians. They could be immobilized if they were concerned about every note played being perfect. How can they bring themselves to play on a crowded corner? Because they are more concerned with their charitable mission, their ideas, than how they sound or appear to the public. Cosmetic concerns tend to hamper our decentering and force us back into an infantile egocentrism. In fact, this kind of centering upon our own person can work against us. Have you ever noticed how when someone is going to take your picture and commands, "Smile!," you find your smile being forced and unnatural? When, during a speech, you concentrate on your smile, the same thing can happen, the smile can look forced and false. The same holds true for posture and gestures in public speaking. When speaking, concentrate on the idea or ideas you are trying to have your audience understand, or accept, or enjoy. Substituting idea-consciousness for self-consciousness can help you achieve a naturalness and an ease which some overly egocentric public speakers never acquire.

Experience

Repeated public speaking experiences will raise your coping quotient, just as repeated ski trips will raise your coping quotient for skiing. The more often you speak in public the easier, or at the very least, the less threatening, it will become. You'll find that the fundamental skills will become increasingly routine and that you will be able to deal with the unexpected more easily and with greater confidence. Most audiences want the same thing out of a public speaking experience—enjoyment and satisfaction: enjoyment of the experience and satisfaction with the quality of the ideas presented. Most audience members arrive at a speech hoping the speaker will succeed and wishing the speaker well in his or her efforts (since if the speaker does well, presumably the audience members will also have had a profitable time). An audience is not usually a many-headed monster just waiting to gobble up some poor speaker but, on the contrary, is composed of individuals hoping for a good (or at least not a boring) time. The fact that audiences are, for the most part, benign should be a comfort for the beginning speaker but should never be used as an excuse for sloppy speech making. As you gain more and more experience, you will find the speaking event becoming more and more enjoyable since your coping quotient will be getting higher and higher. With each successful speaking experience you will become increasingly confident, and this confidence will itself assist in making future speeches successful. Experience guided by preparation and permeated with idea consciousness will help you raise your coping quotient and become a better public speaker.

Relax

It may seem impossible to relax when the very thought of giving a speech makes you anxious. However, you can do a lot to lower your general anxiety level so that it won't interfere with giving an effective speech. Here are some specific relaxation techniques to try:

1. To feel what it's like to be physically relaxed, try the following exercise. Sit down in a comfortable chair. Grip the arms of the chair with all of your strength and at the same time push your feet against the floor, try to feel the floor through your shoes, try to push the floor down an inch or so. Grit your teeth, set your jaw hard, and shut your eyes as tight as you can. Make every muscle tense.
   Now, hold this position for a full 30 seconds.
   Finally, *let go!*
   Slump; let your arms hang by the sides of your chair.
   Rest quietly and savor the luxurious feeling of complete relaxation.
2. Remember some happy moments from your past—a day at the beach basking in the sun, a restful drive through the rolling countryside. Recall times when you had no worries and felt peaceful and relaxed.
3. Listen to some of your favorite relaxing and quiet music. Read a reflective and peaceful poem.
4. While sitting let your head hang forward, limply on your chest. Now roll your head—slowly—only your right shoulder, keep relaxed. Let your head slowly roll backward, then onto your left shoulder, and finally let it come to rest on your chest again. Always stay as relaxed and loose as possible. After just relaxing a few minutes, sit up again.
5. Yawn. Yawning is an extremely effective means of relaxing your throat and vocal musculature. Next time you involuntary yawn try to be sensitive to what's going on—your whole throat tenses up and then relaxes, a true contrast in tenseness. With a little practice putting yourself in the appropriate mood, you will be able to yawn voluntarily. A relaxed vocal musculature almost always makes your voice sound better, reduces tension, and helps you feel more relaxed overall.

The PIER formula can help you build confidence about your ability as a speaker and reduce your anxiety about speaking. Using the PIER formula will raise your coping quotient. It's also helpful to remember that in public speaking, as in many other daily activities, we are often our own severest critics. Our own nervousness may seem almost disabling to us. To others, however, it may not even be noticeable. Your own nervousness may appear to others as enviable energy.

☐ Selecting a Topic

Whether you have eagerly accepted the challenge, become used to the idea, or just given up the fight against the inevitable, you have gotten past the initial concern about giving a public speech and now face the problem of what you are going to talk about. Most new speakers wonder, "What new ideas can I present?" "What do I have to talk about that will interest an audience?" How does one choose a topic? Since topics may either be *chosen for you* (mandated), or freely *chosen by you,* we will consider both kinds.

Mandated Topics

The choice of an overall topic is not always the speaker's decision. The topic may be dictated, or mandated, by the occasion, by the instructor, or by the audience. If you were asked to give a talk at the tenth reunion of your high school graduating class, your speech would pretty much have to deal with something related to that occasion. In a course your speech may be mandated by the instructor, or by an exercise in your textbook. Throughout your school career you will be asked to present papers or speeches in many courses; such presentations are mandated.

In addition, the overall topic may be mandated by an organization or person that has invited you to speak. When responding to an invitation to speak, it is important that you find out as specifically as possible what it is the person or group hopes to see accomplished as a result of your presentation. There are occasions when your host has goals for your speech that are in addition to the audience's goals (the audience may simply wish to be entertained, your host may wish the audience to be entertained but also to learn something). The more detail you can get from the host concerning the host's or group's needs and expectations, the easier it will be for you to prepare your remarks.

As you develop your public speaking experience, you may find that often it is your own past record and reputation that dictates the choice of a general topic. Perhaps you've earned a reputation as an authority on the role of political organizations in undergraduate life, or the place of athletics in a liberal arts college, or how the honors student views required courses, or the value of speech courses for business majors. In each of these instances it is natural that your topic choice will be heavily influenced by your own expertise.

Having a topic mandated may seem somewhat restrictive. However, it has the advantage of relieving the speaker of having to make the overall topic determination and assists in providing an insight into audience expectations.

We have consistently referred to mandated overall, or general, topics. This is because even in the case of mandated topics there are still many aspects of the topic that are up to the speaker's judgment. Given an overall topic the speaker must decide on the specific focus he or she will take in the speech, the specific selection of issues, the degree of support needed, the appropriate use of humor, whether or not to use audiovisual aids, and so forth.

Freely Chosen Topics

Typically, most beginning speakers have difficulty when they have complete freedom in choosing a topic. In some instances the beginner is tempted to talk about what at first seems to be an "easy" topic, such as "How to Shine Shoes." But it is pretty difficult to say anything novel or interesting about shining shoes, and consequently what might seem at first to be an easy subject instead becomes a difficult and boring one.

Ordinarily a speaker should try to select a topic of importance. Important topics are topics that make a difference for an individual or for a group ("Dealing with Death," "Cheating"). Something quite important, such as the problems caused by vanity and pomposity, can be treated in a light manner. Certainly listening to Joan Rivers or Bill Cosby talk about everyday matters can illustrate our own vanity and tendency to take ourselves too seriously. Humorous speakers can take something quite trivial and elevate it to a subject of mirth. Trivial topics are topics that deal with commonplace subjects that usually don't make much difference to anyone ("How to Make a Toothpick," "The Art of Snapping a Shoeshine Cloth"). There are times and circumstances when triviality is the order of the day such as at "roasts" and similar occasions. When choosing a topic, ask yourself how important the topic is to the members of the audience.

A more serious problem for many beginning public speakers is their tendency to choose a topic that is too general. Consider a 5-minute speech on "The Role of Evil Throughout the History of Western Civilization." Perhaps a very long speech, or a series of long speeches could present such a topic effectively—usually after a lifetime of study on the part of the speaker—but it is not a suitable topic for a 5-minute speech by a beginning speaker.

☐ Narrowing a Topic

How can you steer your way between choosing a banal topic and choosing an overwhelmingly large or complex topic. One way is to be precise in your choice of a topic. Narrowing the focus of your topic to fit the audience and the occasion can help you uncover novel and interesting approaches to subjects that at first don't appear promising. The following example deals with picking a topic for a written essay but easily applies to choosing a speech topic. The quote, which helps illustrate the importance of precision, is from *Zen and the Art of Motorcycle Maintenance,* a novel by Robert M. Pirsig (1974). In this excerpt we are listening to the reflections of a college teacher of freshman English in Bozeman, Montana, helping a student pick a suitable topic for a class essay.

He'd been innovating extensively. He'd been having trouble with students who had nothing to say. . . . One of them . . . wanted to write a five-hundred word essay about the United States. He was used to the sinking feeling that comes from statements like this, and suggested without disparagement that she narrow it down to just Bozeman.

When the paper came due she didn't have it and was quite upset. She had tried and tried but just couldn't think of anything to say. . . .

It just stumped him. Now HE couldn't think of anything to say. A silence occurred, and then a peculiar answer: "Narrow it down to the MAIN STREET of Bozeman." It was a stroke of insight.

She nodded dutifully and went out. But just before her next class she came back in REAL distress, tears this time, distress that had obviously been there for a long time. She still couldn't think of anything to say, and couldn't understand why, if she couldn't think of anything about ALL of Bozeman, she should be able to think of something about just one street.

He was furious. "You're not LOOKING!" he said. A memory came back of his own dismissal from the Unversity for having TOO MUCH to say. For every fact there is an INFINITY of hypotheses. The more you LOOK the more you SEE. She really wasn't looking and yet somehow didn't understand this.

He told her angrily, "Narrow it down to the FRONT of ONE building on the main street of Bozeman. The Opera House. Start with the upper left-hand brick."

Her eyes . . . opened wide.

She came in the next class with a puzzled look and handed him a five-thousand-word essay on the front of the Opera House on the main street of Bozeman, Montana. "I sat in the hamburger stand across the street," she said, "and started writing about the first brick, and the second brick, and then by the third brick it all started to come and I couldn't stop. They thought I was crazy and they kept kidding me, but here it all is. I don't understand it."

This is a nice illustration of what we've been talking about. At first the composition student failed to understand that by looking closely at something specific she would be able to sharpen her powers of observation, perception, and creativity. By carefully focusing on a specific target, she could see things that she didn't even know were there, things that started streams of thought culminating in the required essay.

This technique can work for you in picking a speech topic. Suppose you are a psychology major and you are interested in the subject of perception. You only have 5 minutes for your speech and perception is an area within the field of psychology that has a large body of literature and theory. It would be impossible to cover the whole subject of perception in 5 minutes. However, you could illustrate the application of some principles of perception to the audience. You could either tell them about or demonstrate the exercise where someone runs through the class waving a gun and someone else in the class falls to the floor. How many people saw the person waving the gun shoot the person who fell to the floor? You could make the point that we often see what we expect to see regardless of what actually took place. Even this simple demonstration would have to move very fast to allow enough time for you to make sense of it in your speech—but it could be done in 5 minutes if carefully planned, rehearsed, and presented. This would be just one point about perception, but a point that might make a real impression on your audience. Or suppose your major interest is in human language. In a 5-minute speech you could help the audience understand the impact of language on their everyday lives simply by describing some common objects in different ways, a steak becomes a "piece of dead cow," a mushroom a "fungus." What to some is "religious commitment," to others is "fanaticism." Where some see "overtures to peace," others see "war mongering." What to some is simply "doing it the easiest way," others classify as "cheating."

The interaction of *speaker, audience,* and *occasion* are the most important determinants of a speech topic. We've already discussed the speaker and will do so throughout the text. Later on we will discuss the occasion as it relates to topic choice. Now let's talk at greater length about the second element, the audience.

☐ Audience Analysis

Audience analysis is a very powerful factor in successful public speaking. On the basis of an adequate analysis a speaker may choose to change almost everything about the speech—the topic, the support provided, the length of the speech, the style of language, the use of humor, even the style of delivery. The audience analysis can affect the speaker's choice of general purpose (inform, convince, persuade, entertain) or the way in which the general purpose is expressed in the speech's specific purpose (discussed in Chapter Five). If you succeed with your audience, you succeed as a public speaker. If you fail with your audience, you fail as a public speaker. You speech may be filled with good ideas, clothed in elegant and appropriate language, delivered with verve and sincerity—but if the audience doesn't like it, if the audience doesn't consider itself informed, or convinced, or persuaded, or entertained, then the speech, as a public speech, is a failure. There is no point in arguing with the audience. If, after you are finished speaking you become aware that the audience has rejected your speech, there is no point in telling them that they really missed the point, or that they didn't understand the wisdom of your remarks. You have finished your speech and the audience has made their judgment. If you are lucky, you may get another chance to talk to the same audience (such as in a classroom setting) and try to succeed where first you failed. Usually, it's a one-time shot and you get one chance to succeed.

You need to know as much about your audience as you reasonably can. The more you know about them the better you'll be able to tailor your speech to their needs and expectations and the more likely you'll succeed as a public speaker. What is the best technique for learning about your audience? Through decentering. You already know the fundamental secret for good audience analysis. Decentering. We talked about decentering in Chapter Two, pp. 33–35. Decentering involves taking the perceptual and conceptual viewpoint of others, and it is a uniquely human capability. Another technique we can use in audience analysis is empathy. *Empathy* involves taking the emotional point of view of some other creature; it is a capability we share with other animals. When we can feel the sorrow of someone else, or his or her pain, or joy, we are using empathy. Whereas decentering is mainly perceptual and conceptual, empathy is dominantly emotional. By using both decentering and empathy you can make some important analytical judgments concerning your potential audience since you can consider both how they feel about something emotionally and how they think about something conceptually.

Your audience is made up of people, and people are fascinating. Part of what makes them so fascinating is the blend of endless variety with enduring similarities that we find in them. There has never been and there will never be two people with exactly the same experiences, values, moods, appearances, knowledge, likes, and dislikes. Yet even with all their differences people still share important similarities. They all need nourishment in order to survive, they all need shelter and protection from animal predators (whether of our own or of a different species). In order to grow up physically and emotionally healthy, all individuals need affection and acceptance from others as well as the opportunity to fully develop their own capabilities. These common needs and desires create basic similarities among people regardless of their age, sex, race, or nationality. Yet the forces of differentiation are also at work from the moment of conception. Differences of food, parental affection, cultural norms, education, varying personal experiences all punch and pull those similarities into the wonderful and startling diversity that is humanity.

An additional factor that influences both similarity and diversity is spoken language. All normal human infants vocalize, acquire speech, and then manifest their speech in one of thousands of languages. The characteristics of vocalization and speech create a base of similarity which both shapes and is shaped by the specific language spoken and makes public speaking such a universally important technique of influencing human behavior.

Use decentering to know as much as possible about your fellow humans since the better we know them the better we will be able to understand their point of view and to empathize with them. Learn more about people through conversation, observation, and the vicarious experience that you can gain through various print and electronic media. Watch people and how they react to the various experiences they are having. Are they reacting much as you would react, or differently? If differently, why? Try putting yourself in their place, seeing things from their point of view. If you are going to speak to an audience composed of members of a nationality different from your own and you don't know much about that national group, find out about them. Read, go to a restaurant that serves their national dishes, ask among your friends to see if any of them has insights into the group. If your audience is a religious group, find out how their religion is similar to and different from (contrasts with) your own. If your audience is composed of people of one political conviction, find out what the members of that political group believe and what issues are of most concern to them. The advantages of speaking several languages also become obvious when analyzing your audience.

Because different languages code experiences somewhat differently, the more languages you are familiar with the better you will be able to see how the same things look differently to different language groups. Finally, if you are speaking to a class composed of majors in a specific area, such as business, or speech communication, or psychology, try to assess how people with that particular interest will relate to topics you know something about and which you are interested in sharing with others.

In addition to the techniques already mentioned, there are sources of general information about the population. *Demography* is the statistical study of human populations, their size and density, their distribution, and their vital statistics. Demographic information is available in the reports of the United States census, and in volumes such as *The Statistical Abstract of the United States, World Almanac,* and *Reader's Digest Almanac and Yearbook.* Such general information can be useful in assessing the overall composition of an audience and how that might affect your speech topic. Suppose you are interested in giving a speech on bilingualism, the idea of having a student population learn in two languages while going to school. Demographic data can give you a good idea as to what language other than English would likely be spoken in various locations you might speak. People's economic level often affects how they look at various government programs such as public transportation or welfare. You can find fairly specific regional economic information through demographic sources.

Public opinion surveys are also sources of audience analysis information. Survey results may include up-to-the-minute information on how the survey population feels or thinks about current world and national questions, the national economy, civil rights, womens' rights, what TV shows they are watching, what products they buy. Newspapers and magazines often feature public opinion surveys along with interpretations of the survey results. Some survey organizations even provide toll-free telephone numbers which you can call and hear a taped report of current survey questions, responses, and analyses. We have just called one number (The Merit Opinion Center) and heard a 5-minute report on how the U.S. survey population feels about President Reagan at the midpoint of his term of office. The results are broken down into a number of categories including respondent age, economic level, educational background, and type of employment.

Thus far we've been talking about analyzing general audience characteristics. In an actual public speaking situation it is likely that you will be able to zero in on a more specific audience. Your public speaking opportunities are not going to be limited to a public speaking course. You will take other courses in which you will be requested to make presentations. You are probably a member of a number of groups—religious, political, athletic, study—any of which might ask you to speak on some topic or other. If you accept any kind of office in a group (president, secretary, treasurer) you will have reports to make. In addition, as you gain experience and expertise, you may well be invited to speak before other organizations. Suppose you are contacted for a speaking engagement. You want to know the general composition of the expected audience. You would like to be aware of the audience's *knowledge* or familiarity with your topic. Knowing something about the audience's *interests* and *concerns* could help you in speech preparation. The audience's *attitudes, values,* and *predispositions* will also affect their expectations and should be of interest to you. Here are some questions to ask the person contacting you. The answers to these questions will assist you in audience analysis and topic selection.

- Is this an educational session for the audience? (Do they expect or want to learn something?)
- Is this a motivational situation for the audience? (Do they want to hear something that makes them feel good?)
- What result does the arranger of the speech hope to achieve as a result of your speech? (Sometimes the person setting up the speech has goals, like increasing worker productivity, of which the general audience is unaware.)
- Are you expected to speak on a specific, preselected topic?
- How long is the speech supposed to be? (Many programs run on very tight time schedules. It is important to know how long you will be expected to speak and to keep very close to the time requested.)
- Will there be time for questions and answers following the speech? (It's better to know from the outset whether or not you are going to be expected to answer questions from the audience. If you are, you might want to read the suggestions in Chapter Eight on situational speeches.)
- How many are expected to be present? (Differences in audience size should make a difference in presentational style—more about this in Chapter Seven.)
- What is expected to be the approximate proportion of males to females in the audience? (This is a simple question which helps the speaker make decisions regarding the type of illustrations that might be most suitable.)
- What is the general educational level of the audience?
- Who have been some of the speakers who have addressed this audience in the recent past, and upon what topics? (The answer to this one can give you a good idea of the kind of programs that this audience seems to enjoy. It also alerts you to possible overlap with previous speakers' presentations.)
- Can arrangements for audiovisual aids be made if you need them?
- How will the room be set up? (Will you be expected to speak from a head table during a banquet? Or will the room be set up in typical classroom fashion? These answers will give you some idea of any physical problems that could affect your coping quotient.)
- Where will the speech be given, on what date, at what time, and when would they like you to arrive? (The answers to most of these inquiries have self-evident importance. This last question, for example, lets you know if there may be prespeech festivities to which you are invited. You should always plan to arrive at least a half hour before you are scheduled to speak so that you can get a feeling for the audience and for the speaking situation.)

Even though you are a beginning speaker, there may be times that you find yourself being asked to speak in a situation where some money may be involved. Here are two questions which you might ask if such a case materializes.

- Is there an honorarium? ("Honorarium" is the word usually used to refer to a speaker's payment. An honorarium is given in cases where it is not customary for a specific price to be set and the amount paid is governed by tradition and good taste. These days most speakers are not shy about mentioning a specific dollar amount for their services—but the traditional name "honorarium" still hangs on. Service clubs such as Rotary, Lions, Kiwanis, and most charitable organizations seldom offer honoraria. It doesn't hurt to ask this question if there is a real possibility of a fee being involved. Sometimes you may be asked what you charge and you should have an answer ready—always err on the low side since you can always raise your fee if you get too busy.)
- If there are expenses involved (such as travel or overnight accommodations), whom should you bill for repayment?

Keep careful notes on the questions you ask the arranger and on the answers given. You will probably use these notes in the process of speech preparation.

Whereas questions are useful in getting information about your audience, the absolutely best information would be having some firsthand experience with the group. For instance, if you are a member of a class and if you are speaking before the class, you have loads of direct experience upon which to draw in your audience analysis. If you haven't had direct experience with the audience, then talk with someone who has. If you know someone who knows someone, ask. If you have names of some people who have spoken to this audience in the past, call them up and ask about the group. Always remember that people see and hear things differently. Secondhand information although valuable should always be carefully evaluated and not taken as cold fact.

Your personal predispositions and assumptions can have an important effect on how the audience receives your speech. Judgments you've made about certain economic groups (the very wealthy, the terribly poor), or ethnic groups, or religious groups may reflect your own background, biases, and prejudices, but may not be consistent with reality. Don't take your own experience as inalterable fact; test it, especially if you sense the possibility that your view may be skewed or that there are other equally acceptable viewpoints. If you think the eating habits of a culture are "gross" because they are different from your own and if you let this erroneous judgment appear in your remarks, you may lose your audience completely. Even the best speaker may make the mistake of presuming knowledge in cases where the situation, although appearing quite similar to past situations, is quite different. For example, you may have spoken to a group of marketing people before, but this time you will be speaking with people from the business's manufacturing division. People from marketing and manufacturing, even though from the same organization, are often quite different in their interests and orientation.

Sometimes when you give a public speech, you may have more than one audience out there. The people who invited you may have different expectations from those of the general audience. Sometimes you can't meet everyone's expectations and you have to decide early exactly which part of the audience you are going to try to reach. For example, you may know that in a speech in front of

Speakers May Face a Variety of Audiences at Any One Time (© Sepp Seitz 1980, Woodfin Camp & Associates)

the class that the class members would really enjoy learning about the internal workings of a traveling musical group. You may also know that your teacher is unalterably hostile to topics dealing with gossip. The class members compose the major part of your audience, but the teacher may have unique importance as an audience member. How are you going to handle these conflicting audience expectations? There are instances where a speaker is brought in by management for the express purpose of bringing about a greater degree of unity among members of the work force. The audience, composed of the employees, is coming to the speech to be entertained and given encouragement and enthusiasm (a motivational speech). In this case there are two audiences and two expectational sets for the speaker to work with. Fortunately these two expectational sets can both be met rather easily, but such is not always the case.

It is not always easy to assess audience expectations. An audience may want to be entertained, but still hope to learn about some new behaviors they can use successfully at home or on the job. An audience may take itself very seriously and look down its collective nose at the use of humor in a speech; they may expect a speaker on a serious topic always to be serious. Or the listeners may expect (or hope) that a serious speech be spiced with a little humor from time to time. Information about these kinds of audience predispositions can be gotten from speakers with past experience with the group or from members of the group whom you talk with sometime in the stages of speech preparation. As a speaker you need to determine what the audience is expecting. A speaker may have some very hard decisions to make concerning his or her obligation to meet audience expectations. There may be times when you find that an audience expects to hear you say something which you seriously believe to be inappropriate, unwise, wrong, or not in the audience's best interests. The fact that a speaker knows the audience's expectations does not mean that the speaker is automatically obligated to meet those expectations. But a speaker should be aware that unmet expectations may easily turn into demands. You may be appearing before a group expecting to hear a motivational speech but on the basis of conviction you may have decided to deliver a speech heavy with important information and quite low on motivational enthusiasm. At least in this case you know that you will have to spend some time in the early part of your speech altering the audience's expectational set.

Often the expectations of both speaker and audience are shaped by the occasion. Graduation ceremonies are not usually considered the proper occasion for a speaker to do nothing but entertain, whereas a retirement party is not usually considered the appropriate occasion for a speech that is totally lacking in humor. Decentering, empathy, and careful audience analysis can provide important information about audience expectations.

A public speaker plays a powerful role and good audience analysis contributes greatly to this power. People are often moved by a speech to change their way of doing things, to look at matters differently, and sometimes to alter their whole approach to life. Public speaking is a very serious responsibility and the speaker should take this responsibility seriously from the outset. A public speaker should always be ethical; that is, the speaker should avoid consciously misleading or using the audience so as to produce results beneficial for the speaker or the speaker's organization but detrimental to the best interests of the audience members. When performing audience analysis the ethical public speaker should be sensitive to the interaction of ethics and expectations on the part of both speaker and audience.

By this point in the process of immediate preparation you have gotten some control over public speaking anxiety by learning how to raise your coping quotient, you have thought about your topic choice and started thinking about audience analysis. It is now time to consider the overall form which your presentational style is going to take.

☐ Public Speaking Modes

The term mode refers to the manner in which a public speech may be delivered. The common modes of public speaking are the impromptu mode, the extemporaneous mode, the manuscript mode, and the memorized mode.

Impromptu Mode

In the *impromptu mode* the speaker is called upon on the spur of the moment and must rely on remote preparation entirely because there is no time to put together an outline or rehearse.

Every conversation is an opportunity for practicing impromptu speaking skills. Your efforts to present ideas clearly, interestingly, and with animation will be useful on those occasions when you are called upon to use the impromptu mode of public speaking. Skill in impromptu speaking is extremely useful, and you should take every opportunity to develop this skill.

Extemporaneous Mode

In the *extemporaneous mode* the speaker uses both remote and immediate preparation, carefully plans the speech, prepares an outline, and rehearses. Adequate rehearsal enables the speaker to recall the major structure and sequence of ideas. However, the speaker does not memorize extensive passages nor read from a prepared, word-for-word manuscript. The illusion of spontaneity and instantaneous audience adaptation characterizes the extemporaneous mode.

Because it is carefully planned and yet flexible and immediate, the extemporaneous mode has become the most popular speaking mode for most of today's public speaking situations. It allows the speaker to give the illusion of spontaneity, and to continually adapt the speech to the audience during actual delivery. Whereas the impromptu mode is spontaneous by its nature, it requires practice to give the illusion of spontaneity when speaking extemporaneously. Today's audiences have become so accustomed to the characteristics of the extemporaneous mode that even if a speech is being read from a manuscript, or delivered from memory, audiences still expect the speech to sound as if it were being delivered extemporaneously. It is this expectation, at least in part, that is responsible for the devel-

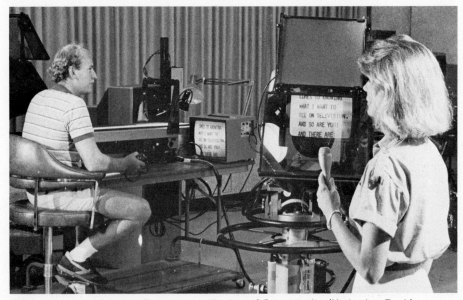

A Teleprompter Gives the Speaker the Illusion of Spontaneity (Katherine Buck)

opment of the teleprompter, a remarkable technical apparatus that allows a person giving a manuscript speech on television to appear as though no notes or manuscript are being used.

Manuscript Mode

In the *manuscript mode* the speech is written out word for word and often delivered by reading from the manuscript.

Speeches are given in this mode when it is essential that there be no possibility of misquoting the message later. Sometimes the manuscript mode is also used when there are strict time limitations as are imposed on television or radio programs. Perhaps the most obvious example of use of the manuscript mode is presidential speeches, which are almost always widely quoted in the news media. The manuscript mode might also be used when a corporate executive wants to be able to distribute his or her remarks to people who were unable to be present at the time when the speech was delivered or when the speech consists of material of unusual technical complexity.

Preparing a speech to be delivered from manuscript requires remote and immediate preparation, preparation of an outline, and rehearsal. Then talk through your speech using a tape recorder. Listen to the recording and then try to capture your oral style when writing it out word for word. The use of a personalized oral style will contribute to making the manuscript delivery seem closer to the extemporaneous delivery. More about the differences between written and oral style will be discussed in Chapter Six, where we treat the subject of style in more detail. It is sufficient at this time to note that certain characteristics of oral style can help make the speech seem fresher and more spontaneous. These include:

Short and simple words
Short and simple sentences
More use of questions
More personal pronouns
More contractions of words
More use of colloquial expressions
Frequent use of transitions
Repetition
Internal summaries
More direct adaptation to the immediate audience

Memorized Mode

In the *memorized mode* the speech, in its entirety, is usually written out word for word, memorized, and delivered from memory.

In earlier times, and even today in some cultures, the memorized mode has been and is the preferred mode of public speaking. The decline in the use of the memorized mode hasn't been due to any defects or shortcomings of the mode itself as much as to the popularity and availability of the printed word. Before the invention of writing all speeches were delivered from memory, and before the invention of print most speeches were delivered from memory. However, we have now become so dependent upon having notes available, or having ready access to printed copies of materials, that we have let our memories almost atrophy. Socrates, in Plato's essay *Phaedrus,* talks about the effects of writing on memory:

> If men learn this [writing], it will implant forgetfulness in their souls; they will cease to exercise memory because they rely on that which is written, calling things to remembrance no longer from within themselves, but by means of external marks. What you have discovered is a recipe not for memory, but for reminder. And it is no true wisdom that you offer your disciples, but only its semblance, for by telling them of many things without teaching them you will make them seem to know much, while for the most part they know nothing, and as men filled, not with wisdom, but with the conceit of wisdom, they will be a burden to their fellows.

☐ Writing, Speaking, and Memory

Writing, and its extension in printing, has benefited all of us and we should be grateful for the ability. But writing has altered the manner in which literate people think—we depend too much on memory stored outside of ourselves rather than within ourselves. Writing occurs sequentially or linearly, and memory of writing is also linear. Oral thinking has its own characteristics. The speaker who seems to speak from the depths of his or her own experience and his or her own internal knowledge projects an authority and expertise that is seldom matched by the speaker speaking from notes or manuscript. There is some current speculation that computers are closer to oral than to written memory in terms of their storage and retrieval capabilities and that the use of computers may induce a return to the attributes of oral memory (Bolter, 1984).

The qualities of spontaneity and audience adaptation that audiences consider the hallmarks of the extemporaneous mode actually derive from the self-confidence of the speaker who knows the speech material so intimately that the speaker's words seem to well up spontaneously and under such control that the speaker can immediately adjust ideas to the audience. These qualities are those of a speaker whose material has entered his or her memory as the result of experience and repeated use. In Plato's *Phaedrus,* Socrates asks: "Isn't there another kind of word . . . in the soul of the learner, able to defend itself and knowing whom to speak to and when to be silent?" Phaedrus answers: "You mean the living word of knowledge which has a soul, and of which the written word is properly only an image" (Park, 1980–1981, p. 61). If *you* desire to speak with the authority and power of someone whose words flow from the intimate knowledge and recall of experience and repeated use, then memory is an invaluable help. Memory is a talent worth cultivating.

☐ General Purpose, Mode, and Audience Analysis

At this point you may wish to consider how your general purpose (inform, convince, persuade, or entertain) and the mode (impromptu, extemporaneous, manuscript, or memorized) may interact with the results of your audience analysis. Most likely you will be using the extemporaneous mode of presentation, but if the occasion is one which calls for a careful record, you may wish to prepare a word-for-word manuscript. You will probably use elements of memory in either case. An informative speech to a scholarly audience may call for a transcript to which the audience may refer in pursuing their own research. A persuasive speech to a more general audience may call for a perceived level of commitment on your part, an understanding of and familiarity with your subject matter, that would make a manuscript or even extensive and visible notes undesirable. A very short speech seldom calls for a manuscript. (However, we should note how fortunate we are to have a written record of Lincoln's notes for his Gettysburg Address since there were no recording devices available at the time of its delivery.) Speeches to entertain almost always are given without extensive notes much less a manuscript. They may, however, be memorized. Reflect on your general purpose, the available modes, your particular audience, and make a decision.

Adequate Work Space Is Important When Preparing a Speech (© Timothy Eagan 1980, Woodfin Camp & Associates)

☐ Putting It All Together

As you go through the processes of remote and immediate preparation, keep careful notes. It is frighteningly easy to have a good idea, a great insight, a "eureka" experience and then, in the rush of ongoing activities, to completely forget it. Then you rack your brain and your unexercised memory trying to recall the idea only to find it gone for who knows how long. Far better to make notes as you prepare. Get a pile of blank sheets of paper (we use standard 8½ × 11 white paper, the least expensive we can find), clear a nice broad work surface—like a kitchen or dining room table, or a large desk—get some ballpoint pens, two black and one red, and start to get your speech preparation down on paper.

1. In the top center of your first sheet write down your general topic, and under it print *Remote Preparation* (see Figure 3.1). Now look at the topic and start thinking about what you already know about your topic from your own past experience. Write one idea to a line and number each line, leaving space between each entry. When you've exhausted your remote preparation material, make sure to leave some space in case you remember something else later on. Also remember

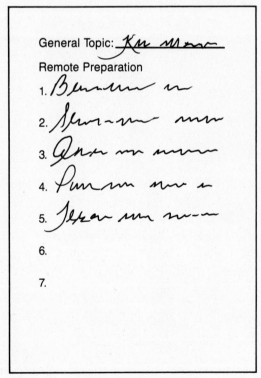

Figure 3.1 Remote Preparation Notes

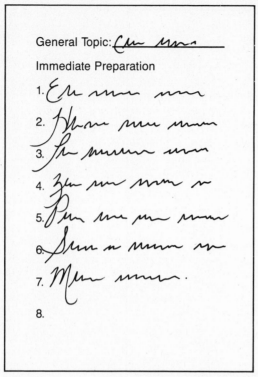

Figure 3.2 Immediate Preparation Notes

to number each sheet. When you have completed your listing of ideas from remote preparation, put those sheets to the side and put another clean sheet in front of you.

2. In the top center of the new sheet again write down your general topic and under it print *Immediate Preparation* (see Figure 3.2). Again, listing one idea or note to a line and leaving space between lines, write down the critical elements from your audience analysis. Put down everything that will help you in understanding the audience and in adjusting your topic, general purpose, and mode to the audience's needs and expectations. Go back to the section on audience analysis in this chapter and work your way through the chapter, making notes as you go along. Be careful not to use single words all the time since you will forget exactly what a single word was meant to recall. This isn't the time to save on paper and ink. When you think you've got down everything from your immediate preparation, remember to leave some space for things you remember later. Keep on numbering the sheets consecutively in the upper right-hand corner. Put your immediate preparation notes under your remote preparation notes, put the packet to the side, and get out another clean sheet.

3. Write your general topic in top center and under it print *Brainstorming* (see Figure 3.3). Now just sit back and reflect on what you've already done and

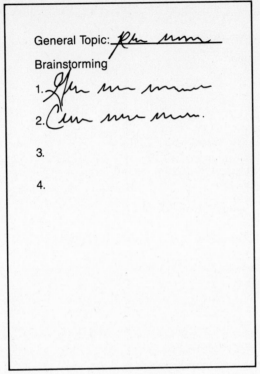

Figure 3.3 Brainstorming Notes

see if any additional thoughts occur. If so, and they fit under either remote or immediate preparation, enter them on the appropriate sheet. If they don't fit under earlier materials, then write them down here, again a single item to a numbered line.

Time for another clean sheet.

4. In the top center write your general topic and under it print *Needs Further Research* (see Figure 3.4). Now go through everything you've written so far and carefully note those areas where you think you need to provide further information, clarification, support, or examples. One idea to a numbered line. Remember to number the sheets. You will use this particular material as you research your speech, a topic covered in the next chapter.

Get out another clean sheet.

5. Top center print *Preliminary Outline*. Along the left-hand side, a few spaces under your heading, print *Topic:* and next to it write your general topic. Drop down a few spaces and again along the left side print *General Purpose:* and next to it write your general purpose for this speech (to inform, convince, persuade, or entertain). Again, drop down a few spaces and along the left side print *Preliminary Specific Purpose.* Your first draft, or preliminary, specific purpose is the result of trying to specify what response you want to get from this specific audience

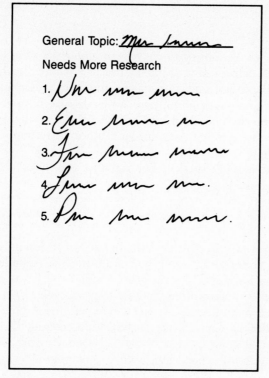

Figure 3.4 Additional Research Notes

with this specific speech on this specific occasion. It is the product of applying your general purpose and topic to this audience. At this point you are just making a first approximation of a fully formed specific purpose. So next to the words *Preliminary Specific Purpose* note down a few things that you think your audience might do as a result of your speech.

Look over your material and start listing items in what seems to you the order of their importance in terms of your speech purpose and topic. You needn't find a place for everything you listed on the completed sheets—in retrospect some items may seem silly or superfluous, just leave them out. You can always go back later to your notes and see if there is anything else you want to include.*

Now get everything into one pile and start the research process described in Chapter Four.

---

*If you are using a computer with a good word processing program, you can speed up the process of "putting it all together" that we have just discussed. Use a blank disk, or one with plenty of space (there is nothing more frustrating than losing all of your work to a "disk full" error). Remember to save your material frequently. Fool around with rearranging your points as you put them down. Where the instructions above call for a clean piece of paper, just enter the formatting command that starts you on a clean page. At the end, save everything to disk and then run a printout to use when following the research process described in Chapter Four.

☐ Summary

In this chapter we have continued to move you along the time line that will culminate in the actual delivery of your public speech. We have discussed the areas of speech anxiety, topic choice, audience analysis, modes of presentation, the consideration of a preliminary specific purpose for your speech, and the steps in putting everything you've done so far into order so that you might move on to performing any necessary research. Stage fright is a normal response to the stress of the unpredictable. It is only bad when it is uncontrollable. Some degree of anxiety is beneficial to a public speaker. You can raise your level of coping (your coping quotient) with the unpredictable by using the technique of PIER: preparation, idea, experience, and relaxation. Audiences are almost always rooting for the speaker and want very much for the speaker to succeed in giving an effective speech.

You should always try to pick a worthwhile topic. If dealing with a trivial topic, you should try to treat it in as worthwhile a manner as possible. Remember to narrow your topic so that it is manageable within the limits of your own experience, the audience's expectations, and the time available.

Audience analysis may cause you to alter almost everything about your speech. The fundamental technique for audience analysis is decentering. Decentering focuses on the conceptual point of view of others, while empathy focuses on the emotional point of view of others. Use both decentering and empathy in the process of audience analysis. When analyzing your audience, try to assess their expectations for the speech. Remember that frustrated or unmet expectations may turn into demands. The speech occasion often affects the expectations of both speaker and audience.

Having completed your audience analysis, you should consider how you are going to achieve your general purpose with this specific audience, including what audience outcomes you would like to see as a result of your speech. Without going into great detail write down the audience outcomes you would like to see as a result of your preparation; this is your preliminary specific purpose.

The modes of presentation are impromptu, extemporaneous, manuscript, and memorized. Today's audiences generally prefer the extemporaneous mode. Be attentive to the differences between oral and written style, and consider the value of the appropriate use of memory in public speaking.

Exercises ■

1 Prepare an essay reporting on how professional public speakers handle the problem of stage fright. Consult available literature and if necessary interview, either in person or by phone or letter, three professional public speakers. If you interview people, it is important to plan ahead of time the questions you will ask. Keep notes of their responses.

2 Prepare a speech in which you take a seemingly trivial topic and develop it in a worthwhile manner.

3 Making use of decentering and empathy prepare an audience analysis of:
a Your classroom audience
b A group of senior citizens (over 65 years of age) meeting to discuss social security benefits
c An audience composed of homeowners from the neighborhood around school meeting to discuss neighborhood safety

4 Prepare an audience analysis. Your overall topic is compulsory military service for both men and women. Your general purpose may be to either inform or to persuade (specify which). The speech can be no longer than 10 minutes. In your analysis provide a specific purpose, a title, and a brief statement of how the analysis was conducted and the result of the analysis. Make use of decentering and of demographic techniques. Analyze the following audiences:
a The undergraduate student council
b The school's parents club
c The university faculty organization
d Your public speaking class
e Your high school alumni club
f The local chapter of one of the veteran's organizations (such as the American Legion, etc.)

5 Prepare a full preparation outline for a 3-minute informative speech on the topic "thought and speech." This original outline is for a speech to be delivered in class. Using audience analysis adapt your outline for presentation to a pscyhology class, a marketing class, and a philosophy class. Indicate on the outline exactly how the speech would be altered for each of these audiences based upon your analyses.

6 Using an outline for a speech you have already delivered in class, adapt that outline for any one of the following audiences. Indicate on the adapted outline the methods of audience analysis used and the exact areas of adaptation based upon your audience analysis.
a A high school speech class
b An elementary school assembly
c A neighborhood citizens organization
d A local service organization luncheon (such as Lions, Women in Business, etc.)

7 Prepare a speech on the subject of memory in which you demonstrate all four modes of public speaking.

8 Together with two classmates, organize and present a 15-minute panel discussion on how mode may interact with the treatment of a public speaking topic.

Bibliographic References ■

Bolter, J. David: *Turing's Man: Western Culture in the Computer Age,* The University of North Carolina Press, Chapel Hill, N.C., 1984. Some insights and reflections on a topic which will become increasingly important.

Park, Clara C.: "The Mother of the Muses: In Praise of Memory," *The American Scholar,* vol. 50, no. 1, Winter 1980–1981, pp. 55–71. A delightful essay on an almost forgotten topic.

Pirsig, Robert M.: *Zen and the Art of Motorcycle Maintenance,* William Morrow, New York, 1975. Not much about motorcycle maintenance but lots about the interaction of values and self-analysis.

Plato: *The Collected Dialogues of Plato,* Hamilton and H. Cairns (eds.), Princeton University Press, Princeton, N.J., 1963. Especially the dialog "Phaedrus," pp. 475–525. A classic discussion of public speaking with some fascinating insights on memory.

Recommended Readings ■

Clevenger, T., Jr.: *Audience Analysis,* Bobbs-Merrill, Indianapolis, 1966. A short, thorough approach.

Higbee, K.: *Your Memory: How It Works, How to Improve It,* Prentice-Hall, Englewood Cliffs, N.J., 1977.

McCroskey, J. C.: *An Introduction to Rhetorical Communication,* 4th ed., Prentice-Hall, Englewood Cliffs, N.J., 1982. Chapter Two, "Stage Fright: A Normal Problem," pp. 23–38. A treatment by one of today's foremost researchers of communication apprehension.

Osborn, M.: *Speaking in Public,* Houghton Mifflin, Boston, 1982. Chapter Five, "Selecting and Analyzing a Speech Topic," pp. 101–116. Additional insights on topic selection.

Winans, J. A.: *Speechmaking,* Harper & Row, New York, 1938. A classic general text.

Zelko, H. P., and F. E. X. Dance: *Business and Professional Speech Communication,* 2d ed., Holt, Rinehart and Winston, New York, 1978. Chapter Six, "Using a Manuscript," pp. 146–164. Professor Zelko gives abundant information on the whys and wherefores of preparing a manuscript speech, including a discussion of the differences between oral and written style.

Research

Chapter Four

"Research is simply the manner in which men solve the knotty problems in their attempt to push back the frontiers of human ignorance."
Paul D. Leedy, *Practical Research: Planning and Design*

You have a general topic, a general purpose, you've done some prespeech audience analysis. You've begun to narrow your purpose for speaking by stating more specifically what you would like to accomplish through your presentation. Although you may not be ready to solidify your specific purpose, the more you can detail what audience response you want your speech to achieve, the more you protect yourself from doing unnecessary or irrelevant research.

☐ Research Defined

Research, defined as "careful or diligent search" and "studious inquiry or examination" (*Webster's New Collegiate Dictionary*, 1979), can be a time-consuming, albeit interesting, process. There are basically two problems that a speaker faces by overresearching a topic: The time commitment can be overwhelming, and there is a human tendency to want others to know how much we know and we might attempt to "stuff" a 5-week course into a 5-minute speech. Neither of the above problems are meant to discourage you, the speaker, from doing the necessary and appropriate research of your topic. They are mentioned, instead, to encourage you to specify, for yourself, your purpose for speaking. Once you have designated some goals for yourself and for your speech, you can go back to your sheet headlined NEEDS MORE RESEARCH (Chapter Three, "Immediate Preparation," page 70). Read through your REMOTE PREPARATION, IMMEDIATE PREPARATION (which at this point is primarily your audience analysis), and BRAINSTORMING sheets (see pages 69–70). Keeping in mind the specific purpose you have begun to formulate, carefully list those areas that you feel need support, as well as those areas where you think you need more information.

The benefits of the process of a preliminary specific purpose and the consequent topic-narrowing procedure accrue to both the speaker and the audience. The speaker saves herself time by not researching those aspects of her general topic that are not pertinent to the speech at hand. Additionally, the audience is not overloaded by a massive amount of information in a short time period.

Let's look at an example of a person giving a 4-minute speech on the general topic of stained glass artistry. This topic could include the history of stained glass, the different types of glass, how stained glass is made, the varied construction methods of a stained glass window, the tools needed. It's a very broad topic to attempt to cover in 4 minutes. By combining an awareness of the speaker's own knowledge, audience analysis, and the time allotted for the speech, the speaker starts to intrapersonally specify that she wants the audience to understand the technique of glass cutting at the end of her 4-minute speech. This initial attempt to formulate a specific purpose has helped her to avoid researching the history of stained glass or types of glass—topic areas irrevelant to a speech on glass cutting.

□ Research and Thought

Avoiding unnecessary research has some very pragmatic advantages, as discussed above. However, once you have pinpointed the topic areas that need further examination, the research process itself has advantages for the speaker. Besides the fact that there are practical, situational, bottom-line benefits of research that allow for a more effective presentation, research can be personally enjoyable and fulfilling in the sense that research is a way of acquiring knowledge.

In an earlier section of the book, while discussing public speaking and power, we stated that words are often considered our greatest tool for the acquisition of power. Words—symbols—are also our greatest tool for the acquisition of knowledge. Words or symbols are what allow humans the opportunity to search, store, research, and reevaluate phenomena. Perhaps it is because of the intermediary of knowledge gained through words that we acquire power. Whether or not *interpersonal* power is derived from knowledge could be argued. Certainly *intrapersonal* power, power within oneself, is enhanced by one's acquisition of knowledge.

We have stated that the primary function of human communication is mentation or thought. We have also stated, and believe, that the primary goal of a public speaker should be to ethically expand the conceptual horizons of the audience. Before a speaker can broaden the conceptual horizons of others, he has to assess the inventory of his own conceptual warehouse. Research is the instrument and the medium through which we can acquire knowledge, enhance our own mentative-conceptual powers, and thus expand the mentative powers of others. Furthermore, research helps us to fulfill our ethical responsibilities to our audience.

□ When Research Is Needed

The purpose of research is to aid the speaker in explaining, clarifying, and/or supporting his ideas, assertions, or assumptions. Often, in order for a speaker to achieve his specific purpose, and to appear a credible source, support materials derived from the research process are needed. Declarative assertions or assumptions are generally accepted in our day-to-day conversations by those who know us. You as a speaker cannot count on the same accepting behavior from your audience. Nor should you expect it! A speaker has the ethical responsibility to her audience to provide support for her assertions, to explain her assumptions, and to clarify her ideas. The research process provides the speaker with the data needed to answer the *who, what, why, where, when,* and *how* questions that the audience might pose.

When trying to decide what facets of your topic need further research, start with yourself. What is your drafted preliminary specific purpose? What information needs to be included in your speech in order to achieve your preliminary specific purpose? How does your knowledge of the topic match with the knowledge required to reach the goal of your speech?

Previously, we spoke of a *Needs More Research* sheet of paper. One way of visualizing the content of such a sheet would be the following. Imagine that you have two 8½ × 11 inch pieces of plastic (like the transparencies that are used for overhead projectors). Write your preliminary specific purpose, in black, at the top of one transparent sheet. Now list, in red, from most important to least, the items of information that are necessary for you to attain the goal you've set in your specific purpose. Take your second transparency and overlay it on the first. Go down the underlying list, item by item. If you feel that you have the necessary and sufficient degree of knowledge to speak as an authority on that item, rewrite that item in black, directly over the red writing. When you have completed your examination of the list and of your personal knowledge, the items that remain in red (those that you have not rewritten in black on the overlay) are the items that contribute to the content of your *Needs More Research* sheet. Although the procedure just described may be more time-consuming and cumbersome than necessary, our intent was to provide you with an imagined visual example.

The point is not so much how you go about your "knowledge required/ personal knowledge possessed" match, but that such a match is the first step in the decision of what and where you, as a speaker, need to do research.

If a speaker was speaking to herself, the "further research" query could stop here. Silly as it may sound, if a speaker stops at this point and only examines those areas that she is personally unsure of, she might as well speak to herself. Framing a specific purpose calls for a desired response from your audience. In order to achieve that response the speaker must research her audience as thoroughly as possible.

We discussed analyzing your audience in Chapter Three. A quick review of the concept is in order, however. Audience analysis is based on the theoretical principle of decentering. We try to decenter—move away from ourselves as the center of everything—and try to conceptually take the point of view of another or others. We often can decenter to another person if we know that person and are around him a lot. Familiarity and repeated interaction can facilitate decentering. As a speaker, you won't always "know" your audience. You may not see them face to face until 5 minutes before you are to speak. But you can "know about" your audience, you can analyze your audience, you can decenter to your audience by researching your audience.

Inquire about the general demographic makeup of your audience and use demographic reference books to learn more about your population. Suppose, for example, that most of your audience is in the 25 to 40 year age range and resides in metropolitan Denver. Go to an almanac and learn some facts about Denver, about the employment opportunities in Denver, about the percentage of Denver-ites who fall into that age range. Try to determine your audience's knowledge of the topic, their attitude or predisposition toward the topic, their interest in the topic, and their expectations for you as a speaker on your specific topic on a given occasion.

There will be times when, with the right sources and by asking the right questions, you can learn a great deal about your audience before you speak to them. There will be other times when despite your efforts you learn very little about your audience prior to meeting them and you have to do some on-the-spot analyzation. Whichever is the circumstance you find yourself in (and we hope it is the former), it is important to remember that the conclusions or inferences that you make from your analysis are based upon data *about* the people and not the people themselves. Stereotypes become such because they tend to exhibit predict-able behavior and/or a set of associated characteristics. Nonetheless, be prepared to be flexible with your assumptions regarding your audience. Research is a means of "knowing about" your audience. Until you have the opportunity to "know" your audience as well as "know about" them your knowledge is not comprehen-sive.

Now let's talk about how you can use your audience research for your topic research. You have completed a knowledge required/personal knowledge possessed match. Juxtapose this with your audience's knowledge of the topic. Are there areas where your audience—or some member of your audience—has more information or experience than you? Occasionally this happens and it is important to be aware of the possibility. It is always preferable to know more than your audience about a topic. Research can help you to know more, but there may be an instance when no amount of research possible will equip you for an expert in the audience. While an awareness of your audience members' knowledge is essential for the research and planning of your speech, it is used to gear your speech toward the norm of your audience, not toward the one unusual or expert member.

During your analysis of your audience you assessed their interest in your topic and their attitude toward the topic. If you find, through your research, that your audience is more interested in the tools used in glass cutting than the actual cutting process, you can put more emphasis on tools. If your audience has a slightly negative attitude toward your topic because they don't see the usefulness for them of cutting stained glass, try to move them toward a neutral or positive attitudinal position by showing them the uses of glass cutting in household repair as well. Some additional research on cutting tools or household repair projects may be needed by the speaker, but the extra time and effort can only contribute to a more successful presentation.

The use of your audience analysis information and of your decentering ability is instrumental in trying to pinpoint potential audience questions, concerns, or areas of confusion. The speaker has to consciously try to decenter to the perspective of an audience member and ask himself, "If I were listening to a speech on this topic, would I accept that statement? Would I want further proof or support? Would I understand that point, or is it too abstract? Would I need some concrete examples?" The answers to these questions are indicators of areas that may require more research on the speaker's part.

The use of your personal knowledge appraisal and your audience research, as a means of assessing the need for research, has a direct, positive outcome for the audience and both a direct and indirect benefit for the speaker. A speech, much like a piece of clothing, that has been tailored to the knowledge, interest, attitudes, and expectations of the audience; that answers potential questions; that clears up ambiguities; that supports it tenets with credible research data is going to "fit" the audience better than a speech "off the rack." The direct benefit to the audience is hearing a speech that they are interested in, that they can understand, and that they can learn from. You as a speaker have helped to broaden their conceptual powers in an ethical, nonmanipulative way.

As an indirect benefit for the speaker, a speech that has been adapted to the audience has a far better chance of being successful in terms of the speaker's specific purpose. The positive effect on a speaker of a successful presentation lasts longer than the applause. Because of the interaction of the levels of human communication, the person-to-person level supplies the intrapersonal level with positive feedback. Positive input to one's intrapersonal level of human communication has a positive effect on one's self-concept and self-esteem which can be long-lasting.

Adequate research, using whatever resources necessary, has a direct benefit for the speaker as well as an indirect one. Although perhaps not as long-lasting as a positive shift in self-esteem, the feeling of comfort with the extent of your knowledge on a topic has the almost immediate result of anxiety reduction for a speaker. If we briefly return to the PIER formula, you can see that

- Research can help *prepare* you for the unknown.
- Research directs your consciousness toward the *ideas* in your speech.
- Research leads to more effective and enjoyable speaking *experiences*.
- Research gives you an adequate knowledge base and creates a climate conducive to *relaxation* during the presentation.

To summarize, a speaker has a responsibility to his audience to provide support, explanation, etc., within the context of his speech. The determination of which aspects of the speech need research, or further research, is made by the speaker assessing her own knowledge of the topic, and by her analyzing the audience and decentering to their point of view. Fulfilling the assessed research requirements provides the audience and the speaker with positive conceptual and behavioral results in an ethical manner.

☐ Research Sources

There are basically two categories of research sources from which a speaker can draw support materials for a speech: (1) subjective sources and (2) objective sources.

Subjective Sources

Sources categorized as subjective are characterized by direct personal involvement, where the emphasis is on the individual's internal judgment of a given phenomenon rather than the objective attributes of the phenomenon. For example, you are shopping for a Christmas tree. After scouring four tree lots you find the tree that is "right." The "right" tree is a subjective judgment that may or may not be dependent on the physical attributes of the chosen tree. Traditional Christmas trees have certain physical characteristics that are pretty constant: They have a trunk, limbs, space between the limbs, some variety of needle on the limbs, and a shape that resembles an inverted cone. Because of an individual's personal experience and involvement, a subjective judgment is superimposed upon the tree's physical characteristics. Your definition of the "right" tree may be—and probably is—different from your neighbor's definition. Luckily for tree growers and tree sellers, every tree is "right" for someone.

Again, subjective sources of support for your speech are those that are defined by an individual's involvement with and judgment of an event, somewhat removed from the event itself. Some examples of subjective experiences that could conceivably serve to substantiate the ideas or points in your speech follow.

Personal Experiences

Alfred North Whitehead is reported to have said "We think in generalities, we live in detail" (Peter, 1979, p. 493). Who you are, what you do, where you live, where you've traveled, what your interests and hobbies are, how you or your experiences are unique, all provide detailed data that can supply a speaker with examples, illustrations, anecdotes, and analogies.

Observations

By listening and watching we can learn a tremendous amount. We can also mentally collect and store events that we have observed to draw upon as support material for future speeches. Observations can provide factual and hypothetical examples or literal and figurative analogies, as well as anecdotes.

Interviews

The form of interview that most people are familiar with is an employment interview. However, in a generic sense, an interview is an interpersonal communicative interaction that can have various forms and/or purposes. Interviews can take place face to face, over the phone, or through the mail (i.e., questionnaires), and they can involve either or both information getting and information giving. Subjective support that can be derived from interviews includes testimony, quotations, or a compilation of data resulting directly from the interview or questionnaire (for example, if you have interviewed 10 people regarding their favorite breakfast cereal, your data might show that 8 out of 10 people prefer corn flakes for breakfast).

A rule of thumb, when beginning research for your presentation, is to start within yourself and then move to outside sources. Your research started with what we have termed "remote preparation." All of your life experiences, the events and people you have observed and spoken with, are potential sources of subjective support. The authors can only recommend that you look within yourself, initially, and make use of your remote preparation as your first research source. We also encourage speakers to become more consciously aware of their future experiences and to sharpen their powers of observation. Write down some of the things you have seen and/or heard. Remember day-to-day personal happenings as well as out of the ordinary events. You will be building your personal storehouse of support materials.

A speaker can extract examples from formal interviews she has personally experienced in her past. Sometimes the speaker feels the need to conduct further interviews for her upcoming speech. Some brief guidelines and suggestions regarding interviews are in order.

Face-to-face interviews will probably be the type of setting most speakers will seek out. In a face-to-face interaction you gain visual, nonvocal information as well as the vocal message of the interview. This nonvocal information can be important with regard to the emotional meaning of the information you're requesting.

A speaker can either interview numerous people randomly, without regard for their knowledge or lack of knowledge on the chosen topic, and get the opinions and reactions of the "person on the street," or go to one or more authorities on the topic. If you are interviewing people randomly, remember to choose a location where you will get a good cross section of people, a shopping center or public building, for instance. If you are a college student and interview students in your student cafeteria, you have probably received responses from people involved in the educational process, probably within a pretty narrow age range, and perhaps from the same socioeconomic group—a relatively homogeneous sample of respondents. A homogeneous sample is acceptable as a research base, but the speaker must be aware of his data base and the problems of generalizing responses of the college students to the general population. It is preferable for you to have some standard questions that you ask everyone so that you have a standard basis for comparison of responses. Of course, at the conclusion of the interview you can ask if they have anything further to add to their comments, which allows for personal variability.

If the speaker chooses to interview an authority, the speaker must define "authority" and determine how to find one. An authority is a person who is believed by many to have comprehensive knowledge and experience with a specific informational area or topic. One might consider the parents of 11 children to be authorities on childhood diseases. Perhaps they are. Nonetheless, an even more experienced and impressive authority for most audience members would be a pediatrician. Furthermore, the better known the pediatrician, the more weight her comments would carry with the audience.

A speaker can locate authorities through several means. If you are looking for a pediatrician and you have no children, ask someone you know who does. If you don't know anyone with children, look in the yellow pages under physician specialties or call a local Children's Hospital. You can get additional names of informed authorities from the authorities you have already interviewed. Also, if you have done some library research, you might find the name of an authoritative source from the print materials you've read.

Once you have located your potential interviewee, you will need to call and make an appointment. It would be inappropriate, and probably unsuccessful, to assume that you could just walk into a pediatrician's office and that she'll have time to talk to you. When you call for an appointment, identify yourself, give your purpose for calling, and inquire whether the interviewee would like references who will substantiate your research purpose. When you do have the interview, conduct it in a professional manner. Know how much time you have and work within the time limit. Know exactly what information you need, rather than saying, "Can you tell me about childhood diseases, Doctor?" It will be helpful if you write out for yourself the specific questions that you have. If the authority tells you that she can be quoted, inquire if you can tape record the interview so that the quotes are accurate. When the interview concludes, thank your interviewee for the time and the information. It is also a nice gesture to follow up the interview with a short note telling the interviewee how the speech went and again thanking her for her contributions.

Telephone interviews essentially follow the same procedures we've discussed, but they lack the visual component of human communication. At times, due to time limitations or the geographic location of your authority, they may be necessary. A telephone interview might also be preliminary to a face-to-face interview as a way of ensuring that a speaker is interviewing the best source of specific information. At one time or another, we have all been given the name of a person who is supposed to have the answers we need, only to find out that that person can't help us but Ms. Someonelse can.

Written interviews, or questionnaires, to one or many people lack the personal, visual, and vocal components of human communication, but they are a means of reaching many people in diverse locations and getting responses that can then be compared. The basic problem for a speaker with a written interview is the time factor. A response can be long in the coming and may never appear at all. If a speaker is relying upon support materials from a written interview, he had better allow plenty of time.

Use of the subjective category of support materials has some concrete advantages. A speaker can research a topic within her own house, office, or classroom. The use of personal materials injects a speech with a human touch. Individual examples can add an emotional tone to a speech while testifying to the credibility of the speaker.

Similar to a good news/bad news joke, however, the bad news about the use of subjective sources can be found in a quote by the eighteenth century English poet, Alexander Pope, in his *Moral Essays* (1720–1735) when he said

> To observations which ourselves we
>   make,
> We grow more partial for the observer's
>   sake.

A similar message comes from a contemporary humorist who says, "It is impossible to experience one's death objectively and still carry a tune" (Woody Allen as quoted in Peter, 1979, p. 134). The bad news about the use of subjective sources of support for your speech is that they are so personal, perhaps so idiosyncratic, and they certainly contain the elements of individual bias as well as possible error, that your speech may still contain what appears to the audience as unfounded assertions. Although the sole use of personal information may be appropriate and sufficient for a speech entitled "My Pet Peeve," most topics will require support sources other than those derived from direct, personal experiences. Those "other" sources fall into the category of objective sources.

Objective Sources

Objective research sources may be distinguished from subjective sources. The adjective "objective" is defined as "emphasizing or expressing the nature of reality as it is apart from personal reflections or feelings" (*Webster's New Collegiate Dictionary,* 1979). Materials that are considered objective have an emphasis on the attributes of a phenomenon rather than an individual's like/dislike of or agreement/disagreement with the attributes. For a speaker to strive to search for objective materials is to say that he is trying to determine the "facts"—what is present in reality (not only in his mind), what can be perceived similarly by independent others, and what can be verified scientifically if necessary.

The distinction between objective and subjective as clearly separate categories of support sources becomes somewhat academic if one argues that whenever a person perceives an objective item, subjective elements are introduced. As soon as you read a report of a flood in the newspaper, your definitions of the language used, your emotional state when you read it, etc., affect how you might relay the event to your friend who has not read the report. The authors can only remind a researcher of his ethical responsibility to the audience and encourage his continual attempt to be objective when seeking and reporting objective materials.

A sampling of sources and information that can provide a speaker with objective verification for his presentation includes studies (e.g., correlating a speaker's sex with a speaker's credibility); statistics derived from reputable sources (e.g., "The U.S. Department of Census reports . . . "); analogies or examples from literary or film sources; published or taped interviews, to name only a few. Objective research can be found in either print or nonprint form, and in both nonlibrary and library locations.

Nonlibrary Materials

Because we become so accustomed to our home environment, some obvious sources of objective support material become obscured. Most households contain one or more *dictionaries,* which include sections on the English language, biographical names, geographical names, and foreign words and phrases. A *Roget's Thesaurus* provides a speaker with synonyms and antonyms. A book of quotations, such as Bartlett's *Familiar Quotations* or *Peter's Quotations* can be a source used for speech introductions or conclusions. Quotes are also useful to make a point or to illustrate an idea from differing personal and/or historical perspectives.

101 Famous Poems, or some other poetry book, can be used in ways similar to a book of quotations. Another very handy use for a poetry book is for voice and/or gesture exercises. If a speaker believes he has a relatively monotone, expressionless voice, reading poetry aloud can be used to develop his vocal variety. If the speaker looks like he is in a straitjacket, or frozen behind the lectern, physically acting out a poem can be a loosening up activity that encourages the use of gestures. Similarly, reading story books to young children can be used for voice and gesture exercise.

Books, both textbooks and literary works, can supply objective information to a speaker. General information books, such as the *Guinness Book of World Records,* the *Reader's Digest Annual and Yearbook,* and *Information Please Almanac* are filled with potentially useful facts and figures. Periodicals that are helpful to a speaker range from the daily newspaper to popular or technical magazines.

Although it is likely that many of the print sources mentioned above are already part of your home library, all can be purchased in paperback form. They can also be found in your local public library.

Two principle nonprint sources of objective information located within most homes are the radio and the television. These sources provide up-to-the-minute coverage of local, national, and international events, as well as educational programs.

A speaker's next move in the research process is to his school library or public library.

Library Materials

While we will list several library sources that a speaker might utilize (an exhaustive list would be as long as the chapter itself), initially the most helpful library source of library information for a speaker/researcher is the reference librarian. If you have any doubt as to where to look for specific support materials, the librarian is the person who will direct you.

Library print materials provide a varied source of data for a speaker. A sample of some commonly used materials follows.

I. *Books* on the topic you are researching can be found by using the card catalog. The card catalog is a list of a library's holdings arranged alphabetically by author, title, and/or subject. (See Figure 4.1.) The card catalog offers a wealth of information to a researcher, although much of the information will not be current. There is often a time lag from when the book was written until it is actually shelved in a library. The timeliness of a speaker's support materials is sometimes vital, so note the publication date of card catalog sources. Many public and private libraries have moved to a computerized catalog system. The screen or hard copy representation of the computer information provides the same data as the traditional card format. U.S. government documents and publications and United Nation publications are often not represented in the card catalog.

II. *Reference books* and the reference area in a library contain a library's basic collection of research materials. This is the area in which you will find *dictionaries, almanacs, atlases, directories,* and general and specific *handbooks* and *encyclopedias.* In this area you will also find the following.

A. *Biographical resources:* A library's biographical works include volumes such as *Who's Who in America, Who's Who in the World, Who's Who of American Women,* and *Who Was Who in American History.* There are biographical

Human communication theory.

Includes bibliographies.
1. Interpersonal communication—Addresses, essays,
lectures.   I. Dance, Frank E. X.
BF637.C45H85   001.54   81-20054
ISBN 0-06-041481-2   AACR2

Figure 4.1 Card Catalogue Reference

resources other than the *Who's Who* series and such holdings will vary among libraries. Biographical materials provide speakers with condensed biographies of currently or historically famous persons.

B. *Indexes and abstracts:* Libraries provide lists of books, articles, documents, reviews, studies, statistics, etc., and direct a speaker/researcher to their location. Some lists include abstracts of articles, and others direct the researcher to the location of the current data on a given topic. Frequently used indexes and abstracts include the following:

1. The *Readers' Guide to Periodical Literature* is a cumulative index to general interest U.S. periodicals. Listings include *Consumer Reports, Ebony, Field & Stream, Gourmet, Ms., National Geographic, Psychology Today, Reader's Digest, Scientific American,* and *Vital Speeches.* The guide is arranged alphabetically by subject and by author. Reviews of books, movies, TV programs, drama, dance, and records are indexed. This guide also notes which indexed periodicals are available for physically handicapped persons on talking books, magnetic tape, or in braille.

2. *The New York Times Index* is a guide to the *New York Times* newspaper on microfilm. This indexes local, regional, state, national, and international news articles, as well as editorials, letters to the editor, and entertainment reviews. Newspapers provide timely information on a subject and often allow a researcher to trace an event's evolution. Additional newspapers that are indexed are the *Washington Post,* the *Wall Street Journal,* and occasionally the local newspaper.

3. *Resources in Education Index* abstracts journals that contain literature related to education.

4. *Psychological Abstracts and Sociological Abstracts* are two distinct publications that abstract literature related to psychology and sociology, respectively.

5. *Humanities Index* is a publication that indexes journals whose subject matter includes classical studies, history, philosophy, and the performing arts. The *Social Science Index,* similar in format yet distinct in content, indexes articles in the areas of geography, economics, and sociology.

6. *Index to Journals in Communication Studies* indexes articles from journals in the speech communication discipline. This index can lead a public speaker to research studies and articles in the area of human communication in general and public speaking in particular.

7. *Digest of Public General Bills & Resolutions* lists, in an annual volume for each congressional year, Senate and House bills and resolutions. Each bill/resolution is indexed by subject, and by sponsors and co-sponsors. Finally, there is a "Factual Description" section in each digest that translates the legal terminology of each bill and resolution to language easily understood by a lay person. The translations themselves could serve as support material for the general speech topic of "jargon."

8. *Congressional Information Service* (CIS) annually indexes catalogs and abstracts and summarizes publications issued by Congress.

9. *American Statistics Index* (ASI) is an abstract guide and index to statistical publications of the U.S. government. It includes social, economic, demographic, natural resource, and additional interest area data. A real highlight of the ASI is the inclusion of a "Suggestions for Making Information Searches" section which illustrates types of information available through ASI and gives search suggestions to the researcher. A "Sample Search" is also included in this index.

The ASI index primarily provides statistical information to researchers; statistics can also be obtained from any of the sources listed above. A speaker using statistical support material should use it carefully and ethically.

Suggestions When Using Statistical Materials

- Determine whether the statistics you are going to use actually support a point or are being used for effect. Using numbers to emphasize a point is acceptable as long as you aren't being manipulative.
- If you use statistics to compare, use the same measurement units in your comparison, i.e., pounds of sugar eaten per year should not be compared with ounces of sugar eaten daily unless the speaker also translates the ounces to a fraction of a pound of sugar eaten daily. Your comparison will be more effective and your audience will not as easily be confused as when you change your units of measurement.
- Unless you need exact numbers, round off your figures to the nearest whole number, tens, hundreds, thousands. Too much detail will lose your audience.
- A translation of statistics can sometimes make them more easily understood by your audience and at the same time provide emphasis through redundancy or repetition. For example, translate percentages into whole number ratios, such as "90 percent, or 9 out of 10" and "65 percent, or 2 out of 3."

- Make sure that your statistics come from a reliable source and that you understand what they mean.
- Finally, don't overdo your use of statistics. Statistical material is supposed to be support for your speech ideas, not the primary content of your speech.

   C. *Bibliographic computer searches:* Some public libraries as well as school libraries provide computer searches of a topic. Through the use of key words, the computer searches a file or an index, such as *Psychological Abstracts* or *ERIC.* Available computer files will vary with libraries. Advantages of computer searches are time and accuracy. Also, more than one topic can be searched at the same time, or an interaction of topics can be searched. A disadvantage is cost. The on-line hourly rate of computer files is variable and some corporate files can get quite expensive. The reference person doing the computer search for you will probably be able to give you a cost estimate, so ask before beginning a computer search.

 III. *Special collections* designate materials separate from a library's main collection. Special collection materials might include rare books, items of historical value to a region, and bequests that have value to the community.

 IV. *Interlibrary loan* departments figuratively expand your library's walls across the nation. If a library has an interlibrary loan department, it can locate, borrow, or photocopy material that you need from another library.

  V. *Nonprint materials* can be located within a library, an organization's Media Services department, or both. Nonprint sources of support are films, slides, videotapes, audiotapes, special education kits or games, and microform. Microform is the general name for miniature photocopies of print and graphic materials. If a library has a microform collection, it will also have microform viewing facilities. Photocopies can usually be made of microform materials. Nonprint library materials can be used for personal research information by a speaker, or they may be physically used within the speech itself.

☐ Recording Your Research Support Materials

You have put a lot of time and effort into the research you have done, but it is all for naught if you have not adequately recorded the information you have accumulated. The primary purpose of research is to provide support for the ideas that a speaker is communicating to his audience. In order to be a credible source, a speaker must be correct when reporting his support materials, and accurate and ethical when crediting the source of the material.

    Note taking from visual sources can be done either on cards or full-size paper. Those persons who use cards note one idea or topic per card. Those who use paper note all relevant aspects of an entire article, book, film. An advantage of cards is flexibility. When a speaker begins to outline her speech, the cards can be arranged in piles according to the ideas they support. An advantage of the use of full-size paper is cohesiveness. A speaker is less likely to take a statement out of context if other parts of the article are there to provide context. Also, you don't have as many separate bits of note taking to keep track of. Whichever method is used—cards or paper—is left to the researcher. Use the method that works best for you.

On the card first list the topic or aspect of the topic being researched and then the following citation information:

1. author(s) or editor(s) name(s)
2. title of the book or article, noting volume, edition, etc.
3. place of publication, publisher, date of publication
4. chapter or pages, if not the whole work
5. abstract, summary, or direct quotation
6. library call number, if a library source

Recording from nonprint sources can be by taping and transcribing, or by asking if a direct transcript is available. If you are going to quote an individual, try to verify the exactness of your note taking or recording. If you are summarizing or paraphrasing or emphasizing another's remarks, note that fact. Include in a nonprint citation:

1. the name of the person
2. the person's qualifications
3. the occasion, date, and place
4. how and where the person could be contacted in the future (see Figure 4.2)

The recording of your research support should be accurate and complete. Citations of support materials are your bibliographic references. They are just as important to a speech as they are to a written term paper.

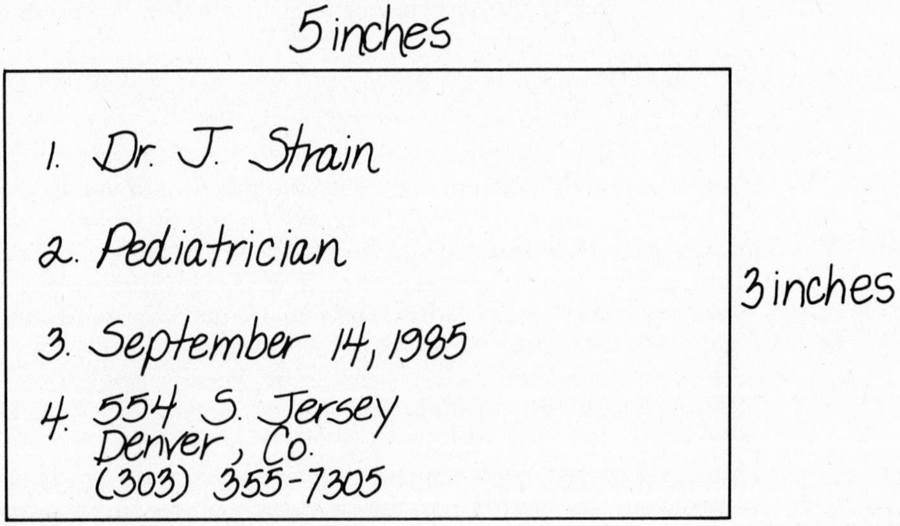

5 inches

1. Dr. J. Strain

2. Pediatrician

3. September 14, 1985

4. 554 S. Jersey
   Denver, Co.
   (303) 355-7305

3 inches

Figure 4.2 Nonprint Citation Card

☐ Evaluating Your Research Support Materials

While a speaker is engaged in the research process, and again after the process is completed, she has to evaluate the support materials that have been collected. Validity and reliability are two concepts that can be used to test and evaluate one's research.

Research support is *valid* if it genuinely examines the phenomenon that the original researcher intended to examine and if a well-grounded conclusion was correctly derived from the researcher's presuppositions. For example, you read an article in which a researcher administers a test that measures anxiety level of passengers on an airplane and of passengers on a train. He scores the tests and finds that airplane passengers have higher anxiety levels than train passengers. He concludes that flying is more anxiety-producing than taking a train. Is this conclusion valid? Does he (the original researcher) know for sure that the mode of transportation caused the anxiety of the passengers? Perhaps, by some quirk of fate, most of the airline passengers were going to a critical business meeting, or were adoptees who were going to meet their biological parents for the first time. Perhaps most of the train travelers, on the other hand, were on vacation and were very relaxed because they were leaving their work behind. Was this researcher validly measuring anxiety as a result of mode of transportation? Another example that surfaces regularly with regard to validity is whether or not tests validly measure intelligence, or do they measure a person's facility with language, ability to read, cultural experiences, or ability to perform in a high-pressure situation.

A speaker/researcher has to assess the validity of his support materials. Look for a definition of the behavior being examined in a study. Is the researcher defining "anxiety" the way you define it? The way it is being defined by others? If you define cooperation among children as not hitting each other and your friend defines it as sharing toys and another friend defines it as a child's doing what he is told to do, are you all validly observing and reporting on "cooperation" or on differing cooperative behaviors in children?

Reliability refers to consistency and stability. A person who has stable and consistent behavior is a reliable person. You can rely on that person always to be on time—or always to be late, whichever the case may be. Consistency does not imply correctness. One can consistently use a ruler that is only 34 inches long and call it a yardstick. If you measure the width of a room today, you will say the room is 3 yards wide. If you measure the room tomorrow and next week with the same erroneous ruler, you will say the room is 3 yards wide. Your measurement is consistent, but it is not correct. The room is only 2⅚ yards wide. The "yardstick" you have used is reliable—it is consistent—but it is not valid.

When you, as a speaker, are evaluating your research, ask yourself if it is reliable. If the study was replicated would it yield the same results? Then ask if the results are valid as well as reliable. If your research is valid, then it is also reliable. However, even if your research material is reliable, it is not necessarily valid, as was the case with the 34-inch ruler.

We have discussed subjective and objective sources from which a speaker can draw evidence and support for her speech. Without stating that one category of sources is preferable to the other category, we have tried to pinpoint the advantages of each. During the research evaluation phase a speaker has to find the appropriate balance between subjective and objective sources, keeping in mind the audience, the occasion, and the topic. Subjective sources of support add a personal touch to a speech, but they can be unreliable. We tend to see the same things differently at different times depending upon our mood, our experience, or our personal involvement. Subjective sources of support often lack consistency. Again, if our sources are not consistent—reliable—how valid are they?

A speech filled with objective sources of support can be intellectually convincing, but may lack a human element that makes the source credible or the audience emotionally persuaded.

Although humans do test their commonsense theories and observations for their reliability and validity, they tend to do so selectively. Attempting to do objective research, using objective sources, is a step toward testing and validating our personal perceptions. Each speaker has to strive to find the optimal subjective/objective balance that is supportive of an effective presentation.

A further consideration while evaluating your support sources is whether or not you will need audio or visual aids for their presentation. Some materials, by their very nature, require visual as well as vocal presentation. The use of a film or videotape may be necessary to support a point in your speech. Complicated or detailed material, such as a series of statistics, may need to be presented on a slide or a chart. Remember that audio or visual aids are nonprint sources of research support, and if appropriately used they can be as valuable as print sources to both the speaker/researcher and the audience.

One of the final evaluative judgments a speaker needs to make is "how much research is enough research?" You have assessed your own knowledge of the topic, analyzed your audience and their knowledge, interest, attitudes, and expectations, and tried to cross-match both with your preliminary specific purpose. A speaker's final decision as to when enough is enough has to be a personal judgment, but the process of decentering encourages the addition of an objective element to a subjective decision.

By this point in this chapter you may be feeling overwhelmed by what sounds like a tremendous amount of work in order to put together a public speech. Remember that not every presentation will require extensive library research. But if your goal as a speaker is an effective presentation, you will have to work to attain that goal. Furthermore, research, inquiry, and examination are mind-expanding activities that are not a waste of time. This sentiment is expressed by the twentieth century essayist Norman Cousins, who states "It is nonsense to say there is not enough time to be fully informed. . . . Time given to thought is the greatest timesaver of all" (Peter, 1979, p. 494).

☐ Summary

Research is defined by behaviors that include careful examination, studious inquiry, and diligent search, and it involves a time commitment on the part of a speaker. Beginning to detail your desired audience response describes a speaker's initial attempt to formulate a preliminary specific purpose. A specific purpose is your safeguard against overresearching a topic or researching irrelevant aspects of the topic.

Because we believe the primary function of human communication to be mentation or thought, and because research is a way of acquiring knowledge and enhancing our own mentative powers, the research process can be a personally fulfilling one. Once a speaker has expanded his own mentative abilities, he can ethically expand the conceptual horizons of the audience, which is the primary goal of a public speaker.

Within the context of a speech, a speaker has the added responsibility to his audience to provide support, explanation, and clarification for his ideas. A speaker determines which aspects of the speech need research, initially, by assessing his own knowledge of the topic. Then, by analyzing his audience and assessing his audience's knowledge of the topic, he can more easily decenter to their point of view. A self-assessment and an audience assessment, cross-matched with your specific purpose, point to those areas that require more examination.

Once you have pinpointed the areas that require research, there are basically two categories of sources from which a speaker can draw support materials for a speech: (1) subjective sources and (2) objective sources. Subjective sources include a speaker's personal experiences, her observations, and interviews she is or has been involved in. If a speaker is going to arrange an interview as a means of garnering information and support, there are different types of interviews, formats, and interviewer responsibilities of which she should become aware.

Objective research sources can be found in either print or nonprint form, and in both nonlibrary and library locations. Nonlibrary materials are those information sources that you might have in your home, such as a dictionary, a thesaurus, books of quotations or poetry, general information books and periodicals, plus a television and/or radio. Library materials include books on your topic, reference books (general reference as well as specific indexes and abstracts), bibliographic computer searches, special collections, and perhaps an interlibrary loan department. Most libraries also have nonprint materials—films, slides, microform—that are accessible to a speaker/researcher.

Objective and subjective sources from which a speaker can draw support for his speech are in opposition, by definition. A speaker, however, need not choose one category of support over the other. Depending upon the speaker, audience, topic, and occasion, it is preferable to find the balance between objective and subjective sources that will most effectively contribute to a successful presentation.

The primary purpose of research is to provide support for the ideas that a speaker is communicating to his audience. In order to be a credible source, a speaker must be correct when reporting his support materials, and accurate and ethical when crediting the source of the material. Whether you are note taking from print or nonprint sources, the citations of your support materials are bibliographic references and should be accurate and complete.

Finally, you have determined your research needs, completed the actual research process, and carefully recorded your support information. While you are researching and certainly when you have finished, it is imperative that you evaluate support materials you have collected in terms of their validity and reliability. A concluding evaluation of your materials will assist a speaker in the decision of how much research is enough research. In other words, have you responsibly explained, clarified, supported, and illustrated your ideas sufficiently to achieve your specific purpose?

Exercises ■

1 Take a tour of your local or your school library. Construct and deliver an interesting 3-minute speech describing the research materials and services available for use by a public speaker.

2 Ask an "authority" (e.g., a nursing home administrator) to suggest a topic (e.g., characteristics of the aged) for you to research. Research the topic and discuss the results of your research with the authority. Discuss the strong points, weak points, sources, etc. of your research.

3 Interview a person who currently occupies the career position to which you aspire. Construct and deliver a 5-minute speech in which you describe the position and the education, skills, experience needed to attain that position. The information for your 5-minute speech should be derived primarily from your interview.

4 Using the bibliography from another person's speech, locate and verify the accuracy and completeness of their support sources.

5 Research two famous speeches—e.g., J. F. Kennedy's inaugural address and M. L. King's "I Had a Dream." Analyze, compare, and contrast the use of subjective and objective support materials.

Bibliographic References ■

Bartlett, John: *Familiar Quotations,* 13th and centennial ed., Little, Brown, Boston, 1955.

Peter, Laurence J.: *Peter's Quotations,* Bantam Books, New York, 1979.

Webster's New Collegiate Dictionary, G & C Merriam Company, Springfield, Mass., 1979.

Recommended Readings ■

Kerlinger, Fred N.: *Foundations of Behavioral Research,* Holt, Rinehart and Winston, New York, 1964. Chapters 24 and 25 are especially interesting for their discussion of the concepts of validity and reliability.

Osborn, Michael: *Speaking in Public,* Houghton Mifflin, Boston, 1982. See pp. 129–135 for a further discussion of interviewing.

Selltiz, Claire, Lawrence S. Wrightsman, and Stuart W. Cook: *Research Methods in Social Relations,* 3rd ed., Holt, Rinehart and Winston, New York, 1976. Further comments on validity, reliability, questions, and interviews.

Zannes, Estelle, and Gerald Goldhaber: *Stand Up, Speak Out.* 2nd ed., Addison-Wesley, Reading, Mass., 1983. A good resource for their discussion of library card catalogs and the Dewey decimal system.

Appendix to Chapter Four

Aids for Your Speech (or Give Your Speech a Hand, a Chart, a Slide)

"All our knowledge has its origins in our perceptions."
Leonardo da Vinci

A public speaker has a responsibility to his or her audience to provide support, explanation, and clarification for his or her ideas. Research support materials were discussed in Chapter 4. The purpose of this appendix is to examine the forms of speech support known as speech aids.

Anything a speaker uses to illustrate or support a point in the speech, other than his or her own physical body and voice, may be considered a speech aid. The reason we say "other than his or her own body or voice" is because an *aid*, by definition, is an assisting or supporting device. An aid provides illustrative material in addition to the basic components of the presentation. A speech's basic components are a person (speaker) orally presenting material (the speech) to an audience. Any supplemental components that are used by a speaker in achieving the speaker's specific purpose are speech aids.

The primary purpose of aids is to provide additional print or nonprint information that can be used to support, explain, or clarify.

When Is an Aid Appropriate?

The speaker's decision to use an aid requires an examination of the speech material and an analyzation of the audience. The use of speech aids is appropriate when they will help the speaker to achieve his or her specific purpose in a fashion not available through the use of the speaker's unaided body and voice. There will be speaking occasions when your voice and your gestures will prove to be an insufficient means of accomplishing your speaking goals. On such occasions it is helpful to present your ideas through additional modes of human communication.

The systems through which people send and receive information are called *modes*. Modes of human communication are tied to a person's sensory abilities and therefore include the following systems: vocal (or oral), auditory (or aural), visual, olfactory (the sense of smell), and tactile (the sense of touch).

Sometimes the material contained in a speech becomes more easily understood, clearer, or more believable, if it is presented through several modes. For

TABLE 4.1 Comparison Chart [Figures with asterisks include interest rates and gross income. (Courtesy of Pat Persinger, Arapahoe Community College.)]

Own	Rent
$700/month	$550/month
$8400/year	$6600/year
$7800/tax deduction*	$-0-/tax deduction
$2500/tax saving*	$-0-/tax saving

*Given specific gross income, tax bracket, interest rate.

example, one of our students gave a speech in which he tried to convince the audience that it costs less to buy a home than to rent a home because of the tax deductions allowed to home owners. He told the audience that deductions on interest and property taxes actually reduce house payments. He argued that renters, on the other hand, receive no tax deductions for renting and therefore do not reduce their monthly payment. After orally comparing home owning and house renting, he produced two visual aids to support his thesis (see Tables 4.1 and 4.2).

This student's aids visually supported the auditory message. For most of the audience members, the speech became more concrete, more readily understandable, and more persuasive. The use of aids, in this instance, was appropriate because they helped the speaker achieve his specific purpose in a way that would not have been possible with this audience without the use of the aids.

When you, as a speaker, analyze your speech material, try to decenter to your audience's position and ask yourself some questions:

- Is the speech information too abstract?
- Is the material very unfamiliar to the audience?
- Is the material complicated or very technical?
- Do I need to present a lot of statistics?
- Do I need to draw comparisons that may be difficult to understand?
- Do I need to create a mood or tone or effect while presenting my information?
- Can I reach my specific purpose without the use of speech aids?

If you answer "yes" to any or all of the above questions, the use of a speech aid may be appropriate. Remember, however, to always approach these questions

TABLE 4.2 Actual Costs (Courtesy of Pat Persinger, Arapahoe Community College.)

	Own	Rent
1. initial/year	$8400	$6600
2. tax savings	2500	-0-
3. net cost	5900	6600
4. actual/month	500	550

from a particular audience's perspective since what may be unfamiliar or complex to one audience may be familiar and simple for another.

Any speech aid is inappropriate if it needlessly duplicates the oral presentation. If you can take away an aid and it does not hurt the effectiveness of the presentation, the aid is unnecessary and inappropriate.

Always remember that speech aids are extensions of you as a speaker, not substitutes for your actual speaking. Test your choice of an aid against the part it will play in helping you achieve your speech's specific purpose.

☐ Kinds of Aids

Visual aids are the most frequently used. However, depending upon one's specific purpose, other types of aids may be more appropriate. If you are talking about different types of music, it might be of value to have recorded excerpts of classical, jazz, country western, and rock music. This would be an instance of an *audio* aid being of more assistance than a visual aid. Audio aids might also be played quietly in the background during a speech so as to create a mood, or for some other special effect. *Tactile* aids appeal to an audience's sense of touch. A speech on the communication systems of the handicapped could give the audience an opportunity to feel a book printed in braille. Also, speakers who bring objects (e.g., coins, cultural artifacts) to use as visual aids in their speeches are simultaneously providing tactile aids if they allow members of the audience to hold and examine such materials. What better way to illustrate a speech on "The Many Moods of Perfume" than by providing scents for your audience to sample. Or, if you are giving a speech on how to bake a cake, the smell of a freshly baked spice cake can add a desired effect. These are examples of *olfactory* aids.

The speech aids discussed thus far are used quite literally: They are intended as near-exact representations of the orally presented speech material. *Figurative* aids are illustrative in a metaphorical way. A figurative speech aid suggests a likeness between objects or ideas that are normally considered unlike. An example of a figurative aid, in a speech entitled "What Your Footwear Tells About Where Your Head Is At," would be using several pairs of shoes, of different styles, to illustrate different personality types; e.g., wingtips = aggressive and business-oriented, jogging shoes = energetic and inner-directed, spike heels = impractical and other-directed. The use of figurative aids can be fun and creative if constructed thoughtfully, and can provide concreteness for otherwise abstract concepts.

Visual aids can be either projected or unprojected. Unprojected visual aids are not dependent upon a light source to project an image. Chalk boards, magnetic boards, charts, models, objects, and pictures are examples of unprojected visual aids. In contrast, projected visual aids require a light source to project their visual image. Slides, films, and overhead transparencies are examples of projected visual aids. Table 4.3 enumerates the advantages and disadvantages of using either unprojected or projected visual aids.

TABLE 4.3   Basic Types of Visual Aids Used in Public Speaking

I.   *Unprojected visuals:* Any visual which does not rely on an artificial light source to project an image. Examples include: flip charts, blackboards, posters, models, objects, photographic prints, etc.

Advantages	Disadvantages
1. Relatively inexpensive	1. Not appropriate for a large group
2. Readily available	2. Using a blackboard often requires a speaker to face away from the audience (unless the information is written on the board ahead of time)
3. No mechanical or electrical parts to break down	
4. Can be used in a lighted room; therefore the speaker and audience can see each other, their notes, etc.	3. Blackboards and easels for charts are not always readily available
5. Easy to use	4. May be cumbersome to transport and handle
6. Can be prepared ahead of time by the speaker	5. Difficult to create mood or to inspire
7. Allows the audience the freedom to individually examine your materials either before and/or after your speech	
8. Doesn't require an elaborate setup	

II.   *Projected Visuals:* Any visual which relies upon an artificial light source to project an image. Examples include overhead transparencies, slides, videotape, filmstrip, film

A. Overhead Transparencies

Advantages	Disadvantages
1. Can present information in systematic developmental sequences	1. Equipment is subject to availability and breakdown
2. Uses easy-to-operate projector	2. If using more than one transparency, they may easily get out of order or sequence
3. Presentation rate controlled by the speaker	3. Difficult to create mood
4. Frequently requires only limited planning	
5. Can be prepared by a variety of simple, inexpensive methods by the speaker	
6. Can be used with large groups	
7. Can be used in a lighted room	
8. Information can be added to transparencies during the presentation	
9. Easy to revise and update	
10. Easy to use, store, and rearrange for various uses	
11. Information can be shown using a pointer on the transparency to direct attention to detail	
12. Overlay sheets can be moved so as to rearrange elements of a diagram or problem	
13. Transparencies can be masked to conceal information	
14. Additional transparencies can be superimposed as overlays onto base transparencies in order to separate processes and complex ideas into elements and present them progressively	

TABLE 4.3   Basic Types of Visual Aids Used in Public Speaking (*Continued*)

15. Motion can be simulated on parts of a transparency by using the effects of a polarized light on special plastic with a polaroid spinner
16. Three-dimensional objects can be shown from the stage of the projector—in silhouette if the object is opaque or in color if the object is made of a transparent color plastic
17. The material to be presented as transparencies can be inexpensively duplicated on paper so that it can be used as a handout

B. Slides

Advantages:

1. Easy to use, store, and rearrange for various uses
2. Prepared programs give polished support
3. Sound and slide changes can be incorporated into one package which is synchronized to run by itself
4. Can be used to establish mood, capture attention
5. Image size can be easily changed (with proper lenses)
6. Can be easily revised and updated
7. May be adapted for group or individual use
8. Results in colorful, realistic reproduction of original subjects
9. Can be used with large groups
10. Can be purchased from a number of sources
11. Can present information in systematic, developmental sequences
12. Presentation rate controlled by speaker

Disadvantages:

1. Slides from an outside vendor may be expensive
2. Equipment is subject to availability and breakdown
3. Room lights must be turned out for proper visibility
4. Can get out of sequence and be projected incorrectly if slides are handled individually
5. Slides may jam in projector
6. Must be used in a room which can be darkened
7. May be difficult to produce yourself

C. Videotape

Advantages:

1. Is capable of easily showing motion
2. Can be used in conjunction with computer-generated graphics
3. Can be used in a lighted room
4. Program can be prepared ahead of time to run by itself
5. Is easy to transport a single video (assuming the player, monitor/TV are provided) and set up on location
6. Can be used to show close-up detail
7. Prepared programs can be purchased

Disadvantages:

1. Can be expensive to produce or purchase
2. Production usually requires assistance from an outside source
3. Provides a small picture—therefore audience size must be small or else you must provide a monitor/TV for every 20–25 people
4. Equipment is subject to availability and breakdown

Because they are most often used, *visual* aids have a greater chance of being misused. Again, regardless of the kind of aid used, aids are extensions of the speaker, not substitutes for a speaker or for a poorly constructed speech. The less dependent you are on external additions to the speech, the more in control you will be. The more dependent you are on aids, the more you are open to unexpected problems.

☐ Sources for Aids

A speaker using speech aids can make them, rent them, or buy them. If you design your own aid, consider the following suggestions:

Visual Aids

1. Your aid should be large enough to be seen by all members of your audience. (See the charts at the end of this appendix regarding letter sizes for projected and unprojected materials.)
2. Keep your aid simple. If your aid includes too much information, your audience may get confused or read ahead. If necessary, divide the information into a series of aids.
3. Attend to the colors you use. Some colors (e.g., some shades of yellow) have very low visibility and are difficult to see from even close up. If you are contrasting points, use contrasting colors. Don't let your color choice contradict the corresponding spoken text. (E.g., If you say that a corporation is operating $2000 "in the red" and you have a chart that shows that figure, print the $2000 figure in red, not blue.)
4. Your aid should look neat. Unless you are a good printer, use stencils for words. Make sure the text runs straight across and not downhill or uphill.
5. If you need to draw people and you are concerned about your artistic skill, draw stick figures or schematic representations.
6. When you present information obtained from a source outside of yourself (e.g., graphs from the Department of Education or statistics from a newspaper article), cite the source of your information (see Chapter 4 on research and note taking).

Audio Aids

1. If using a record or tape recording, be sure the sound is clean and of good quality.
2. Adjust the volume during the taping so that the entire audience can hear the aid without straining. Avoid extremes of too quiet or too loud.
3. If you use a cassette tape recorder and you tape several different segments to use in one speech, note the starting and stopping point of each segment on the recorder's counter. If you need to shorten the listening time of a segment

or skip a segment, you can use the counter numbers to help you smoothly move on to the next section of the audio aid.

4. When you use an audio aid as background, arrange it to coordinate with the spoken text of your speech. (You don't want a military march when you are talking about something intended to be soothing and quiet.)

5. Be certain that the recording is not too lengthy. Your audience may start to drift away if they have to listen to an overly long recording.

If you choose to rent or buy your speech aid, ask your instructor for assistance. If you are searching for specific, or specific types, of films, slides, graphics, statistics, recordings, start with your school librarian or a public librarian. Educational institutions often have media departments staffed with knowledgeable and helpful people. The resources are out there, but you will have to put forth the effort to locate them.

☐ Guidelines for the Use of Speech Aids

Certain precautions are necessary regardless of the type of speech aid that a speaker may use. We have grouped such overall suggestions in the "general" category below. Following the general guidelines are specific suggestions for using visual, audio, tactile, and olfactory speech aids. Read the general guidelines before moving to the section that discusses the specific sensory aid that you wish to use.

General Guidelines

1. Have you *first* planned your speech and *then* decided on appropriate speech aids?

2. Have you checked the room before the presentation? Can you locate the lights, outlets? Are you satisfied with the seating arrangement?

3. If you need any equipment (e.g., chalk, erasers, pens, paper, chalk board, electrical equipment), have you made arrangements for the equipment to be where you want it when you want it to be there?

4. If equipment is being provided, did you check whether all the needed parts were included (e.g., a long enough extension cord, a screen, an extra bulb)?

5. Are you prepared for the equipment not to work? Not to be there?

6. Can you remember not to use any aid beyond the necessary time? If you are using more than one aid, remember to put the aid away when it is no longer needed.

7. Can you make transitions back and forth between the speech and your aids?

8. Do your aids take your attention away from your audience? It is important to talk to your audience and not to your aid.

9. Have you rehearsed your speech with your aids? Can you handle the aids so that they do not become a distraction?

10. During rehearsal have you timed yourself? A speech + aids usually = more presentation time.

Visual Aids

1. Are your aids large enough for the audience to see them?
2. Are your aids positioned so that they may be easily seen by all members of the audience?
3. If you are using the chalk board, have you written or drawn your information ahead of time so as not to take away time from your speech?
4. If you have written on the board ahead of time, have you covered the information with a pull-down screen or blank paper that may be kept in place until you want your audience to see your aid?
5. Do you have chalk and an eraser available for your presentation?
6. When using flip charts, do you have wall space and masking tape in case you want to tear off a sheet and tape it to the wall for display while you move on?
7. If your aids are not projected, do you have some way of displaying them without having to hold them up? Clips? An easel?
8. If you need to refer to a specific part of your aid, do you have a pointer? A pointer blocks less of the aid than does your arm.
9. Have you positioned charts on the same side as you are handed—right-handed, charts on right side? This way when you point to your aid you won't have to cross your body with your pointing arm or have your back to your audience.
10. If you are using a series of aids, are they in their correct order?
11. If you are not using your own projection equipment, have you made the necessary arrangements for the equipment to be in the right place at the right time?
12. Do you have the correct projection equipment for your aids?
13. If you are using projection equipment, do you know how to operate it?
14. If you are using a slide or movie projector, does it have remote controls for operation? If not, have you made arrangements for an operator to be present?
15. Do you plan to distribute handouts, or pass around any objects? Carefully consider the best distribution pattern.

Audio Aids

1. Is your recording at the volume necessary for all to hear it without being too loud?
2. Are the acoustics of the room suitable so that a recording may be heard without an echo?
3. Is your recording cued for easy location and movement from portion to portion?
4. Does the speaking situation require that you use a microphone? What types of microphone are available? Which best meets your needs?
5. Have you adjusted the microphone for position? Voice level?
6. If you need additional amplification equipment, have you arranged for it?

Tactile Aids

1. Have you properly cleaned and prepared the items to be handled by your audience?
2. Have you prepared directions for your audience regarding the proper handling of objects to be passed around?

Olfactory Aids

1. Are you using a number of fragrances? Remember, too many scents begin to blend together for most people and the individual scent may lose its usefulness as a separate aid.

Two final suggestions: If you have decided that a speech aid is necessary in order to accomplish your specific purpose, keep the aid as simple as possible.

If you can accomplish your specific purpose on your own, avoid the use of aids. The use of external additions to the speech setting causes the speaker to forfeit some control of the situation to other people or be at the mercy of mechanical or electronic devices. Murphy's law states: "If anything can go wrong it will!" This can be especially true when using speech aids.

Organization and Outlining

Chapter Five

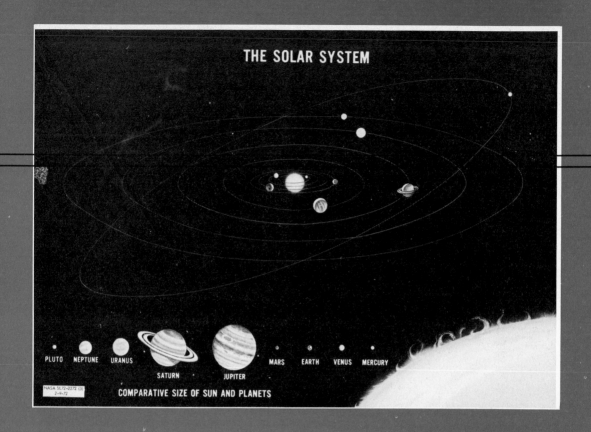

THE SOLAR SYSTEM

PLUTO   NEPTUNE   URANUS   SATURN   JUPITER   MARS   EARTH   VENUS   MERCURY

COMPARATIVE SIZE OF SUN AND PLANETS

NASA 5L72-2272 (3)
2-4-72

"Organized thought is the basis of organized action. Organization is the adjustment of diverse elements so that their mutual relations may exhibit some predetermined quality."
Alfred North Whitehead, *The Organization of Thought*

☐ Organization

The impetus to organize things seems to be innate in human beings. The seemingly natural and almost involuntary urge to organize suggests a human delight in unity and harmony, a preference for order rather than chaos. Human beings generally prefer some degree of predictability to total uncertainty. We are uncomfortable when faced with evidence of organization destroyed, as when we view the carcass of an animal killed on the highway. For most of us chaos and anarchy are repugnant. We seek order, we seek organization.

This human organizational imperative has been the subject of reflection by philosophers and scholars for centuries. In the sixth century B.C., the Chinese philosopher Lao Tzu and the Greek philosopher Heraclitus were both testifying to the need for human beings to bring order out of the conflicting elements humans face in their daily lives, to bring some kind of unity out of disunity, to bring some kind of harmony out of discord.

Robert Nozick, a contemporary American philosopher, when discussing human values says, "Values are organic unities; something is intrinsically valuable in accordance with its degree of organic unity" (1981, p. 446). Humans create values by a process of integration, of creating harmony, of bringing unity out of diversity. Given the importance of ethics in all human communication this position also suggests that the negative personal value and unethical social reality of lying may well derive from the manner in which a lie distorts and destroys the inherent revelatory unity of an act of spoken language.

When faced with something seemingly so disorganized as to defy interpretation we are often asked by others, or ask ourselves, "Can you make any sense out of that?" If we are asked to pronounce the word "cho—pho—use," or the word "pol—opo—nies," we are likely to make a few errors until we reorganize the letters into more recognizable and familiar patterns and see in them the words "chop house," and "polo ponies."

It is even true that if we, as individuals, fail to consciously organize an act prior to its performance, we still are so desirous of organization that we will impose organization upon the act after its enactment. Consider the case of works of abstract art. Many of us look in admiration but simultaneously try to "make sense" of the artwork, searching for organization, seeking for patterns. The same "search after organization" typifies some efforts at poetry analysis. It is also difficult for us to accept historical events as purely random, we search for reasons and for patterns.

Perhaps this human tendency to organization is a response to the contrasting physical tendency toward disorganization, toward the increase of entropy in the universe. All animals try to reduce entropy, or uncertainty, through communication. Human animals have the added advantage of being able to utilize spoken symbols in their communication. Spoken symbolic communication enhances the human capacity for reducing uncertainty and for introducing organization where earlier there had been disorganization (Boulding, 1956; Dance and Larson, 1976, pp. 55–58; Hewes, 1975, pp. 76–81).

Human communication, enhanced by spoken language, allows us to communicate across great expanses of space, and over great lengths of time. This is true of spoken language alone and it is even more true of spoken language when it is transformed into another medium such as writing or print or electronic codes. For most of history, and today for most people in the world, spoken language is either the only or the predominant form of human language. Writing, print, and the accompanying literacy are acquired characteristics, parasitic upon spoken language and far from universally distributed among our fellows.

The reason we stress the dominance of spoken language is that public speaking is essentially a spoken language behavior. When public speaking becomes predominantly a written language behavior, we then have an "essay on its hind legs," rather than a "speech." As we have discussed in Chapter Two, there are substantial differences between oral style and written style and these differences substantially alter the substance and the form of a public speech.

Spoken language brings with it a structuring of individual thought processes. In a preliterate society the characteristics of spoken language affect the social thought processes as well. It is difficult for those of us who have been literate for most of our lives to sympathize or understand the effects on thought of the absence of writing and print. We live in what Ong has called a secondary oral culture, a culture in which literacy has altered our oral thought processes (Ong, 1967). However, each one of us has at one time lived in a primary oral culture when we were infants and children prior to our acquisition of the ability to read and to write.

What kinds of things are true of a primary oral culture, how is thought affected by the presence of spoken language without an accompanying presence of written or printed language? If you speak, but don't write or read, you have a recall limited by the spoken word. Spoken words come into being and simultaneously are passing out of being—they are evanescent. When listening to a speech you are constrained by having to listen to new material at the same time you may be processing the material you have just heard. The complications of an oral argument or of an oral explanation can become very difficult to attend to if such argument or explanation is detailed and lengthy. Ong once observed in a speech that in a primary oral culture an explanation may be quite truncated as in this example:

A is caused by B.
B is caused by C.
C is caused because Athena got mad at Zeus.

On the other hand, when our speaking is extended through literacy, we are able to construct quite convoluted arguments and quite lengthy explanations since our reader can go back and forth in the written or printed text and refresh his or her memory and consider the logic of the argument or explanation without having simultaneously to attend to additional input.

Public speeches are oral experiences. It is preferable to allow an oral "way of knowing" (also called an oral "noetic") to predominate. If you are having difficulty understanding this discussion, let us relate a recent experience. One of us was asked to talk to a preschool class, a group of 3-year-olds. Three-year-olds, even living in a literate society, are members of a primarily oral culture, few 3-year-olds read or write. Combined with their primary orality, 3-year-olds have the short attention span characteristic of young children. The speaker, even with abundant public speaking experience, found this one of the most difficult audiences ever faced. There could be no development of an idea, there could be no presumption of attention—except to the novelty, which soon wore off—there could be no reliance upon a reservoir of past experience on the part of the audience in listening to speeches. It was tough. It was absolutely imperative that the speaker work within the boundaries of primary orality. Such an experience isn't typical of public speeches in our culture—but it was an instructive one. In fact, if you yourself want to gain some experience of speaking to a predominantly primary oral culture, try talking with a similar group. Even when the speaker and the audience are all presumably literate, as in listening to a news broadcast, it is usual that the speaker, the newscaster—reading from a prepared script—tries to the utmost to sound as if the remarks are *not* being read but are instead the spontaneous conversation of the speaker.

As a public speaker in a literate society, you may presume literacy on the part of most of your audience and most of your audiences. However, we advise and encourage you to develop a public speaking style which is dominantly an oral style and which uses audiovisual aids where appropriate but still relies heavily on the techniques attendant upon knowing in an oral manner. Such an oral commitment will manifest itself in your speech preparation from the moment of choice of topic through the determination of a general purpose and the structuring of your specific purpose and the rest of the speech. In a public speech there are certain things which are generally best not attempted—such as the presentation of an extraordinarily long and convoluted argument calling for all kinds of recursive allusions and statistical support. Such an argument, or explanation, is prime material for an essay or a set of written arguments, a "brief," or a book-length exposition.

On the other hand, we should not neglect the advantages of literacy. In public speaking in our culture there is ample reason to make use of audio/visual aids, such as handouts, overhead transparencies, films, slides, and tapes where appropriate.

The manifestation of organization is a pattern evidencing that the speaker has taken a certain point of view concerning the material of the speech. We will talk more about available patterns later in this chapter.

In organizing your speech: Take an "oral" point of view, and use language suitable to an oral style rather than a written style.

You have now completed your remote and immediate preparation and your research. Remember at the end of Chapter Three we set up a means of making a preliminary outline of your material? *Now you should go back to your preliminary outline and add in all of the materials you have gathered as a result of your research.* In your preliminary outline you have listed your topic, your general purpose (to inform, to convince, to persuade, or to entertain), and a simply stated preliminary specific purpose. So far you have (1) found a topic; (2) put down on your preliminary outline everything you know about the topic as a result of your remote and immediate preparation; (3) searched for and found the blank spots in your information; (4) tried through research, to the best of your ability, to fill these blank spots with accurate information.

Now is the time to refine and polish the specific purpose of your speech.

☐ Specific Purpose

Developing a well-constructed specific purpose is most important to the preparation of a successful public speech. In most instances we are more successful in an activity when we adequately plan to be successful. If we have a goal in mind, we usually are able to choose the means for reaching that goal. The more specific the goal, the more specific the means. If you live in Boston and want to go to England, you can choose to get there by ship, by air, by balloon, or perhaps by means that are even more unusual than a balloon. If you live in Boston and wish to go to Denver, as quickly as possible, ship is usually out of the question. The more specific your destination, the more specific the means by which you will reach your destination. If you want to be wealthy, it isn't always easy to determine when you have reached your goal. If you want to acquire $100,000 in savings, the goal itself signals when you have reached it. Your goal can serve to help you in your plans to reach it and can also help you in evaluating your success when you reach it.

A well-constructed and polished specific purpose can assist you in putting together the rest of your speech and can also assist you in gauging the success of your speech after it has been given. When you have finished giving your speech, the members of the audience should be able to tell what it was you wanted to accomplish in you speech. If asked to reflect upon it, they should fairly accurately be able to restate your specific purpose.

The specific purpose refers to the exact outcome the speaker intends and hopes to achieve, with this audience, with this particular speech.

- The specific purpose should be as specific as possible.
- The specific purpose should be stated, if at all possible, in a single declarative sentence.

- The specific purpose should be something that is realistically attainable within the limits of the speaker, the speech, the audience, the occasion, and the time available.

More speakers fail from trying to accomplish too much in a speech than from trying to do too little. Think about the time available, the audience, and the occasion and then try to state your specific purpose as simply as possible. Think about what, when the speech is over, you would like to have had accomplished with the audience. Perhaps you have 15 minutes available and you would like to have your audience understand the importance of organization to human beings. You can't possibly cover everything from Lao Tzu and Heraclitus to the present (using a chronological pattern), so you decide to concentrate your remarks on the role of organization in simply getting through a single day of an individual's life. Your specific purpose might be stated this way:

☐ *Specific Purpose:* To develop within my audience an understanding of how an individual uses organization to get through a single day.
or another choice:

☐ *Specific Purpose:* To develop in my audience an appreciation of how an individual's natural rhythm may be used in organizing the day's activities.
Or suppose you are going to give a talk about the subject of organizing a speech:

☐ *Unaccaptable*
Specific Purpose: To tell about organizing a speech.
By our standards that is a pretty weak specific purpose. Here is a much stronger one:

☐ *Specific Purpose:* To bring about a realization of the importance of organized material for achieving a specific purpose.
Perhaps you have been asked to give a speech in celebration of Flag Day for a local merchant's association. You have 15 minutes available for your speech. How about this:

☐ *Unacceptable*
Specific Purpose: To tell my audience all about flags throughout history.
No. That is obviously too much for 15 minutes, and besides it isn't pointed enough for a celebration of the American Flag Day. This would be better:

☐ *Specific Purpose:* To develop within my audience an understanding of how the first American flag came into being.
or

☐ *Specific Purpose:* To bring about within my audience an appreciation of the importance of the American flag as a unifying national symbol.

The shorter the speech, the more pointed you must be in delineating your specific purpose. In many ways short speeches present a speaker with greater difficulties than do longer speeches. A short speech must be exceedingly well constructed and delivered; a longer speech allows more leeway for handling lapses of memory or errors of presentation.

There are some subjects which simply cannot be very adequately dealt with in a short speech: nuclear fission, the essence of justice—these are topics about which one would wish for a substantial amount of time to speak. There are also topics that are totally unsuited to some audiences. To speak to a first grade class about the problems of retirement—no matter how much time is available, this doesn't sound like a promising topic for that audience. There are topics which we might not be able to speak about given all the time in the world and the brightest possible audience, topics that are beyond the speaker's grasp. Not all of us can speak intelligently about theology or quantum physics or mysticism. The occasion may also block some topics. To choose to speak in praise of the Democratic party candidate at a dinner for the Republican candidate would seem inappropriate.

Take your time in putting together your specific purpose. Rework it, re-phrase it, until it pretty much says exactly what you would like to have happen with this audience as a result of their hearing your speech on this occasion. If you do a good job in stating your specific purpose, you can use the final specific purpose in at least two ways. First, you can use your specific purpose to help decide what goes into the speech and what gets cut out of the speech. Only those things should go into the speech which assist you in achieving your specific purpose. Certainly nothing should be included in the speech which would detract from your achieving your specific purpose. So you can use a well-worded specific purpose as a means of judging which of your materials from your preliminary outline get included in your preparatory outline. Second, you can use your specific purpose as a means of judging whether or not your speech was a success. The degree to which you have achieved your specific purpose, to that degree you have given a successful speech. The degree to which you have failed to achieve your specific purpose, to that degree your speech has failed.

Since the specific purpose is the goal of your entire speech, it is in terms of the specific purpose that you should organize your speech. Now that you have chosen your topic and your general purpose and you have refined your specific purpose, you are ready to organize your speech.

□ The Rule of 30/70

At the beginning of this chapter we pointed out the fact that in general human beings much prefer some degree of predictability to total uncertainty. Actually most of us prefer more predictability than more uncertainty. But we want some of both uncertainty and predictability. If we have too much uncertainty, we get fragmented and disorganized, we get lost. If we have too much predictability, we get disinterested and restless, we get bored. The same is true for an audience— too much unpredictability or uncertainty in a speech and the audience gets lost, too much predictability in a speech and the audience gets bored. In either case of too much, we lose our audience.

Audiences like to hear what is new—but not too new. Audiences like to hear what is novel—but not too novel.

We suggest, based upon extensive public speaking experience as well as upon some indirect theoretical support, that as a rule an audience best handles a speech in which there is approximately 30 percent variety (or uncertainty) and approximately 70 percent predictability. This is what we refer to as the rule of 30/70. The 30/70 rule is not a factual rule; it is a suggested rule of thumb meant to help you (but not to constrain you) in your speech preparation and delivery. Our best recommendation for using the 30/70 rule of thumb is that we have found it to work more often than not in speeches we have given and in speeches we have heard.

The 30/70 rule exists within a time frame. The longer the speech, the more you will be able to fit within the 30 percent variety. What is more, if you are able to stop the input of new material for a few minutes, by using examples, anecdotes, humor, you will allow some of the 30 percent to sift down and be absorbed into the 70 percent comfortable predictability, thus leaving some space for additional novelty in your speech. By using decentering and association you can reduce the threat of novelty by working with devices such as analogy, illustrations, and redundancy (as well as the examples, anecdotes, and humor mentioned above).

The 30/70 is plotted in terms of a baseline. The baseline is arrived at by decentering. You decenter to your audience in order to figure out exactly what the audience would like to know about the topic you are addressing. While decentering to the audience, you also take into consideration how much the audience already knows about the subject. Where the audience is vis-à-vis your subject prior to your speech constitutes the baseline from which you then construct your speech utilizing 30 percent variety and 70 percent predictability.

Another aspect of handling the rule of 30/70 is through patterning—designing a pattern for the presentation of your material. The audience can use the pattern as a framework within which to organize their own perception of your speech; the pattern can reduce the threat of excessive variety by establishing a feeling of patterned predictability.

☐ Internal Organizational Patterns

At the beginning of this chapter we discussed the seemingly innate human imperative to organization. In many if not all things there is present an inherent organizational structure. Patterns manifest themselves all around us. The human body has an organization of cells, tissues, organs, and systems of organs. A flower has an internal organization. There is the organization of the solar system and the organization given to time as a result of the rotation of the sun around the earth. If closely examined, most reality will yield up a hint of its organization to the patient investigator.

The first step in organizing a speech is to examine the topic, the specific purpose, and the materials to see if there might be an inherent, natural, organizational pattern present. Recently there has been a lot of interest in the oriental approach called Zen. In Chapter Three when discussing topic selection for your speech, we quoted from Pirsig's book *Zen and the Art of Motorcycle Maintenance*. In his book Pirsig talks about ways of viewing reality. One of the goals of the Zen method is to enable you to see into the essence, the core of something. In examining your speech material for an inner pattern, allow yourself to simply meditate on what you have thus far pulled together, to reflect on what it—the material—says to you. Consider whether some points seem preliminary to other points, whether some points flow naturally from a consideration of earlier statements within the material—search for any pattern that seems to be imbedded within the material itself. If you do find such a pattern, carefully reflect upon it, uncover it, unpack it, listen to what it says to you and how it says it. The pattern that is part and parcel of the subject is often the most effective pattern for communicating the subject to others.

The examples of the natural organization of the body, of a flower, and of the solar system are but a few among many. Even when considering such a modern-day artifact as a personal computer, one can find an internal organization which is true of all examples of personal computers, an internal organization which could be used as a means of organizing a speech on the subject. Suppose you are going to give a speech on the topic of computers, with the general purpose to inform, and in which your specific purpose is as follows.

☐ *Specific Purpose:* To assist the audience in understanding the essential components of a personal computer.

What are the essential components of a personal computer? At the very least such an instrument would have to provide the capacity for input, processing, and output and this usually means there will be a keyboard (an input device), a central processing unit (the heart of the computer), and some kind of an output device such as a TV screen or a printer. An organizational structure for a speech begins to become apparent. You will have to tell the audience what a personal computer essentially does and the hardware (equipment) it needs in order to do it. The degree of detail you can present is related to the sophistication of the audience, your own understanding, as well as the available time. This, by the way, would be a speech which could profit greatly from visual aids.

Another topic might be a team sport such as football, baseball, hockey, or polo. Any team sport, if you think about it, has certain common elements, elements which could be used to structure a speech describing the sport to an audience.

Even though most things have some kind of natural inner organization, you may for any number of reasons choose not to take the time to discover that inner organization, or even if you have discovered it you might choose not to use it. In such a case you may well wish to superimpose upon the topic an external organizational pattern.

□ External Organizational Patterns

As we know, human communication doesn't work by transfer but by association. Good use of association is the result of a well-developed capacity for decentering. The key words for choosing an appropriate external organizational pattern for your speech are *decentering* and *association*. Decenter to your anticipated audience members and try to perceive which external organizational pattern might be most successful in helping them associate their past knowledge and experience with the material you are presenting in your speech.

From the many available external patterns we have chosen a group that seem most generally useful.

1. **Deductive (from general to specific).**   Suppose we go back to our earlier topic of flags. In using a deductive pattern, we could move from a general treatment of flags as representative emblems to a more specific treatment of the flags of different countries.
2. **Inductive (from specific to general).**   If we were using this pattern, we could start with a description of the flag of the United States of America and then move to a consideration of flags in general. The inductive pattern is the opposite of the deductive pattern.
3. **Simple to complex.**   Flags come in varying degrees of complexity involving colors and geometrical patterns. A speech could be organized so as to first treat the simplest form of a flag and then progress to more involved patterns

Flags—a Topic That Can Be Organized in Many Different Ways (© Joel Gordon 1982)

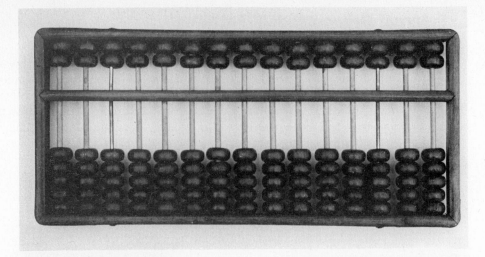

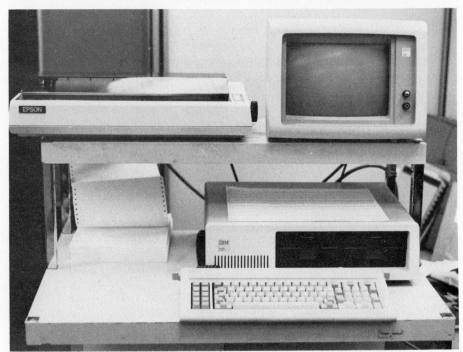

One Could Arrange a Talk about Computers Chronologically, Starting with the Abacus and Moving to the Most Recent Developments in Computers (The Image Works)

of colors and symbols. In our earlier example of a speech on personal computers we could start with the simplest configuration for a personal computer and then move to include more elaborate setups. The same pattern might work nicely for a speech on hi-fi systems. This is a reversible pattern—you could also organize your speech moving from complex to simple (our decentering should warn us that this reversal is not always a good idea).

4. **Part to whole.** Although somewhat similar to simple to complex, this is not the same pattern. For example, you might wish to discuss just one program you can run on a personal computer (and it might be a fairly complex program) before considering overall uses of a personal computer. If your topic was the music of Beethoven, you might first treat his symphonies before considering his works as a whole. This is a reversible pattern since you could also organize your speech moving from the whole to the parts. Using Beethoven again, you could first discuss his overall contributions as a composer and then talk about his symphonies in particular.

5. **Cause and effect.** In giving a speech on a suggested change in legislation, you could first state the proposed new law and then go on to show that the effects would be upon the general population if that new law were passed. This is a reversible pattern. You could discuss current problems of crime, giving specific examples and then trace them back to show what has caused them to multiply.

6. **Problem/solution.** Although this might sound a lot like the cause and effect pattern, they are distinct. You can have a problem/solution which are unrelated to cause and effect. For example, most mathematical problems are not thought of as being "caused." For some social problems the cause is so remote that it is not discernible. In fact the cause of some social problems might simply not have any bearing on a current solution to the problem. Your speech might deal with the problem of getting adequate distribution of a new product: First you detail the problem and then you set forth your suggested solutions to the problem. You may wish to consider the problem of hunger in some countries and then suggest possible solutions to that problem. This is a reversible pattern. You could begin your speech with a proposed plan of action and then show how that proposed plan of action would solve some current and bothersome problem.

7. **Temporal.** This is a very easy and useful pattern. It is sometimes called a chronological pattern. You can simply organize your materials in terms of their order in time. Let's go back to the topic flags. We can first talk about the earliest flags and then move on to discuss how flags have evolved over the centuries. Obviously this is an easily reversible pattern. There are innumerable topics which can be organized around the three general headings of past, present, and future. A speech on mass media would be such a topic. Many beginning speeches on topics such as "How To Change the Oil in an Automobile" are organized around a first step, second step, third step temporal or chronological pattern.

8. **Spatial.** This is another easy and useful pattern. Suppose you wanted to give a speech informing your audience about Colonial Williamsburg in Virginia. You could discuss the layout of the original city starting with the Governor's Palace and then take the audience on a simulated tour of the reconstructed village. If you were dealing with the arms race in the world, you could move geographically in your presentation. If you were discussing the architecture of a new building, you could arrange your speech based on the different parts of the structure. If you were speaking on the subject of wine, you could discuss California wines as compared with the wines of Europe.

9. **Topical.** This is a pattern which is often used as a catchall when you can't discover a pattern more appropriate to the needs of the audience. A topical pattern, sometimes called a string-of-beads pattern is a pattern organized around general subject matter headings. You might organize a speech around topic headings which have a meaning just for you, such as "Why I am interested in this subject," "Why I think you should be interested in this subject." Although a topical pattern can at times be a good one, you should avoid using it as a substitute for more careful analysis of a pattern better meeting the needs of decentering and association for your subject, occasion, and audience. Some patterns which at first thought may seem to be topical may have another underlying pattern. We have heard a speech on stage fright organized around the five stages of dying. Although the speech was quite effective, the speaker was in error in considering it a topical pattern since the five stages of dying were originally organized in a chronological pattern by the author, Dr. Elisabeth Kübler-Ross.

10. **Contrast.** By now you have a good idea of what is meant by the concept of contrast. You can organize a speech by contrasting the status quo, the situation as it is, with the situation as it might be or with the situation as you would like to see it. You can contrast a symphony with another form of musical composition. You can contrast the present American flag with the flag of 100 years ago. You can contrast how you felt when giving your first speech with how you feel giving the last speech in the course.

□ Pattern Combinations

Our previous discussion of the external organizational pattern called "contrast" is an example of combined patterns. When using contrast, you can also organize temporally or spatially. This is true of the other patterns as well. You could organize your speech using a combination of problem/solution and spatial by treating the problem of hunger in different parts of the world. Although we would recommend that in your early speeches you confine yourself to a single pattern, as you gain confidence in your public speaking you will want to try out some pattern combinations if such combinations best meet the audience needs as dictated by decentering and association. The same holds true of combining internal and external patterns. There is an internal organization to the human body, but you may also wish to treat the evolution of that organic organization across time.

□ Patterns for Impromptu Speeches

Since impromptu speeches by their nature seldom allow sufficient time for extended pattern analysis, you can use brief forms of some of the external patterns for organizing your impromptu remarks. Here are some suggestions for organizing patterns for impromptu speeches. As you look them over, you will readily see their relationship to some of the more extended patterns treated earlier.

1. past, present, future
2. partition, development, review
3. advantages, disadvantages
4. need, plan, application
5. what it is, what it does, how to use it

☐ Outlining

An outline is a voluntarily designed artificial representation of the innate organization you have uncovered in your material or of the external organization you have superimposed upon your material. Outlines are after the fact representations of our organization. If we have followed an oral thought process in our speech organization, our outline will provide us with a representation of that organization. The outline is a gift of our capacity to write, and it is a tremendous aid to both thought and recall.

There is a tendency when outlining to force our oral organization into a written framework. For example, you may read or be told that if you have a point "A" in your outline, then you simply must have a point "B," that logic calls for such a presence. Perhaps so in written logic, not necessarily so in speech. When the testing point is the achievement of your specific purpose, point "A" may be just right, enough, stop there. While the written framework may assist us in seeing the relationship among the various elements of our speech and in correcting glaring errors, we should not allow the outline to change the nature of our speech from a predominantly oral experience to a predominantly written experience. The outline also provides us with a written record of our speech, a record that can come in very handy when we are interested in giving the same speech again some time after the first delivery. Without an outline, a carefully prepared and organized speech may be well delivered and well received but will rapidly lose its shape from disuse after its original delivery. An outline is to your speech as your skeleton is to your body: they both help keep things in shape.

Your outline is something like a roadmap. You already know your destination, but your outline helps you visualize the means of arriving at your destination. Whatever is true about an oral way of knowing, it is also true that the more modalities we are able to involve in our learning, the better our learning may be. If we hear our speech internally while preparing it and then if we see our speech in written outlined form, we will have a greater likelihood of remembering when called upon to deliver the speech.

You already have prepared your preliminary outline, the listing of your materials gathered as a result of remote preparation, immediate preparation, and research. You are now going to prepare your preparatory outline. Your preparatory outline is the most complete outline you will put together for your speech.

It is from your preparatory outline that you will rehearse your speech and finally put together your speaker's notes.

The Preparatory Outline

You now have on hand your preliminary outline, including your refined specific purpose and your organizational pattern. Your preparatory outline is going to include everything you are going to use for your speech. The asterisks on the preparatory outline form indicate transitions and will be discussed later in this chapter. The preparatory outline form will look like the one shown in Figure 5.1.

The material in the upper right-hand corner will help the outline get back to you in case you mislay it and will guarantee that you won't forget the place and date of the speaking engagement.

General Purpose and Specific Purpose

You can take the general purpose and the specific purpose directly from your preliminary outline and write them into your preparatory outline. Be certain to put down the final form of your specific purpose as worked through earlier in this chapter.

Title

A title may seem to be a relatively unimportant consideration, yet it sometimes can make the difference between someone coming to hear you speak or staying at home to watch TV. Spend a little time choosing an appropriate and catchy title for your speech. You have spent a lot of time preparing this speech, the little bit extra to find the right title will be well spent.

- The title should give some indication of the subject.
- The title should pique the curiosity of the listeners.
- The title should be as concise as possible.

Imagine that you are going to give a speech dealing with the subject of the improper administration of public transportation in major metropolitan areas in the Midwest. This is quite a mouthful to begin with, and not very intriguing either. How about this as a title for this speech: "Ride a Crooked Rail!" There is time enough in the speech itself for you to spell out the meaning of your title, but with a catchy title you at least have some hope of the audience approaching the speech occasion with some degree of curiosity.

Time

This means just what it says—how long the speech is supposed to be. You can use a notational convention from geography and use the symbol ['] to refer to minutes. So the notation 45' next to time would mean that the speech is supposed to be a 45-minute presentation. Timing is often a most important consideration in planning and presenting a speech.

_____

Your name
_____

Name of group for whom the
speech is being given
_____

Date upon which speech is
being given

General Purpose:

Specific Purpose:

Title:

Time:
_____

Introduction
  I.
      A.
          1.
          2.
*

Body
  II.
      A.
*
III.
      A.
          1.
          2.
      B.
*
IV.
*

Conclusion
  V.
      A.
      B.
*
                         **
_____

Expandable material
Expendable material
Bibliography

Figure 5.1 Sample Outline Format

Introduction

At the very outset of your speech you have the involuntary attention of your audience. The fact that someone is speaking where there was no one speaking before causes the audience members to attend at the outset. *The introduction of the speech needs to convert that involuntary attention to voluntary attention.* Although the audience starts listening because of novelty, they must choose to continue listening because of the material of the speech and the presentational style of the speaker. The introduction allows you your first opportunity to use decentering and association to involve the audience in your speech. The introduction usually accounts for somewhere between 10 and 15 percent of your total speaking time.

When first outlining your introduction, leave yourself some leeway for change. As you go through the process of outlining your whole speech, you may find some things you would like to add to or delete from your outline. So be open to adjusting your introduction even after you have completed the rest of the outline.

If you have been properly introduced to the audience by the toastmaster or the master of ceremonies or by someone especially charged with introducing the speaker, then your authority for giving the speech should be clear to the audience. It sometimes happens that the audience doesn't know or understand why you are entitled to speak on the subject you have chosen; they may be unaware of your credentials. If such is the case, then you have to build into your speech introductory materials that will give the audience reason to believe that you are a qualified speaker on the topic. Building your own credibility is a task that calls for delicacy and good taste on your part. You should try and present evidence that you are a credible speaker on the subject but you must, at the same time, not give the impression of undue egotism and self-satisfaction. Perhaps some allusions to your past experience with the subject, low key but definite, will do the job. All in all it is preferable to have this job done by someone else when you are being introduced. The best way to handle it is to prepare some notes for the person introducing you and to include the materials on your credibility in those notes. Still, you should be aware that sometimes the burden of establishing your credibility will fall on you.

During your introduction you should also be trying to sense the mood of the audience; you should be sensitive to audience feedback from the very outset of your speaking.

In our culture an expectation has been developed that a speaker will use humor in his or her introduction. Often this is worth doing *if* the humor is appropriate and *if* you are comfortable using humor. Certainly your first few words should allow time for the audience to settle down and give their voluntary attention to you the speaker.

Your speech's introduction should contribute directly to the achievement of your specific purpose.

A good introduction:

- captures the audiences' attention and interest
- helps the audience understand how the subject relates to them

- tells the audience about the background of the topic and possibly the specific purpose of the speech
- leads the audience into the main body of the speech

Body

This is the main part of your speech. This is where you provide the material which is going to assure that you achieve your specific purpose. Test every point in your body by asking yourself whether or not that point, and its attendant support, is going to move the audience from where they were at the beginning of the speech to the point of supporting and accepting your specific purpose. Everything in the body—main points, supporting material such as examples, illustrations, quotations, audiovisual aids, humor—should contribute directly to the ultimate realization of your specific purpose. Remember earlier we mentioned that more speakers fail because they include too much material than because they include too little material. Three main points are generally enough for an audience to remember and process. Certainly there are occasions when you might only have one point, but beware of including many more than three main points. The body of the speech should contain the greatest amount of substantive content and should consume the greatest amount of your speaking time—perhaps as much as 90 percent of the time. It is in the body that you bring to bear the full power of your decentering, association, logic, evidence, and proof.

If you are giving a long or a fairly complicated speech, you will want to include in your body some internal summaries. Clear transitions from point to point will also help the audience maintain understanding of the flow of your speech.

Throughout the body keep using your powers of observation to test the audience feedback.

A good speech body:

- covers only the material most likely to move the audience to support your specific purpose
- usually includes about three main points
- evidences thorough preparation, support, and logic

Conclusion

The conclusion provides you with an opportunity to summarize your main points, recall their importance, and apply them to the needs and interests of your audience. If you have done a good job in your body of the speech, the conclusion should present few difficulties. You have led the audience carefully through every important point in support of your specific purpose. Unspoken questions which you sense have been bothering the audience have been answered and now the time has come to bring the speech to an end. Your conclusion should "pull together" the preceding materials and apply them to *this* audience. Generally the conclusion should not introduce new substantive materials. However, while delivering your speech you may sense that a point made earlier needs to be restated—do it in the conclusion, with force.

Although we will mention this again when considering the delivery of your speech, it is worth pointing out here that it is important that you have your conclusion especially well rehearsed, you want to be able to concentrate fully on working with your audience during the conclusion—not looking at your notes or searching for just the right words. With this in mind you should be especially diligent in outlining your conclusion, giving attention to what you wish to say as well as to how you want to say it.

The conclusion, like the introduction, should be fairly short, accounting for somewhere around 10 percent of the speaking time. Beware of "false" conclusions. American audiences are intolerant of lengthy and flowery conclusions which promise much and deliver nothing. When you say you are going to conclude, do so!

A good conclusion:

- summarizes and applies your materials to *this* audience on *this* occasion
- reinforces any point you feel calls for restatement
- moves quickly and forcefully

Transitions

On the outline form given earlier in this chapter there are some asterisks. The asterisks are meant to indicate transition points in your speech. Transitions move you from one point to another, they assist you in going forward, and they assist the audience in seeing the relationships among the various points being made in the speech. Transitions are the rails upon which memory rides. Your transitions may be either vocal or nonvocal. You can move from point to point with a vocal transition that says something like "Now, what follows from what I've just said is . . ." and off you go to your next point. You can even say something as straightforward as "My next point is. . . ." However, you can also move from point to point with a simple change of posture, a facial grimace, a gesture (watch how professional comedians signal that they are moving along in their monologues—Jack Benny used to do his transitions by simply pausing, he was a pause virtuoso). You can make a transition by moving from one place on the platform to another, by coming out from behind the lectern, by going back behind the lectern. By shutting off your visual aid, by turning on a visual aid. What is important is that you be aware of how vital good transitions can be to an effective speech and that you plan your transitions in your first speeches. Between your main points, on your preparatory outline, *write out your transitions*.

The double asterisks (**) on the outline format indicate the transition at the bottom of your preparatory outline page or note card. Just put a few words at the very bottom of the page, words that will give you a start onto the thoughts on the next page. This will help avoid the choppiness of a full stop whenever you reach the end of a page or card of your preparatory outline or your notes. When you are watching professional performers, listening to professional platform speakers, watching and listening to political speakers, or reading a novel—pay attention to how the speaker or author moves from point to point. Some novelists, like Charles Dickens, can take you across great spaces and through large expanses of time with just a sentence or two—and they do it very smoothly. Consider how you can make a transition work for you in your speaking.

Since transitions are sometimes like stage directions or instructions on how to move from point to point, you don't always want to call them to the attention of the audience. Perhaps you should consider highlighting them with a transparent marker pen so that you will cue in on the transition quickly but will be warned that the material thus highlighted is *not* necessarily to be orally presented to the audience.

A good transition:

- moves the speech from point to point smoothly and without calling attention to itself
- can be words, gestures, movement, audiovisual aids, or any other suitable device
- should be carefully prepared and included in the outline

Expandable Material

At the end of your outline, after the conclusion, draw or type a couple of lines, leave a few spaces so that you know that the outline proper is completed, and then next to the words *expandable material* include a few lines which you could use if you found that your speech was going too fast and wasn't going to meet the time limits imposed by the audience or the master of ceremonies. There is no reason why, if your speech has gone well, and you feel you've accomplished your specific purpose, that you can't finish early—but on some occasions it is important that you fill the alloted time. Perhaps the overall program calls for an event following you, an event that is timed based upon your concluding on time and not earlier. (Recently one of us gave a speech following which a marching band was to burst through the doors at the rear of the auditorium and march through the audience playing a rousing fight song. It was important that the speaker concluded at the agreed-upon time so that the program could move along quickly.) You might also find that you simply misjudged the speed with which the material would go and that you could use the extra few minutes to make a point supporting the specific purpose, or for an additional example. Some notes on such material should appear at the end of your outline—just in case.

Expendable Material

You can of course find that things have been going much slower than you expected and that you need to cut some material out of your speech. While planning and rehearsing your speech, you should consider what points, examples, supportive material, humor, visual aids could be sacrificed if you needed to move along faster in order to stay within your time limit. Make notes at the end of your outline reminding you of where you could cut if such cutting is called for. You may even consider putting some kind of colored ink marks within the outline, designating those places where you could cut copy if necessary.

Bibliography

You've spent a lot of time preparing this speech. Keep notes of where you found your materials and put a bibliography at the end of your outline. There will be times when someone in the audience challenges your supporting data, or just wants to know where he or she could find more material on the subject. At such times your bibliography comes in quite handy. Again, if you go back to give the speech in the future, you will be pleased that you have a list of your references available. Follow a standard bibliographical form in putting together your outline references, like the reference form of the Modern Language Association (MLA) or of the American Psychological Association (APA) or some other widely accepted style sheet.

Outline Formatting

From time to time we have mentioned that your outline might be on either pages or note cards. In many ways this is simply a matter of the speaker's taste. Once you become comfortable with speaking in public (as comfortable as anyone ever becomes), you can make a decision as to which format you find most suitable for your style. We prefer, and most of the speakers we either know or have heard prefer, to use full paper pages, usually 8½ × 11, for the preparatory outline and speaking notes. If you find yourself speaking on TV, your notes may be transferred to huge cue cards which are held up outside of the sight of the audience, or your notes may be placed upon a teleprompter or some other such device. Generally we suggest using full-size paper and typing or printing your material. There are special typefaces available for speech outlines; one such typeface is IBM's Orator Typing Element which can be easily spotted and read from a greater distance than ordinary typefaces.

By the way, it is worthwhile when you have completed your preparatory outline to make a couple of copies of the outline. You will find yourself marking the outline up and it is nice to have a clean copy available if needed.

We are presuming that you are going to type out your preparatory outline on regular sheets of typing paper or on a computer word processor.

- Follow the outline form given on page 123 of this chapter.
- All formatting considerations have as their goal to make clear and memorable your material and organizational pattern.
- Your outline formatting should serve to aid your mentation, memory, and delivery.
- Use regular bond, not onionskin paper (it's too noisy).
- Use one side of the paper only.
- If possible use a special typeface created for speech notes.
- Leave adequate margins.
- Double-space your material.
- Use a fresh ribbon, or at least a ribbon that produces easily readable impressions.
- Use full sentences in your outline. (Later on in your speaker's notes you may

choose to use key words if you have the speech sufficiently rehearsed; we'll talk about that later.)
- Remember to consider color-highlighting your transitions.
- Leave enough room in your typed preparatory outline for adding short notes to yourself concerning the use of audiovisual aids. For example, note materials you would like handed out during your speech, or exactly when an overhead transparency is called for.
- Leave enough room in your typed preparatory outline for noting any special stories or humor you may wish to include but which come to your attention after your outline preparation.

As we have been discussing outlines, we have automatically been discussing word outlines. There is an alternate outlining method in which drawing, or visual images, are used instead of words. René Descartes, the French Enlightenment mathematician and philosopher, suggested in his writings that it is a worthwhile exercise to try and reduce abstract concepts to a visual drawing. Modern advertising practice often uses visual "storyboards" in putting together advertising campaigns and presenting such campaign proposals to clients. While we agree with Descartes that it often helps objectify and clarify abstract concepts to give them a form other than words, we are less sure that visual outlining is as helpful a practice as is word outlining. There is some evidence that visual image outlines often collapse concepts in such a manner as to obscure the finer points of an argument (Hample and Dallinger, 1984). In the very act of clarification so much reduction takes place that the complexity of many points is lost. The effect can be that the speaker viewing an outline composed of graphics or images may be unable to move from the reduced image back to the complex argument necessary to make the speech point. Current neurophysiological research suggests that visual images are given abstract meanings by being processed through the auditory cortex of the human brain. If such is the case, then we need to ask what someone hears when they see a visual image. Until we know more about the process of converting visual images to abstract concepts, our suggestion is to usually prepare a word-sentence preparatory outline.

Testing Your Preparatory Outline

As we mentioned earlier, your preparatory outline tests and enhances your mentation, your thinking. Your preparatory outline also tests and enhances the application of your decentering and association by putting in place the means by which you have chosen to link your ideas with your audience.

Following are questions to ask yourself as a means of testing how well you have done the task of putting together a preparatory outline for your speech.

Have I included all the material I need, including supporting material, explanations, and examples, to move the audience from where they were at the beginning of my speech to where they need to be if they are going to accept my specific purpose?

Is my preparatory outline complete enough that if I put it aside for some time I will still be able, upon picking it up, to deliver the speech?

Is my preparatory outline internally consistent? Is my logic clear and noncontradictory throughout? Do my evidence and supporting materials truly bear upon the points I am trying to make in order to achieve my specific purpose?

Does my preparatory outline show that I have done my best, through decentering, to use association in communicating my ideas to this audience upon this occasion?

Does the outline indicate that I followed the 30/70 rule in putting it together?

Does my outline indicate that I have searched for and developed an organizational pattern for my material?

Does my outline follow acceptable outline form?

Is my outline clearly formatted? Are transitions easy to spot?

If you recall, in Chapter Three the acronym PIER was suggested as a memory device for those things a speaker can do to raise the coping quotient and thus to control excessive nervous energy and direct that nervous energy to the goal of better public speaking. By this time you have really been working on the "P" and the "I" in PIER, the "P" referring to preparation and the "I" standing for the substitution of idea-consciousness for self-consciousness. All this work will begin to pay off as you move to the next stage, the stage of rehearsal.

☐ Summary

Organization helps us predict what to expect. If things are totally disorganized, prediction is almost impossible. Human beings generally prefer some predictability to total uncertainty. Spoken language aids organization since it structures thought processes in particular ways. Since public speaking is essentially a spoken language behavior, we should take an oral point of view when organizing a speech.

The specific purpose refers to the exact outcome a speaker intends and hopes to achieve with a specific audience as a result of a particular speech. Developing a well-constructed specific purpose is most important to the preparation of a successful public speech since it affords you a benchmark by which to test the inclusion of other materials in the speech. Everything in the speech should contribute to the successful achievement of your specific purpose. If something doesn't so contribute—delete it!

The rule of 30/70 is helpful when organizing a speech and should also be considered when putting together your preparatory outline. What is the proportion of predictability to uncertainty in your presentation? Patterns, which may be either internal or external, can assist you in reducing needless uncertainty in your speech. The keywords which you can use in determining your pattern selection are decentering and association.

An outline is a representation of your speech's organizational pattern. Part of your outline is the title of your speech—take time to devise an appropriate and catchy title for the talk. The three main parts of your speech (and thus of your outline) are the introduction, the body, and the conclusion. Transitions, the rails upon which memory rides, are important to the flow of the speech and can usefully be included in your preparatory outline. Follow the recommended outline form illustrated on page 123. Use formatting to assist your organization and recall, and upon finishing your preparatory outline—test it!.

Exercises ■

1 Here are a number of topics. Your speech audience is a high school graduation. Your speech is to be 20 minutes long. You have been invited to give the graduation speech because it is the high school from which you graduated and the principal thinks it would be helpful to the graduating seniors and those attending to hear from a recent graduate who is successfully enrolled in a college program. For any three of the topics given below, prepare a general purpose and a well-constructed specific purpose.

a. civil rights
b. communication
c. computers and the future
d. continuing one's education
e. education vs training
f. energy conservation
g. the future
h. love
i. solar energy
j. spoken language
k. work vs labor

2 Your audience is composed of a neighborhood civic improvement association. The group has both men and women members; most members are college graduates and are between 25 and 50 years old. Using the same three topics you chose in exercise 1, rewrite your specific purpose for this audience.

3 Using two of the specific purposes from either exercise 1 or 2, devise titles for your speeches.

4 Pick a topic from exercise 1 and the audience from either exercise 1 or 2. Develop a specific purpose and an organizational pattern for the speech. If you use an internal pattern, tell how you arrived at it. If you use an externally imposed pattern, tell how it meets the criterion of association.

5 Prepare a 3-minute speech on the topic of how spoken language affects mentation. Your speech should have a fully developed preparatory outline.

Bibliographic References ■

Boulding, Kenneth: *The Image,* University of Michigan Press, Ann Arbor, 1956. A readable and interesting short books on humans and their ways of organizing.

Dance, F. E. X., and C. E. Larson: *The Functions of Human Communication,* Holt, Rinehart and Winston, New York, 1976. Especially the material on organization, communication, and entropy on pages 55–58.

Davenport, G. (trans.): *Herakleitos and Diogenes.* Grey Fox Press, Bolinas, Calif., 1979.

Hample, D., and J. M. Dallinger: "Mental Imagery and Logical Terms," unpublished paper presented to the Speech Communication Association, Chicago, November 1984.

Hewes, G.: "Comments on Mattingly's Paper and on Lavalois Flake Tool," in *The Role of Speech in Language,* J. Kavanagh and J. Cutting (eds.), MIT Press, Cambridge, Mass., 1975. pp. 76–81. A fascinating discussion of planning and its relation to tool making and human organizing.

Nozick, R.: *Philosophical Explanations,* Harvard University Press, Cambridge, Mass., 1981.

Ong, W. J.: *The Presence of the Word.* Yale University Press, New Haven, Conn., 1967. The premier work on the manner in which spoken language affects our ways of thinking. The source for the phrase "oral noetic."

Pirsig, R. M.: *Zen and the Art of Motorcycle Maintenance,* William Morrow, New York, 1974. Some interesting commentaries on the interrelationship between Zen and organization.

Tzu, Lao: *Tao te Ching,* D. C. Lau (trans.), Penguin Books, Baltimore, Md., 1978.

Recommended Reading ■

Thompson, W. N.: *Quantitative Research in Public Address and Communication,* Random House, New York, 1967. A dated, but still valuable, resource for data and studies on organization and outlining.

Rehearsal

Chapter Six

"Rehearsal: a private performance or practice session prior to a
public appearance."
Webster's New Collegiate Dictionary

The word "rehearsal" suggests the kind of polished, theatrical performance many of us find extraordinarily threatening. Rehearsal is really just another name for practice, the kind of practice that precedes a public performance. Public speaking obviously takes place in public and rehearsal is an entirely adequate name for the practice associated with preparation for effective and successful public speaking.

We recommend the kind of rehearsal that will raise your public speaking coping quotient by reducing your anxiety about novel aspects of the public speaking situation. The more familiar you are with the public speaking situation, prior to actually standing to deliver your speech, the more you will find yourself comfortable with the experience. As we mentioned in Chapter Five, we are often undone by too much uncertainty—it is nice to have a cushion of predictability upon which to fall back.

The most successful rehearsal technique for public speaking is simulation. Simulation involves creating a situation as close as possible to the actual anticipated public speaking experience. Simulation is used in many situations for the purpose of getting ready for a public performance. Most athletes simulate the situation in which their activity is going to take place; from football scrimmages to baseball practice they engage in simulated practice. Pilots and other airline personnel undergo extensive and very realistic simulation procedures involving mock-ups of the actual aircraft and instrument panels identical to the ones that will be used in actual flight. (There are even software packages for personal computers that allow non-pilots to engage in exciting and fairly accurate simulations of takeoffs, in-flight patterns, and landings of a variety of aircraft.) Corporate executives involve themselves in activities which simulate actual corporate decision-making situations for the purpose of developing appropriate skills. Simulation is valuable for public speaking practice.

Throughout this book we have mentioned the helical development of good public speaking. You start at one point in the refinement of your skills and you continually move onward by refining well-established patterns and in building more successful techniques. We are most interested in the mentation, the thought, that underlies public speaking and is expressed in public speaking. Good simulation practice has as its final goal the internalization of the thoughts of the speech and then as its second goal the development of a high level of comfort with the act of making those thoughts available to the audience in the most effective manner.

□ Mental Rehearsal

A few years ago there was a lot of interest in the "inner game" of various sports: the inner game of skiing, the inner game of tennis, the inner game of basketball (Galwey, 1974). The search for the inner game of something is similar to the Zen approach to searching for the essence of an activity or of a concept. From the moment you know you are going to give a speech, you can be practicing the inner game of public speaking. You will be *thinking* about the topic, the audience, the occasion, the experience. The tools of mental rehearsal, of mental simulation are imagination, analysis, reflection, and anticipated feedback. You can practice mental rehearsal anywhere since it is not bounded or constrained by time or place. As you go through the earlier steps of constructing a preparatory outline, you should be mentally rehearsing the speech. Mental rehearsal is very helpful and you will find that by anticipating the event in all of its particulars you will be constantly polishing your speech as you simultaneously raise your coping quotient. Think about how you can associate this topic with the needs and interests of your audience, of how you can make this topic so much your own that you are completely comfortable with the subject.

Physical simulation involves as much as possible of the actual activities of the speech presentation. The tools of physical simulation include the completed preparatory outline, a familiarity with the room in which you are going to deliver the speech, the use of recording devices so that you can hear and see how the speech is going to be presented, the hands-on use of the audiovisual aids you intend presenting in the speech, the anticipation of the manner in which your thoughts will motivate your physical movement and gesture, and the practice of the motivated gestures.

Both mental and physical practice have as their goals the reduction of undue uncertainty and the raising of your coping quotient. Rehearsal is not intended to produce artificiality in your speaking. Actors rehearse for the purpose of making their performance look *un*rehearsed. Audiences are critical of an actor whose technique intrudes upon the performance, whose technique calls attention to itself instead of to the thoughts and emotions being portrayed. Similarly, a public speaker must rehearse in order to appear unrehearsed, in order to appear spontaneous.

□ Physical Rehearsal

You should try and simulate the actual public speaking situation as closely as possible. This means that you should visit the room in which the speech is going to be delivered and administer a "SALT" test in order to get a feeling for the size of the room and the seating arrangement: the S in the acronym SALT; A, the acoustics of the room (if the room is empty, say something out loud to get a sense of the acoustics, if the room is occupied and there is talking going on, listen to the way things sound); L, the lighting and the arrangement of furnishings within the room (if you intend to use aids that call for electrical power, check the availability of outlets); and T, the temperature of the room. Many speeches fail because the room is so warm that the audience falls asleep or loses its concentration regardless of the speaker.

If you can actually practice your speech in the same room in which you are going to deliver the speech, do it! If not, create as close a simulation as possible. In whatever place you rehearse build a simulated speaker's stand or lectern (you can use a pile of books upon a student desk, or an inverted wastebasket on the desk to simulate a lectern). You want to get comfortable with the use of the lectern to hold your outline or notes rather than to hold you up physically. Think about the kind of clothes you are going to wear for the presentation. If possible rehearse one or two times while actually wearing the clothes you will be wearing for the speech. You want to reduce as many uncertainties as possible. Wearing suitable clothes, in which you feel comfortable and which are appropriate, to a public performance is important. Unless you have to wear a special outfit for the speech (if, for instance, you were giving a speech demonstrating a particular sport—like fencing—you might wish to wear the clothes worn in fencing), the appropriate clothes for a public presentation are the clothes you would wear on a business occasion.

Since, it is impossible to have the entire audience present for the rehearsal, you will want to simulate an audience. Try to see them in your mind's eye. Use devices that actually give you someone to talk to—even if that someone is yourself. It is this need for audience simulation which makes rehearsing before a mirror worthwhile. You can use a mirror to see how you look while speaking, you can use a mirror to practice your eye contact. A mirror is almost a "freeze frame" of a videotaped rehearsal. The problem with a mirror as a freeze frame is that in a mirror your body image is reversed, you gesture with your right hand and in the mirror it looks as if you are gesturing with your left hand; this can be confusing.

Use a tape recorder in rehearsal. Listen to how you sound. Do your spoken words convey the thoughts you wish to convey? Are your words easily understood or are you slurring some of your sounds, for instance, dropping the final endings off of words ending in "g", saying "singin" instead of "singing," or leaving out certain syllables, saying "mir" instead of "mirror." Perhaps you tend to transpose certain sounds in some words, saying "larnyx" instead of "larynx," or "calvary" instead of "cavalry." Perhaps you are going too fast, or too slow. All these vocal aspects can be picked up by listening to a tape recording of your speech.

Don't be overly critical, too much preciseness can be as distracting to your audience as sloppiness. Are you placing your vocal emphasis on the right words or does everything you say sound equally important? Remember that you want to call attention to your ideas rather than to your voice, articulation, and pronunciation.

If you can rehearse in front of a videotape recorder (VTR) you will find such an experience most revealing and helpful. You will need someone, a close friend perhaps, to run the VTR unless you have access to a VTR with a remote control capability. All in all it would be better to have someone else run the VTR so that you are free to concentrate on your rehearsal. Perhaps your school or business has an audiovisual department that will provide VTR facilities for rehearsal. A VTR, unlike a mirror, allows you to see how you actually will appear to someone other than yourself. On a VTR you can check your gestures, your posture, your movements, your eye contact, your vocal aspects, your nonvocal communication, all at the same time. Remember our comment in Chapter Four on how many visual images are translated into auditory images when assigning meaning? When you watch yourself on a VTR, consider how what the audience *sees* translates into what the audience *hears*. (You may think that your tie or your scarf is stunning while the audience may judge that particular item of clothing an inappropriate choice for the occasion—thus distracting them from your ideas and holding them back from full support of your specific purpose.) For more information on getting the most out of a VTR experience, consult the appendix on the VTR in this book.

In mental rehearsal you should usually say the words silently, but fully formed, to yourself. This is the kind of rehearsal most of us do when we are trying to memorize something word for word. In physical rehearsal you should always practice *out loud*. A sound understanding of the requirement for out loud rehearsal requires a brief consideration of some spoken language theory.

☐ The Levels of Speech Communication

In Chapter One we mentioned the levels of speech communication: I, the intrapersonal level where one person is both the sender and the receiver of the message; II, the interpersonal level where one person is trying to communicate a message to another person or to a few other persons and; III, the person-to-persons level where one person is trying to communicate a message to more than just a few other persons all at the same time. The levels are interrelated in that while you are engaged in interpersonal speech communication, you are simultaneously engaged in intrapersonal speech communication. Similarly, elements of intrapersonal and interpersonal speech communication are also present when you are engaged in person-to-persons speech communication. In other words when you are engaged in conversation (level II) you are always talking to yourself (level I), at the same time and when you are giving a speech (level III) you will find that you are talking to yourself (level I) and also sometimes carrying on a conversation (level II) with someone in the audience during the actual speech delivery. Imagine a situation where you are speaking on the meaning of friendship and your own best friend is in the audience. You may find yourself speaking to your own best friend while at the same time addressing the entire audience. Another name for the person-to-persons level is public speaking. This dynamic interrelationship among the levels of speech communication is important to understand since the manner in which you talk to yourself will affect the manner in which you talk to others, whether one other or many others. What is more, the manner in which you talk to others may have a doubling-back or recursive effect on the manner in which you talk to yourself. Your own self-monitoring of your public speaking, a self-monitoring which might include hearing yourself sounding quite confident in your public remarks, may enhance your own intrapersonal feelings of self confidence (Dance and Larson, 1976).

Level I: Intrapersonal
Level II: Interpersonal
Level III: Person-to-persons

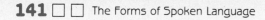

Figure 6.1 The Dynamic Interrelationship of the Levels of Speech Communication

This concept of self-monitoring appears a number of times in this text. You will find it alluded to in the appendix on Evaluation and Listening as well as in the appendix on the VTR and Public Speaking. Self-monitoring is important both conceptually and practically. As Berger and Douglas (1982) point out, self-monitoring has implications beyond public speaking. However, the ability to monitor your own ongoing behavior while actually giving a speech may spell the difference between disaster and distinction. We all self-monitor, but we all do so to varying degrees. For most people it is relatively automatic to self-monitor their conversational behavior. We catch ourselves mispronouncing words and we automatically correct the mispronunciations. But so much is going on when we are giving a speech that our self-monitoring skills seem to become overloaded. Much of what goes into improved public speaking can be directly tied to self-monitoring improvement.

☐ The Forms of Spoken Language

Spoken language is the content of speech communication. When we engage in speech communication we use spoken language. But spoken language and speech communication are not exactly the same thing. Spoken language has two forms, internal spoken language and external spoken language. In much of the research literature, internal spoken language is simply referred to as "inner speech." In this book, for theoretical reasons as well as for reasons of terminological specificity and parallelism, we will use the terms "internal spoken language" and "external spoken language" (see Dance 1982; Sokolov, 1972; Vygotsky, 1962).

External Spoken Language

External spoken language has three characteristics:

1. External spoken language exists in acoustic space. Most simply put this means that external spoken language is spoken aloud, the sounds have a physical existence when uttered. This characteristic carries with it a temporal constraint since we usually talk aloud somewhere between 150 to 200 words per minute.
2. External spoken language is grammatically, or syntactically, expanded. When we talk aloud we express ourselves in the accepted syntactic structures of the language we are using. The syntax of various languages differ in many ways, such as where the verb is placed. When speaking aloud our audience expects us to have subjects and predicates and connectors in the accepted order of the language we are using. This characteristic also carries with it a temporal constraint since it takes some time to put things in their accepted order. The kind

of time sequences being spoken of are quite short, but still noticeable when they differ from audience expectations. The time differences between the speech of a normal person and the speech of someone who has had one too many alcoholic drinks may be short, but they certainly stand out. Just so, the time that it takes to process grammar is short but still longer than when grammatical expectations and constraints are not present.

3. External spoken language is semantically expanded. When we use words with an audience we must, through decentering and association, make an effort to assist the audience in understanding exactly how we are intending the words being used. If we use the word "spring" we must, through definition, illustration, or context, make clear whether we are talking about a time of year, a body of water, or something else. This characteristic also carries with it a temporal constraint since it takes time to use association to make our intended meaning clear.

Internal Spoken Language

Internal spoken language also has three characteristics. The characteristics of internal spoken language are almost exactly the opposite of the characteristics of external spoken language and thus may be contrasted with them.

1. Internal spoken language is silent. When we talk to ourselves we need not articulate or project the words we are using. We are thus freed from the temporal constraint of external spoken language. We talk to ourselves much more quickly than we talk aloud to others. This becomes obvious when we convert our internal spoken language to writing or print. What went very rapidly indeed in our self-talk takes considerably more time to put in writing. Try the experiment of setting a timer for 1 minute and then thinking about a topic—such as justice or charity—for that full minute. When the minute is over try to write down, or speak into a recorder, as accurate a representation as possible of everything you thought of during the 1 minute. Try to include all the nuances or fine points of your reflection as well as the main matter of your thoughts. You will be surprised at how much longer than a minute it takes you to move your reflection from inner spoken language to external spoken language.

2. Internal spoken language is grammatically, or syntactically, condensed or crushed. When engaged in inner spoken language the grammatical constraints of external spoken language are removed. We talk to ourselves in almost pure predication. We don't often need to state the subject of our internal spoken language since the subject is often ourselves. When talking to ourselves we would seldom say something like "I, John Jones, am going to my car." We know who it is that is going to the car, and we ordinarily omit the subject and the connectors and the modifiers. This characteristic of internal spoken language (a characteristic sometimes called ellipsis) frees us from the temporal constraint of grammatical expansion and makes internal spoken language much, much faster.

3. Internal spoken language is semantically condensed or crushed. When talking to ourselves we seldom use words which we don't ourselves understand. You don't usually find yourself asking yourself what you meant by a word you have

used in your own self-talk. When you use the word "spring" in internal spoken language, you know immediately which usage of the word "spring" you intend. Again, you are freed from the temporal constraint of semantic expansion.

As a result of the characteristics of internal spoken language you handle your thoughts so much faster than you would in external spoken language that those thoughts tend to be more ambiguous and more subjective than they would be when spoken aloud. The verbal thoughts of internal spoken language, if they were able to be conveyed to others, would probably be incomprehensible to those others, they would be personally idiosyncratic and fragmented from the point of view of others, and they would exhibit neither decentering nor association.

Because of the differences between internal and external spoken language it is essential that public speaking rehearsal be aloud, that it be expressed in external spoken language. By speaking aloud you test your ideas by the rules of syntactic logic, you slow things down so that lapses of logic become more apparent. Ambiguities which are accepted in internal spoken language are also made more accessible to your attention and can be better dealt with. The rules of acceptable grammar are made manifest and the timing and rate of presentation is raised to a conscious level. In addition, places in your speech where you may have problems of pronunciation or articulation become open to early correction.

By using external spoken language in rehearsal you will be able to take your thoughts and ideas and unpack them by using decentering and association. If you only rehearse your speech in internal spoken language you will open yourself to many distressing occurrences when you finally give your speech to your audience. The closest simulation to the actual speech takes place using external spoken language. *Rehearse out loud!*

☐ Audiovisual Aids

You should carefully rehearse your use of audiovisual aids. You need to check their effect on the timing of your speech and you need to plan transitions that will move you from your spoken words into the use of the audiovisual aid and then back into your speech once again. [For a complete discussion of audiovisual aids, **GOTO the Appendix to Chapter 10.**]

Always remember that audiovisual aids are extensions of you as a speaker, not substitutes for your actual speaking. Always test your choice of an audiovisual aid against the part it will play in helping you achieve your speech's specific purpose.

☐ Transitions

We would like to remind you once again of the importance of well-planned and executed transitions to a successful and effective speech. Plan your transitions and rehearse them. Remember that transitions can consist of movement as well as of words.

☐ Rehearsal and Mode

The only rehearsal for impromptu speaking comes from giving speeches. The more often you speak, the more comfortable you are going to be in speaking, whatever the mode of presentation. Challenge yourself to give a speech on some topic, a short, impromptu speech. This can be done while walking along the street, sitting in your room, or driving your car. The rehearsal we have been discussing in this chapter is most useful for preparing to give an extemporaneous, manuscript, or memorized speech. In an extemporaneous speech your rehearsal will prove invaluable for giving you a feel for the best word choice. Your very muscles will, if adequately rehearsed, help you remember the most felicitous choice of words and phrases for conveying your ideas. There is a kind of "muscle memory" which will come to your assistance during delivery. If you are using a tape recorder or a VTR, always listen for how clearly your ideas, your thoughts are couched in the words you have chosen. Do your words hide or illuminate the ideas? Perhaps you are using too many difficult terms, perhaps you are talking down to your audience. Whenever faced with a choice of talking "down," or talking "up" to an audience— talk *up*. An overestimation of the audience's level of ability is preferable to an underestimation of the audience's level of ability. Flattery is usually preferred to insult. A manuscript speech should be so well rehearsed that the manuscript doesn't get in the way of presentation. A good manuscript speech appears extemporaneous. The same holds true for a well-presented memorized speech; it too should sound to the audience as if it is spontaneous, extemporaneous. What you are striving for in rehearsal, whatever the mode of presentation, is the building of an illusion of spontaneity. The best presented speeches sound as if the ideas and the words that enrobe the ideas are coming to the speaker at the very moment of their utterance.

☐ The Rule of 30/70 Revisited

The rule of 30/70 should be in your mind during rehearsal. You can do a lot with your presentation to reduce the uncertainty of the audience. Patterns of movement, the use of audiovisual aids, parallel word choice for parallel ideas, each of these techniques can be used to help you maintain the rule of 30/70 in your presentation.

☐ Style and Humor

"Style," in the words of the French naturalist Buffon, "is the man himself." Correcting this rather chauvinistic statement to "style is the person" alters neither its meaning nor its value. Our understanding of Buffon's meaning is that style is not something superficially added to a person, something like a costume that is put on for special occasions, but that style emanates forth from the person, comes from the person's being, is representative of the person's essence. A person's style is a totality and it infuses all of the person's actions. We are here most interested in style as it is evidenced in your use of spoken words in public settings, in your public speaking.

The clearest statement of the requirements of good oral style is that the speaker should appropriately present the right words in the right place. This same idea has been expressed by a British juror who said that style consisted of the proper choice of words and then the proper arrangement of those words once chosen.

The proper choice of words depends on the individual's vocabulary and on the individual's precision in identifying the exact concept or idea he or she wishes to convey to the audience. From our theoretical viewpoint it is almost impossible even to identify an idea with precision if the words with which to label and express the idea are absent. Thus adequate vocabulary is in intimate attendance upon conceptual precision. When you consider the additional demands upon vocabulary that are imposed by decentering and association, the need for a rich active vocabulary becomes even more evident. The color vocabulary of an artist usually far exceeds that of the average person. Artists, when describing nature scenes, use color terms such as "teal blue" and "chrome." For most of us our color vocabulary is much more limited or circumscribed. In the same way, physicians have a more varied vocabulary for describing varying states of health and illness than does the typical individual. Within the medical profession this specialized vocabulary lends precision to the description and discussion of a person's health. As public speakers,

The Richness of One's Vocabulary Is Influenced by One's Interests (Hugh Rogers, Monkmeyer Press Photo Service)

words are our stock in trade for the purposes of conveying ideas to our audience. We should constantly work to enlarge and refine our vocabularies. The two methods of vocabulary refinement and enlargement are conversation and reading. We need to converse and discuss on all possible planes.

Our current working vocabulary is our current vocabulary plane. For the sake of information as well as for entertainment, we should discuss and read on our current plane. Our vocabulary would stagnate, however, were we only to use it on its current level. We should also converse with people whose vocabulary usage exceeds our own, and we should read material containing words we are not completely familiar with so that we might enlarge our own vocabulary by learning new words. We should also take pains to frequently converse with those who may not yet have achieved the vocabulary level currently our own. With young children, people just learning our language, people whose verbal experience has been impoverished, this is a way to continue developing your own decentering capacity and to remind you of the verbal adjustments sometimes called for if we intend to use association successfully.

When you hear or read an unfamiliar word, or a familiar word being used in an unexpected manner, make a note of it so that you may look the word and its usage up in a reference book and thus enlarge your own current vocabulary. One of the problems associated with enjoying words and constantly trying to build your vocabulary is finding that other people feel you are making too much use of unfamiliar words. Adlai Stevenson, Sr. was a popular politician in the 1950s who ran twice for the office of President of the United States. Many who heard him speak considered him to be an outstanding public speaker. Yet, if you consider that he lost both presidential campaigns, it would seem that he failed to communicate successfully with a majority of the American voters. In analyzing his defeats there were some who suggested that his failure to communicate with the public at large was often due to his use of unfamiliar words in his speeches. Those who did understand him liked what he said and approved of his views, but those who were somewhat mystified by his word choices were unwilling to put their trust in someone they didn't readily understand. One of Ronald Reagan's strongest attributes is his ability to speak directly and understandably to the majority of the electorate.

The fact that you have a large and precise vocabulary doesn't mean that you should not use it in public speaking. The right word is both the word that is easily understood *and* the word that most accurately mirrors the concept being communicated. If you have the precise word for a concept, even if the word is not one in common usage, use it. But don't stop there. Having used the correct word, the word you wanted to use—now paraphrase that word. Use another word, this time a common one, that means much the same thing but which is more familiar to your audience. For example, you might be talking of brain damage resulting from automobile accidents and wish to comment on traumatic aphasia, an injury affecting the language centers of the brain. By using the most appropriate term and then by paraphrasing the term or by using a more common term similar in meaning to it, you serve your listeners in two ways: (1) you communicate your idea with increased precision and (2) you introduce them to a new word, thus increasing their vocabularies.

Experience is the best guide to proper word choice. But there are some good suggestions which we may use while we are gaining experience. In *The King's English* the authors make some suggestions for a writer's vocabulary. The authors of *The King's English* believe that a good writing vocabulary should have essentially the same characteristics as a good speaking vocabulary. So where you read "writer" in the following quote, just substitute "speaker."

> Any one who wishes to become a good writer should endeavor before he allows himself to be tempted by the more showy qualities, to be direct, simple, brief, vigorous, and lucid. This general principle may be translated into practical rules in the domain of vocabulary as follows:
>
> Prefer the familiar word to the far-fetched.
> Prefer the concrete word to the abstract.
> Prefer the single word to the circumlocution.
> Prefer the short word to the long.
> Prefer the Saxon word to the Romance.

These rules are given roughly in order of merit; the last is also the least [Fowler and Fowler, 1931]. Glen Mills, in his book on speech composition, states: "In general, a speaker's presentation, both in style and in delivery, should be characterized by eagerness to communicate, immediate intelligibility, closeness of contact, informality and spontaneity" (Mills, 1952). The rules for vocabulary drawn from *The King's English* can help you acquire the goals suggested by Mills. Obviously you are not going to have the five rules on an index card and consult the card each time you have to make a word choice. Simply think about the suggestions, try to understand them, watch how good speakers and writers almost automatically use them. Your own use of the rules will, through observation and practice, eventually become semiautomatic.

Vulgarity, profanity, swearing, coarseness, crudeness are all out of place on the public platform. Whatever your thoughts about the appropriateness of these language choices in conversation or among your peers, they are generally avoided in public speaking. What's the point of offending your audience? How can you be certain that everyone in the audience will share your acceptance of unconventional speech? In most situations an audience will react negatively to these language styles—not in all cases, but in the vast majority of cases. There are instances when such language is purposely used for shock value or to meet very special audience or occasion needs, but for the beginning speaker the best course of action is to avoid such usages.

The proper arrangement of these words once chosen calls for your remembering that oral style and written style are not the same thing. Public speaking style—the characteristic arrangement of words by a speaker—is as individual as a fingerprint since it flows from the totality of the speaker's person. It is what distinguishes speaker from speaker and good speakers from great speakers. Style is elusive when pursued and yet is often stumbled upon unexpectedly. Good style may be fostered through imitation of recognized masters of style, but in the long run great style can be achieved only by filtering good style through the essence of your own personality. By imitating Martin Luther King, or Winston Churchill, you may, through long practice, become a first-class King or Churchill imitator; but only by taking what is good in King and what is good in Churchill and then adding to it what is good of your own will you become anywhere near a great stylist in your own right. Here are some guidelines for the proper arrangement of words for oral style.

Remember, as pointed out in Chapter Three, when discussing manuscript speeches that there are important differences between written style and spoken style.

- Auditory and written perception are different.
- Spoken materials, unlike written materials, should be prepared for a well-defined and specified audience.
- Spoken language must be readily understood.
- Spoken language has the assistance of the voice.
- Spoken language, through feedback, can be quickly adapted to the situation.
- Conversational style is usually typified by short sentences.
- Speaking style allows for more repetition than does writing style.
- Whatever you say, say it with as much economy as possible.
- Prepare and rehearse your choice of words and the arrangement of the words once chosen. Don't rely on inspiration.
- The best way to develop a speaking style is to do a lot of speaking. Speak whenever you are invited to speak. Never go into a speech situation unprepared. Always work on your choice of words and the most appropriate arrangement of those words.

When first discussing style, we suggested that the simplest definition was the *appropriate* presentation of the right words in the right places. The appropriate presentation may make all the difference in the world. Again, Ronald Reagan not only has a skill in selecting the right words and in arranging them correctly for his audiences, but he does an excellent job of presenting the words. Another politician, with weak presentational skills, might fail although using the same arrangement of words as Reagan.

Obviously, style has ethical considerations. In no sense are we recommending the acquisition of style as an aid to manipulation. Your style should be elevated by your values and your ethical commitment. In your rehearsal you must attend to the clarity of your presentation: can your words be heard? In your rehearsal you must attend to the pacing of your presentation: are your words, and their arrangement, enhanced by your use of pace and pause?

Humor

Earlier we cited Aristotle's observation on the role of speech in thought. Aristotle was a shrewd observer of the human condition and he enlarged his observations on speech when he noted that among animals only humans speak and laugh. Not only do we laugh, most of us love to laugh. We enjoy enjoying ourselves. The speaker who uses humor so as to enhance the achievement of the speech's specific purpose has a distinct advantage over the humorless speaker. Notice that we didn't say "The speaker who tells jokes . . .", but "The speaker who uses humor. . . ." Jokes are but a single form of humor. A speaker can be humorous in the manner in which he gives an example or recites an illustrative incident. A speaker can be humorous in the manner in which she gestures, or walks away from the lectern, or raises her eyebrows in an expression of facial surprise. The late, great comedian Jack Benny could be funny by just standing still with his hand to his chin. A speaker can be humorous in the use of notes or posture. Humor does not reside in a single joke, or in a one-liner, but in an approach to the subject matter.

The sources of humor are all around us. The great repository of humor is life. Life is absolutely brimming with humorous events. Watch for humor. Keep an eye out for funny happenings, funny expressions, and funny sayings. You must be alert to the manifestations of humor in life, you must watch for them. Obviously it is impossible to do this if you take yourself too seriously. We all make mistakes. Some of our mistakes are silly mistakes, funny mistakes, mistakes that we can laugh at and can bear others laughing at as well. If you have children of your own, you will be constantly finding little children doing funny things, and fun things. If you don't have your own children, then watch the children of others. If you are young enough to have little brothers and sisters—observe them. Children make mistakes and unless spoiled by adults can laugh at those mistakes when they are pointed out to them. Life, the great encyclopedia of sorrow, courage, and challenge, is also the great and never-ending source of humor.

Monitor your own life in your search for humor. Review things that have happened to you about which you have had a good laugh. These are the kinds of incidents others may also find familiar and laughable. Perhaps the incidents involve poking a little fun at yourself. If your speech is going well, poking a little fun doesn't hurt at all. Besides, for many such incidents, who cares? One of us didn't learn to ski until he was in his middle forties and he was very timid about taking any risks that might result in a broken leg or head. After taking a few skiing lessons at Vail, and semimastering getting off the lift (which was a *major* challenge for him), he was skiing down a beginner's slope at Keystone, Colorado. He was in what had become his typical and permanent wedge, going slowly down the right side of the run when from behind him someone shouted "On your right." Since he had all he could do just to stay upright, he made no response to the skiier coming from behind him. Then the voice shouted "On your left." Again he did nothing because he wasn't really capable of doing anything more than he was doing. Finally the person with the voice passed him on the left. This skiier was going down the slope in a full head stand, with a short ski attached to a football helmet and with two other short skis, one in each hand. At one and the same time your author was chagrined (at his own incompetence), impressed (with the skill of the head-standing skiier), and amused at the whole situation. Now this reminiscence is not a joke, it certainly isn't a one-liner, it is an anecdote which the author in question has been able to draw upon from time to time in public speeches where the need has arisen to talk about the difficulties attendant upon acquiring some skills at an age beyond that when those skills are usually acquired. In using the anecdote, the author can usually laugh once again at himself while others in the audience seem to be able to use the anecdote as both an illustration of a point and a source of enjoyment. How about a situation where you are speaking and you aren't sure that everyone can hear you and you ask your audience "Can everyone hear me?" Then you tell them that you are careful when asking that question because on one occasion you said "If you can't hear me, please raise your hand. Someone in the back row raised their hand at which point one of the audience members in the front row stood up and said to the one in back, "I can hear him, and I'll change places with you." Don't be afraid to use yourself as the source and object of a humorous experience, *if* that humorous experience will move along your specific purpose.

Professional humorists are an excellent source of material. Watch Bill Cosby, Joan Rivers, Bob Hope, Woody Allen, listen to them—what do they do, how do they do it? As you will note, it isn't always the words as much as the presentation of the words. They mug, they shrug, they grin, they laugh, they look questioning, they look solemn. Their verbal and nonvocal behaviors reinforce each other—or contradict each other. If you hear a really good humorous bit given by a professional humorist, and that bit fits into your speech and helps you make a point, use it. But *always give credit to the original source*. No one will feel the joke is less funny, or think less of you for your having given credit. When you are listening to a professional and hear a good one, write it down—especially the punch line!

There are also books of humor for speakers. You might feel that it is unfair to go to a book for a joke. Why? You have gone to books for other supporting materials, why not jokes? But you must make the joke your own, you must make the joke fit your speech, for this audience, upon this occasion. The joke must help your specific purpose. There are also periodic publications of jokes and humor for speakers. Many of the jokes you will find in books and periodicals are already too well known to be used right away. But jokes fade, audiences change, and the joke which may be stale today may be quite fresh later on and with an audience of a different age. If you have trouble finding jokes, then don't be afraid to consult such publications. Many speakers have found good humorous illustrations in *The Reader's Digest*.

As mentioned earlier, you should make the joke your own. A joke that has a certain setting when you first hear it can often be *switched* to apply to a situation you want to use in your speech. Perhaps the joke involved stock brokers, just turn it around so that instead of a stock broker it involves a physician, or a professor, or a business major, or a liberal arts major. An old joke tells about a cafeteria that served portions of brains of various professors. The general idea is that by eating the brains of professors you will gain their knowledge. As the story goes, a portion of the brains of a professor of history costs $1.00; of a professor of education, $1.00; of a professor of physics, $1.25; and of a professor of speech communication, $6.00. When asked why a portion of speech communication professor brains costs so very much more, the answer is that it takes so many more professors of speech communication to make up a single portion of brains. Now, some of our colleagues may not think that's too funny—but they can easily switch the names around if they so wish. Don't abandon a story just because it seems to deal with a situation other than the one you need. Try *switching*.

Appropriateness is essential in good humor. Your story should not offend. Good humor, real humor, doesn't hurt. This is why slurs against nationality or race or religion are never really funny. They hurt. They offend. The same is often true of sexual humor. *If you have any doubts about the appropriateness of the joke—do not use it!* Humor, it has been said, is anything that is funny. Cruelty is not funny. Meanness is not funny. There are times that little if anything seems funny.

Max Eastman states that "The first law of humor is that things can be funny only when we are in fun" (1936). This is a wise and helpful observation. Recall how you must reassure some people that what you are saying is meant to be "in fun"? Take time to let your audience know that you are intending them to enjoy your presentation, to be "in fun."

Humor should be rehearsed! Arrange the stories you wish to use in terms of their contribution to your specific purpose and then try them out. Try the jokes out on someone whose sense of humor you trust. Do you think the story is funny in the situation you wish to use it? Vary your timing, use pauses, give your audience time to get the story, to understand it and to appreciate its relevance. Don't run over the punch line of your story.

You need to keep notes of humor. A card file, or a small notebook, is handy for recording the essence of the joke, and especially the punch line.

Humor can be a great help in applying *the rule of* 30/70. When you have given your audience a great deal of new material to digest, it may be time to use humor as illustration or example. The humor will allow time for some of the other material to be assimilated into the 70 percent of predictability and thus open up the audience to the presentation of additional novel substantive material. Remember that humor can be a true story told humorously as well as a one-liner or a joke.

Humor, especially jokes, should always be memorized, well memorized so that they appear absolutely spontaneous. The Lord help the speaker who has to consult his or her notes for a forgotten punch line.

The amount of rehearsal called for depends on your own comfort level with your speech, your own experience as a public speaker, the importance of the speech or of the occasion, and your own interest in becoming an ever more proficient public speaker. As you gain speaking experience you will zero in on exactly what parts of your speeches need the most rehearsal.

In your final rehearsal simulate the final speaking occasion as completely as possible. Even though you may have rehearsed your speech in a number of sessions and a number of times, in the final simulation put the whole speech together and remember to time it and to test it in terms of achievement of your specific purpose. Finally remember the importance of avoiding staleness and of continually communicating the illusion of spontaneity.

□ Summary

Rehearsal means practice, and the best practice is that which most closely simulates the final public speaking situation. Rehearsal goes a long way toward raising your coping quotient to a level totally supportive of your public speaking needs. Mental rehearsal can take place anywhere, at any time, while physical rehearsal has certain time and place limitations because of its need to simulate the actual public speaking situation as closely as possible. It helps if you can rehearse before a videotape recorder so that you can then review your rehearsed performance. Whether or not a VTR is available, *always rehearse out loud*. You should pay special attention to rehearsing your transitions since they provide the track upon which your memory will ride smoothly.

Public speaking style, a reflection of the whole person, involves properly chosen words properly arranged and appropriately presented. Good style doesn't call attention to itself, it is transparent. As a public speaker you should remember that oral style differs from written style in many ways.

Humor is a valuable attribute for the public speaker to cultivate. The absolutely best source of good humor is life itself, the public speaker should train himself or herself as a keen observer of life even as he or she is immersed in actual living. Humor should be memorized. It is almost always fatal to try and read humor from notes. Since for many speakers humor doesn't just "come naturally," it is best to rehearse humor. Switching is a good technique for making humor more personal, for making humor your own. If you have any doubts about the appropriateness of a story or of a joke, don't use it. *If in doubt, don't!*

Check your final rehearsal for time, remembering the tendency to go a bit faster in the actual public speaking situation. As a final check, make certain that your rehearsed speech does all it can to assist you in achieving your specific purpose.

In your rehearsal, as in your final delivery, you should try to cultivate the illusion of spontaneity, the illusion that the speech is being delivered for the very first time.

Exercises ■

1 The best exercise for rehearsal is rehearsing. Rehearse one of the speeches you are going to deliver. Rehearse it mentally. Rehearse it physically. Use simulation techniques. Now, be prepared to give a very short speech to the class on the topic of problems in rehearsal.

2 Consult two or three books or periodicals of jokes for speakers. Take two jokes from the books, jokes you yourself enjoy. "Switch" the jokes to fit yourself and your classroom audience. Fit the two switched jokes into a context. Rehearse them carefully. Deliver them, without notes, to the class. Make certain the jokes are appropriate. If in doubt, don't! Have a handout for distribution after your speech. The handout should include the *original* jokes, with their book or periodical sources.

3 Take a major point from one of the speeches you have already delivered in class. Find an anecdote from your own life to illustrate or explain the major point. The anecdote doesn't have to be humorous but if it is, that's fine. Put together a short speech, the specific purpose of which is simply to help the audience understand how an anecdote, drawn from one's own life, may be used to illustrate a major point. Rehearse and deliver the speech.

Bibliographic References ■

Berger, Charles R., and William Douglas: "Thought and Talk: 'Excuse Me, But Have I Been Talking to Myself,' " in *Human Communication Theory: Comparative Essays.* F. E. X. Dance (ed.), Harper & Row, New York, 1982, pp. 42–60. Some up-to-the-minute reflections on self-monitoring.

Dance, Frank E. X., and C. E. Larson: *The Functions of Speech Communication: A Theoretical Approach,* Holt, Rinehart and Winston, New York, 1976. For further reading on the interrelationships among the levels of human communication.

Dance, Frank E. X.: "A Speech Theory of Human Communication," in *Human Communication Theory: Comparative Essays,* F. E. X. Dance (ed.), Harper & Row, New York, 1982, pp. 120–146. An essay that covers in more detail some of the theoretical materials relating to levels and forms.

Eastman, Max: *The Enjoyment of Laughter,* Simon and Schuster, New York, 1936, p. 3. A serious book on the subject of humor. Mr. Eastman illustrates his points with stories and anecdotes as well as jokes that are so old that they are almost new.

Fowler, H. W., and F. G. Fowler: *The King's English,* 3rd ed., Oxford University Press, London, 1931, p. 11. Some nice style and some nice suggestions on style. Although the book is directed toward written style, many of the observations bear as well upon oral style.

Galwey, W. Timothy: *The Inner Game of Tennis,* Random House, New York, 1974. Here's the book that started all of the interest in the "inner" games.

Mills, Glen E.: *Composing the Speech,* Prentice-Hall, Englewood Cliffs, N.J., 1952. Some fine insights on style in speech composition.

Sokolov, A. N.: *Inner Speech and Thought,* Plenum Press, New York, 1972. For those among you with an interest in the data underlying some of the chapter's observations on the forms of spoken language.

Vygotsky, L. S.: *Thought and Language,* MIT Press, Cambridge, Mass., 1962. One of the classics leading to the argument for always rehearsing aloud. Anyone interested in the theory underlying the study of spoken language should be sure to read this book.

Recommended Readings ■

Linkletter, Art: *Public Speaking for Private People,* Bobbs-Merrill, Indianapolis, 1980. Especially Chapter 5, "The Non-Joke-Tellers Guide to Telling Jokes." The author is a good performer and a good observer so his recommendations are worth taking to heart.

McFarland, Kenneth: *Eloquence in Public Speaking,* Prentice-Hall, Englewood Cliffs, N.J., 1961. Dr. MacFarland was a consummate public speaker, a true professional. This book gives some of his informed observations based upon a lifetime of public speaking practice.

Orben, Robert: *Orben's Current Comedy,* The Comedy Center, 700 Orange Street, Wilmington, Del. A twice-monthly publication of mostly one-line jokes. Bob Orben is a professional comedy writer and one can often find in the publication timely jokes suitable for switching.

Delivery

Chapter Seven

"Speak the speech, I pray you, as I pronounced it to you, trippingly on the tongue;"
Shakespeare, *Hamlet*, III, ii, 1

In Chapter Two we set forth the idea of a coping quotient for public speaking and suggested the acronym PIER as a means of remembering the elements most helpful in building one's coping quotient: P, preparation; I, idea; E, experience; and R, relaxation. By now you have traveled quite a distance in building a solid PIER for your public speaking. You have in hand a fully developed preparatory outline, which means you've done the requisite audience analysis, decentering, research, and effort after association. In the process of selecting your topic and completing your preparatory outline, you've given constant and concentrated attention to the idea, the concept with which your speech deals. You have probably given a number of impromptu speeches and completed some of the exercises at the end of the earlier chapters; you have gained some experience in preparing and presenting. You have also been trying to learn how to relax with the realities of the public speaking situation. Now you are at the moment of delivering your first major speech. This chapter has two parts: Part A focuses upon the speech in its state of readiness for delivery, and Part B focuses upon you, the speaker, and delivery.

☐ Part A: The Speech

Outlines and Speaker's Notes

You have already gone through the process of making a preliminary outline for your speech (Chapter Two) and a fully developed preparatory outline (Chapter Four). You are now ready to make your final outline, your presentation outline, also called your speaker's notes. Your preparatory outline has everything in it you needed for organizing your speech and for recalling your preparation in the event you give the speech again sometime in the future. The speaker's notes, the presentation outline, contain only those things you consider absolutely necessary to have available for the actual delivery of the speech. There should be enough in your speaker's notes to make you feel comfortable with extemporaneous delivery but not so much as to tempt you to read your notes to the audience. You want to have enough in your notes so that you feel confident that you can go to them for help if you need to do so. If you have adequately rehearsed (Chapter Five), you will find that the notes are a comforting presence on the speaker's stand, or lectern, but that you seldom need to refer to them in actual delivery.

We advise that the speaker's notes include your specific purpose, the time allotted for the speech, your introduction, transitions, and conclusion written out in detail, and a simple outline of your main points and supporting material. In addition, your notes, at the very end, should include directives as to what can be cut out to shorten the speech and what can be included to lengthen and more fully support your specific purpose. Writing out your introduction, conclusion, and transitions is simply for your own comfort since, as we have earlier advised, you should have those parts of your speech almost totally memorized as a result of repeated rehearsal. Your goal in your speaker's notes is to continually reduce your dependency upon them. Use whatever memory devices work best for you, rhythm, rhyme, acronyms, etc. Classical memory techniques often advise using visual forms as an aid to memory, for example, assigning each main point in your speech to a separate room in your family home. The hall, or foyer, is the introduction; the living room is your first main point and the various pieces of furniture in your living room can have supporting data assigned to them; and so on through your home and the speech. Some speakers instead use a walk through a well-known park as a visual device (this was supposedly the technique used by Mark Twain for recalling the speeches he would give on his lecture tours), attaching ideas to various physical objects in their park walk. If something like this helps you remember, use the technique. However, the main idea is not to remember the specific words of the speech but simply to assist you in keeping in mind the main structure of the speech and the arguments that will help you finally achieve your specific purpose. You want to know your speech "by heart." This is an interesting phrase since there is an ancient adage that says heart speaks to heart. Your audience doesn't want to be reminded of your efforts to remember your speech, they want to be taken to your ideas with the illusion of spontaneity prevailing at all times.

The physical form of your notes, whether full sheets of paper or index cards, is up to you. We have mentioned that for us full sheets are almost always our choice. There are times when index cards are useful, for instance, if you are speaking out of doors where wind might possibly interfere with the handling of full sheets of paper. Don't crowd your notes. Leave space on your notes between your introduction, transitions, body outline, transitions, and conclusion. If you print, print large; if you type, try to use a typeface and spacing conducive to easily finding your place. Use different colors, underlining and highlighting where helpful.

Leave enough room on your speaker's notes to build in any comments specific to the audience or occasion that arise just prior to your presentation. For example, that portion of the situation which precedes your speech might cause you to think of something that will help the audience identify with you or your topic in a manner that had not occurred to you when putting together your preparatory outline. Jot those things down, in a different color, somewhere on your speaker's notes. Perhaps something appeared in the morning newspaper that bears directly on your specific purpose—no reason to ignore this happening in your speech. Be sure you have your information straight and make a brief note of it on the appropriate place in your speaker's notes. For adding last minute material the self-sticking bright colored note pads prove helpful since their color calls your attention to them so forcefully.

Keep your speaker's notes all together in a file folder. Know where that file folder is—keep it with you. Even though you have your speech well prepared and well rehearsed, it is terribly distressing to arrive without your notes. If you are using audiovisual aids, handouts, etc., make sure you have them with you.

Keep your notes with you, don't put them on the lectern prior to rising to give your speech. What can happen, and has happened to one of us, is that the person introducing the speaker, as that person was leaving the platform, picked up the speaker's notes together with his own notes of introduction. The speaker, thinking that his notes were on the lectern, rose, went to the lectern, and found his notes were gone.

The Introduction of the Speaker

How you are introduced can make a great difference to the success of your speech. An introduction can help you or an introduction can hinder you in your speaking. Ideally your introduction as a speaker should inform the audience why you are qualified to speak to them on this topic on this occasion. The introduction of the speaker should be to the point, relatively short, and should set the audience into the proper frame of mind and mood to hear the speech. There are times, however, when your introduction steals some of your own points or sets audience expectations that are impossible for you to fulfill. If, in introducing you, someone tells the audience that you are "the funniest person they have ever heard," that "the speaker will have you rolling in the aisles," you are being set up to meet almost impossible challenges. These things do happen. It is better not to leave your introduction either to chance or to being prepared on the spur of the moment. Here are some samples of introductions which have actually been given for us from time to time. The first example comes from a time when one of us was asked to fill in at the last minute for a member of the Cabinet of the United States. The host rose, turned to the audience, and said: "Ladies and gentlemen, I don't want you to think that our speaker this evening is the bottom of the barrel, the last choice." On another occasion the host was worried about the speaker's capacity to meet the speaking assignment. The host rose and said to the audience (the board of directors of an international corporation): "Gentlemen, I would like to prevent [—and then gave the speaker's name]." One time one of us gave a speech to a group of university professors, a highly critical audience. The speaker was new to the community, young, not well known, and needed all the help a good introduction could afford. The introducer, who was as nervous as could be, said, "Here's your speaker, who needs no introduction" and sat right down. Perhaps the worst of these stories, all of which actually took place, was when a host went to the opposite extreme. The speaker was supposed to give a 30-minute speech to a large Rotary Club audience. The host gave a 15-minute introduction which told the audience more about the speaker than even the speaker was interested in hearing. By the time the speech started the audience was ready to go home.

In order to avoid these kinds of problems, it helps to prepare your own introductory notes and to send them to the host beforehand or to give them to the host upon your arrival. It is wise to have an extra copy of your introduction with you in the event that the host forgets the copy you sent. Make your notes short. Include your name, your credentials for giving this speech to this audience, and finally the title of the speech. Don't brag. Let your speech be the final evidence of your preparation and suitability for the occasion. Here's a sample:

☐ ☐ ☐ ☐ *Example*

Catherine Tester was born and raised in Brooklyn, New York. Ms. Tester held the highest rank of an enlisted woman in the United States Navy in World War I. She served as commanding officer of the Dolly Madison Post of the American Legion, founded the national charitable organization, The St. Joseph's Guild, and was president of the Woman's Auxiliary of the International College of Surgeons. Her over 50 years of experience in organizing and administering such groups makes her extremely well suited to speak to us today on the topic "The Role of Women in Voluntary Organizations." Join me in welcoming Ms. Catherine Tester.

This brief introduction tells the audience a little bit about the speaker and tells why the speaker is qualified to speak on the topic of the speech. The introduction repeats the speaker's name a couple of times and ends with the title and a final comment that calls for welcoming applause. It will only take you a few moments to prepare your own introductory notes, and that few moments may spare you a good deal of discomfort.

☐ Part B: The Speaker

The moment has arrived: You are going to rise to give a major public speech. Even with all of your previous preparation you are going to feel somewhat nervous. And you *should* feel somewhat nervous. That appropriate nervousness will sharpen your competitive edge, give you the energy that will brighten your eyes, give color to your cheeks, and infuse your whole presence with the spark of attractiveness. The feeling of energy that accompanies your speech presentation is a means of "getting up" for this important occasion. You have done your work well, you have built a firm PIER—now enjoy the flow of excitement, ride with it, enjoy this presentation. Your goal is to give your audience something worthwhile, something they can use, and to do this in a manner enjoyable for them and for you too!

Transparent Delivery

The key concept underlying effective delivery is transparency. Transparent delivery is delivery that doesn't call attention to itself at any point but that allows the audience to apprehend and comprehend the idea which informs your speech. If at the speech's end the audience can only comment on the extraordinary range of your voice, or the richness of your vocabulary, or the elegance of your gestures, or the novelty of your audiovisual aids, you have failed. It is your specific purpose and the idea behind it that the audience should center upon.

The audience should feel that heart has spoken to heart, spontaneously. The primary goal of public speaking is not performance but thought, mentation. Effective delivery is transparent delivery.

The Techniques of Transparent Delivery

Audience contact is essential for transparent delivery. Audience contact has three parts: physical audience contact, mental audience contact, and emotional audience contact.

Physical audience contact refers to the actual visual and auditory contact existing between the speaker and the audience. Being heard is a fundamental requirement of being understood. If you can't be heard, your speech cannot possibly be successful. You must speak with sufficient volume and vigor to be heard by each individual member of your audience.

Nothing is more distressing than to go to a play or a movie where the sound is so low that you cannot hear at all or must constantly strain to catch the dialog. How can you tell whether your audience can hear you? Look around at your

This Kind of Audience Feedback Calls for a Speaker's Immediate Attention (Katherine Buck)

audience. Do some of them have their hands cupped behind their ears like manual hearing trumpets? Are some of their heads drooping in that familiar preslumber nod? Do some have that glazed expression which typifies the chronic daydreamer? If any of these things are so, then there is a good chance that you just aren't being heard. This measuring device is a type of visual feedback. Now pick up your volume—do the heads raise, do the eyes unglaze, do the manual ear trumpets fall away? If so, then your problem was volume and you've solved it; if not, then you must keep on reaching for the solution, having eliminated one of the possible problems. Auditory physical contact depends on your volume and your use of feedback; it means speaking so that everyone can hear you without strain. Beware of going to the extreme of shouting since any sustained and unvarying stimulus, whether loud or soft, will induce boredom. Here, as everywhere, the rule of 30/70 obtains, variety stimulates interest.

Visual physical contact, or "eye" contact, is also important. We who have full use of our eyes seldom reflect on the ways in which seeing helps us. When you walk into a room in which you are to speak, your eyes scan the room for size and furnishings, and this information is unconsciously factored into the decision as to how much volume you are going to need in order to be heard. A large room, more volume; a small room with heavy draperies that absorb sound, more volume; a small room with hard surfaced, bare walls, reduced volume.

Another aspect of eye contact is actually looking at the audience. In conversation when we don't look people in the eyes when we talk to them, certain inferences, usually incorrect, are often drawn. Someone who avoids looking you in the eye, who has "shifty eyes," is labeled dishonest, or is accused of having something to hide. We often tell our children to "look us in the eye." The person who constantly looks away while talking to you often makes you uneasy and arouses your suspicions. You wonder what she has to hide, or why she is so nervous, or why she is bothering to talk to you at all if she so desperately wants to be doing something else. There is much interesting research on the subject of eye contact, gaze, and the effect of various degrees of pupillary dilation on successful human communication (Knapp, 1978, pp. 294–321). Such research, and its application to the public speaking experience, would make an interesting topic for a speech.

Your own eye contact, as a speaker, affects audience response. A nervous speaker creates a nervous audience. If you look away, up, down, out the window, at your shoes, at your fingernails, or always at your notes, you will stimulate tendencies toward nervousness and unrest in your audience. Good audience contact engenders feelings of confidence and interest in both speaker and audience. Eye contact means just that—look your audience members in their eyes—not just over their heads, not at a spot on the back wall, not at their jewelry, neckties, or shirt collars. Pick a specific member of your audience, look at him or her until you feel you have made personal contact, then move to another audience member. Do this with individuals in various parts of the audience. This personal visual contact creates an atmosphere of person-to-person communication, of warmth which assists both speaker and audience in enjoying the speech and in concentrating on the concepts being communicated in the speech. Additionally, this kind of individual audience eye contact helps you build and continue a conversational delivery style. It is easier to "preach" to a large, faceless, group than to a single individual. By centering your eye contact on individual audience members, you create an automatic reminder to yourself that you should try to speak to the individuals in the audience, avoiding preachiness and shouting and cultivating a warm, conversationally oriented transparent delivery. If you speak to a large group, it is going to be impossible for you to establish eye contact with each individual audience member. On the other hand, the distance between speaker and audience created by a large group serves to create an interesting illusion. If you are speaking to a large audience and you establish eye contact with someone in the middle of that audience the angle of contact is so wide that audience members to the sides of the individual at whom you are looking, as well as those before and behind the individual with whom you are establishing eye contact, will experience an eye contact similar to that of the chosen audience member. Because of this illusion you will be able to create a feeling of eye contact in a large audience situation even though you will, in reality, be focusing on a relatively small sample of the audience. So, segment your audience and make sure to establish eye contact with someone in each segment, thus contributing to an illusion of almost general eye contact.

Don't zero in on some audience member and keep eye contact with that single individual for an extended period of time. Such concentrated staring will make the audience member terribly self-conscious and uncomfortable. We all like some attention, but not too much please.

If you are too dependent on your notes, it is impossible to establish and maintain eye contact. This is another reason why it is important to have enough preparation and rehearsal to make yourself continually free of your notes.

Mental audience contact bears directly upon that essential aspect of a public speech, the thought, the mentation that drives the presentation and which, through decentering and association, the speaker tries to communicate to the audience. Mental audience contact means that the speaker and the audience are operating on the same mental "wavelength." Mental audience contact may be said to rely on two qualities: vivid realization of the thought at the moment of utterance and establishing *rapport*.

Almost no one engages in a meaningful conversation when their thoughts are obviously elsewhere. We would be offended if we were talking to someone and realized that our conversational partner was not even attending to the words he was speaking. In a good conversation there is obviously thought driving the words being uttered between or among the conversational participants. This aspect of conversation is absolutely essential to successful public speaking. Public speaking is obviously not conversation. The situation is different in many important ways. However, thinking about what is being said is essential both to effective conversation and to effective public speaking. This emphasis on mind driving mouth and mentation informing spoken language is evident in the treatises of classical rhetoric as well as in the writing of modern teachers of public speaking. James A. Winans, after discussing the concept of vivid realization of thought at the moment of utterance, goes on to encourage public speakers to have a feeling of communication with their audience (Winans, 1938, p. 25).

We believe that a speaker should always be motivated to speak by a desire to help the audience, by a desire to bring to the audience's attention something of value, whether that something of value lies in the domain of information, conviction, persuasion, or entertainment. This desire to help the audience carries with it an ethical commitment as well as a commitment to sharing meanings with the audience, a commitment to communication. Part and parcel of the vivid realization of the thought at the moment of utterance is the creation and sustaining of the illusion of spontaneity. *Think* about what you are saying while you are saying it. Don't put your mouth in motion until you've put your mind in gear!

Giving the same general speech over and over doesn't necessarily result either in staleness or the abandonment of the illusion of spontaneity. Every time you give the speech, you rethink it, you work over the ideas in the speech, you refurbish the supporting material, you work harder and harder at associating the thought encapsulated in the speech with the experiences of the new audience. One of us has persented essentially the same speech over 50 times and has, with each delivery, gained new insights into the main concepts underlying the talk. Before the development of mass communications a speaker could prepare, polish, memorize, and deliver a speech well over 5000 times during a span of 50 years.

☐ ☐ ☐ ☐ **Example**

Russell H. Conwell, lecturer extraordinary, delivered his famous lecture, "Acres of Diamonds," over 6100 times during a 50-year period, and yet Conwell never stopped working on the speech. (Braden and Gehring, 1958, p. 14).

"Acres of Diamonds" is still a very interesting lecture to read and must have been an exciting speech to hear. But if Mr. Conwell were still alive and able to deliver his speech on national network television tomorrow night at 9 p.m., he would, in that one presentation, reach an audience larger in number than the combined audience of all his 50 years on the speaking circuit. This tremendous television exposure would make it quite awkward for him to repeat the speech to new audiences over and over again. Mass media has an insatiable appetite for new material and thus there is a constant need for new speakers, speaking new thoughts or speaking old thoughts in a fresh manner. Whatever the age of the thought, it must infuse the speaker's words as those words are uttered.

The second aspect of mental audience contact may be called *rapport*. The word "rapport" is of French origin and refers to a close and sympathetic relationship. There used to be a night club act in which a performer, blindfolded, could supposedly read his partner's mind. The two performers claimed to be in such rapport that their minds were operating on the exact same wavelength and thus what one thought the other thought as well. This particular act was trickery, but the concept of two minds being in such close accord as to facilitate unspoken communication between them has received much interest from experimenters in extrasensory perception. The establishment of such rapport between a speaker and an audience demands that the speaker be extraordinarily sensitive to audience feedback and that the speaker be prepared to patiently restate a posiiton at the slightest sign of audience doubt or bewilderment. You must *never* give the impression of talking down to your audience or of trying to impress them with your vocabulary or virtuosity. Most audiences appreciate what they perceive to be sincerity and warmth on the part of the speaker. You, as speaker, can do a lot to enhance the possibility of rapport by taking the time to meet and chat with some of the audience members prior to the start of the program during which you will be speaking. Introduce yourself, ask what their expectations for the speech are, make them comfortable, and you will find that they in turn will help make you comfortable. In the process of warming up to your audience and getting them to warm up to you, be as natural as you possibly can since any hint of manipulativeness or falseness will not only turn them off but may turn them against you. Remember to establish and maintain eye contact with your audience since it is through both hearing and seeing that you note the subtle facial and postural cues that tell you how the audience is reacting to your presentation. By being sensitive to such audience cues, you will be able to adapt your content and delivery so as to meet audience expectations and create rapport. All this must be done as naturally, as transparently, as possible. As soon as your delivery becomes so opaque as to call attention to itself rather than allowing the speech's ideas to shine through, rapport is destroyed.

Emotional audience contact is the third, last, and most difficult dimension of audience contact. Emotional audience contact results from the melding of decentering, association, and empathy. You are familiar with the concepts of decentering (taking the conceptual point of view of someone else) and association (trying to associate your thoughts or experiences with the thoughts and experiences of others). Empathy is an *emotional* (rather than a conceptual) identification with someone else. Here are a few examples of empathy. You are watching a roller coaster; you see the car climb up the steep incline, reach the top, hesitate for a moment, and then swoop swiftly, sickeningly down, its passengers screaming and gripping the hand rail. How do you react? If you are average, and if you have ever ridden a roller coaster, your own stomach drops for a second just as if you were taking the ride yourself. You identify with the passengers and with the experience; you have an empathic reaction, a "feeling in with" the feelings of the passengers.

Suppose you are reading a description of someone being abused in a World War II concentration camp. Such a description can be cold and detached and leave you with an unemotional intellectual abhorrence for the event. On the other hand, the horrors of suffering can be described so vividly, with such emotion and compassion, that the description nauseates you, makes you cry, fills you with resentment and indignation, makes you so angry that you resolve to do all in your power never to let such a thing happen ever again. Such emotional and intellectual identification is the result of a careful blend of empathy, decentering, and association.

The speaker who establishes emotional contact with the audience will go far toward achieving the speech's specific purpose. To establish emotional audience contact you need to sharpen your decentering ability, to hone your talent at using association, and to point clearly at appropriate empathy in your speech.

Of the three aspects of audience contact, emotional contact is not only the most difficult but the most dangerous. Misused, unethical, emotional contact can backfire and give the speaker a reputation as an emotional manipulator or a rabble rouser. Be careful of this technique, it can make even the most transparent delivery absolutely opaque. Yet be aware that the appropriate use of emotional audience appeal often makes the difference between a good speech and a great speech. Try to grow into the use of emotional audience contact as you become more and more adept at public speaking.

From the vantage point of actual delivery the order in which the three aspects of audience contact have been presented (physical, mental, and emotional) is the easiest order of increasing control. Theoretically you should be working on mental contact all along, but in terms of presentation you will find it easiest to work first on physical contact—it's the most observable. Always try to synthesize the three aspects in your actual speaking. Good audience contact is certainly one of the characteristics which most frequently distinguishes a good speaker from a great speaker. There are three aspects. The best speakers utilize all three aspects, they have a contact quotient of 3. Beginning with your next speech continually try to raise your audience contact quotient, try for *total* audience contact.

Clothing is part of the overall appearance of the public speaker. Clothing and cleanliness are also factors which an audience takes into consideration when judging a speaker and the speaker's public speech. Personal cleanliness is pretty much taken for granted by an audience, it is truly considered transparent *unless* there is something about the speaker's person which suggests something less than the cleanliness an audience automatically expects. Knapp, in his book cited earlier in this chapter, presents a fine review of the available research on the effects of physical appearance and dress in interpersonal human communication (Knapp, 1978, pp. 152–195). There is, however, less information available on the effects of clothing in public speaking situations. One popular author has done some field research on the effects of clothing in a variety of public speaking situations, including television appearances (Molloy, 1976, 1978). Whether or not you are willing to accept Molloy's research results, he still presents a well-articulated point of view on the topic of appropriate clothing. Although we would rather not make specific clothing recommendations, since clothing choice depends on so many variables (income, culture, business occasion, taste) you can find charts adapting Molloy's work to public speaking situations in Zannes and Goldhaber (1983, pp. 203, 204).

We offer the following advice on clothing. *Dress so that you feel you look good.* If in doubt, ask the advice of someone you and others consider an example of a good dresser. Most of us have a pretty good idea of what we look best in. We know when we feel comfortable, when we feel that our clothing suits us and enhances our appearance. For most of us there are some colors that are more flattering than others. Ask someone whose taste you trust to give you some ideas as what colors seem most flattering to you. If you find yourself with some extra cash on hand, or being asked what extravagant gift you would like, there are even specialists who will consult with you on your color preferences and needs and will draw up a "color profile" which you then use to direct your wardrobe purchases.

Especially in the case of clothing, you do not want to wear something that calls attention to itself so that the audience's concentration is directed to how you look rather than to the ideas you are presenting in your speech.

Clothing styles and clothing colors are also culturally influenced. Whereas black is the normal color of mourning in the United States, white is the color of mourning in some Eastern cultures. If addressing an audience composed of members of cultures other than your own, you should make an effort to learn something about the color and clothing preferences of that group. Knowing about such preferences doesn't necessarily mean that you either can or will match the preferences. But at least you will be aware of them and will have made your own decision as to what you are going to do about them. It is almost always safe to dress as you would for a business occasion. Public speaking is no place to try out your clothing eccentricities. Don't wear overly revealing clothes or overly casual clothing for a formal public speech. Wear clothes that fit you, but not so tightly that your clothes restrict the freedom of your movements while delivering your speech. Again, if you have any questions about the appropriateness of your clothing, ask someone whose clothing opinion you respect and whose advice you won't resent. Be clean, be neat, be appropriately dressed. The word "appropriate" is important since there is always the possibility that you may wish to wear some kind of costume peculiarly suited to the subject of your speech.

Body language is another technique useful in developing transparent delivery. Posture, gestures, and movement are all aspects of delivery. From the moment you are called to the audience's visual awareness, they are taking your entire presence into consideration. Stand up straight! Good posture frees the vocal musculature for its easiest and most flexible use. Good breathing is important in public speaking and good posture makes it easier to breathe correctly. It is difficult to produce good volume when you are slouched over. Walk briskly and firmly to the speaker's stand (don't run). If you move away from the lectern remember to make your movements definite, try not to hesitate or look unsure of yourself. The bodily posture is expressive in itself. You can often tell how someone is feeling just by observing his or her posture. Is he walking with the light step of success, the slump of defeat, the angularity of pain, or the slouch of laziness? Try to keep evenly balanced on both legs rather than putting all of your weight on one leg so that your hips angle diagonally downward. A balanced posture suggests strength and allows the speaker to move smoothly in any direction he chooses.

Gestures include facial gestures as well as gestures of the head, arms, hands, and legs. Smiling is attractive. Unless you are dealing with material that should not be accompanied by a smile (you don't want to smile when talking about nuclear devastation or highway accidents), try to look pleasant. Consider using your eyebrows to indicate a questioning attitude (raise them) or sternness (lower them). But don't be artificial. Gestures are the natural accompaniments of talking. We all gesture when we are engaged in normal conversation. During rehearsal allow yourself to gesture naturally and take note of those natural gestures. If they are natural in conversation and in rehearsal, then they are likely to be natural in public speaking. Try to free yourself from inner strains and tensions, try to develop a spontaneous action that springs from inner motivation. When rehearsing use your natural gestures with full force and vigor. In your final speech delivery allow the theory of remembered action to operate. This theory suggests that if you have used natural gestures and movements in your rehearsals, some of them will carry over into your actual speech. But before this theory of remembered action can possibly operate, there must be some action to remember.

As mentioned earlier, the speaker's behaviors affect the audience's behaviors. If you appear to gesture naturally, if the movements and gestures are appropriate to the ideas being considered, then the audience will not even notice them. The audience *will* certainly notice if you look immobilized by the speaking situation. Gesture is also important to the speaker because it serves as an activity to channel off some of the excess energy that is created by the speaking event. The proper use of gesture channels this energy into useful paths. A well-placed gesture can indicate the tilt of a bridge in the wind, or height, width, or length. Gestures can help convey quantity (there was a mound of mashed potatoes on my plate *this* big) and quality ("I hate the taste of raw fish") and we grit our teeth and make a grimace of disgust. If a speaker is describing something that has elements of both comedy and tragedy in it, the appropriate facial gesticulation can indicate which of these two is being emphasized. A smile suggests one thing, a frown another, a total lack of facial expression a third point of view. When a speaker kids herself with a half grin, it signals the listeners that they too may enjoy the joke. To the audience, gestures indicate the speaker's personality and interest in the topic, the occasion, and the audience. The speaker who approaches the lectern with the lethargic gait of an exhausted pallbearer prepares the audience for boredom. An unsmiling, beetle-browed visage can wilt enthusiasm on the part of the audience. A cocky smirk warns the audience of approaching flippancy and sarcasm. The pleasant, enthusiastic face of a well-prepared and interested speaker heralds an enjoyable experience for the audience. Gestures help indicate to the audience the response they are expected to give. Normally the need for a gesture exists before the gesture. *Create the conditions for the gesture, don't try to create the gesture!*

When using gestures, suit the gesture to the concept. The only time big gestures are acceptable is when they are being used to illustrate or underline big concepts or as a source of humor. Use gesticulation sparingly in the beginning of your speech; let your gestures develop as the speech develops.

If you are seated on the stage while being introduced, you are being observed from the moment you sit down. If your name is mentioned at the beginning of a program and the master of ceremonies or toastmaster nods in your direction, from that moment on some members of the audience will be observing you with curiosity. The way you sit during your introduction, the way you stand, the way you walk to your place, your posture or movement while giving the speech or listening to others speak, all these actions and activities provide the audience with cues about your personality and your preparedness. If you worry about doing the right thing when called to the platform, practice privately a few times. Rise from your seat and walk across the room, turn, and face the imaginary audience. Do this until you feel comfortable; and then relax.

The eye follows movement. The movements which you use while speaking will attract your audience's attention. You can use movement to indicate a transition; just walking from your lectern to a position in front of the audience can tell the audience that you are changing direction in your speech. Know where you are going to move, and what your purpose is in so moving.

Posture, movement, and gesture are all techniques of *transparent delivery;* none of them should call attention to themselves. Each of them should reinforce your specific purpose and the ideas you are trying to convey.

Voice, articulation, and pronunciation are essential attributes of transparent delivery.

The *voice* is the fundamental instrument of spoken language and of speech communication. When used correctly the voice is flexible, responsive, and attractive. When it is used incorrectly the voice may be rigid, rasping, and sometimes repelling. Psychiatrists when making an initial diagnosis can often tell much from the voice of the patient. This type of evaluation is not restricted to psychiatrists. What weary mate coming home from a hard day's work isn't attentive to the spouse's voice in the initial greeting? One vocal quality and pattern gives promise of a pleasant evening, another indicates the opposite. In a phone conversation we can usually tell from the first few words just how the other person is feeling. We often say, or are told, "You don't *sound* well." "My, you sound cheerful today!" "What's happened, you sound frightened?" The voice responds to our total bodily condition and reflects our message and our mood.

A pleasant voice suggests a pleasant person. It is a happy trick of the human mind to place a pleasant-sounding voice in a pleasant-looking person. When television first became popular people looked forward to seeing as well as hearing their favorite radio announcers or radio personalities, only to find that the booming base voice that they imagined coming forth from a modern-day Atlas belonged in reality to a modern-day mouse. The reverse had happened earlier when many silent film stars couldn't make the switch to "talkies" because of a thin voice or faulty articulation.

The voice is an index of personality. If you cultivate a pleasant personality, most often you will have a pleasant voice. If you have a blustering, bullying, braggadocio attitude toward yourself and others, your voice will probably indicate that attitude. If you distrust others and look for the dark side of every happening, here too your voice will be likely to betray you.

Most of us have been born with perfectly adequate vocal equipment which, when properly used, can serve as a superior speaking instrument. Only when we misuse our voice or provide it with a less than pleasing personality does the vocal instrument usually fail us. One respected authority on voice says:

> Bluntly stated, one may have a dull, uninteresting, or unpleasant voice because his voice is defective or improperly used; but he may also have such a voice because he is a dull, uninteresting, or unpleasant person. In the one case, voice training appears to be the proper solution, but in the other case it is obvious that the problem involves much more than merely giving attention to the mechanical aspects of voice production. (Anderson, 1942, p. xviii)

An adequate voice is one that is both efficient and pleasing. The adequate voice serves as a vehicle for transmitting an idea rather than as a showpiece for itself. If, after hearing a speech, you find yourself saying "My, what a beautiful voice!" and at the same time forgetting what the speech was all about, then the speaker's voice failed in its fundamental purpose—that of communicating an idea. The voice of such a speaker is opaque, hides the thoughts of the speech, and fails as a technique of transparent delivery.

If there are no organic (such as cleft palate) or functional (such as a very high pitch resulting from hypertension) abnormalities to be corrected, then the development of an adequate speaking voice, a voice both efficient and pleasing, depends on a combination of relaxation, ear training, and correct breathing habits. An efficient voice is one that can be heard with ease by all the listeners present. The good voice should also be pleasing. It shouldn't grate upon the ears of the listeners but should make it easy for them to give their full attention to the message being conveyed.

For efficient voice production the speaker should be as relaxed as possible. Tension and fatigue hamper good voice production. The voice gains a great deal of its color from the tissues of the speaking apparatus. If the vocal tissues are taut and tense, the voice will probably convey that tenseness. A strained voice is usually incapable of either much volume or much pleasantness. If we are not naturally relaxed then we must try to consciously relax. If you feel unduly tense then go back to Chapter Three and practice the relaxation exercises presented there on page 53. As you grow more accomplished at conscious relaxation you will find methods suited to your personal style. Write those relaxation methods down and prepare your own prescription for relaxation that you can administer to yourself as needed. If you can't spare the time for a full relaxation exercise and you feel the need to relax your voice, try to yawn. A good, deep yawn is often quite effective in reducing tension in the vocal regions. (Yawn in private, you don't want to give your audience any ideas.)

Ear training plays an important role in the formation of an adequate voice for speaking. What we hear, and how we hear ourselves, plays a large part in how our own voice sounds. The voice of a hard-of-hearing person often reflects that person's own reduced auditory efficiency. A person also often adopts the vocal characteristics of his immediate environment. Many people after moving to a different part of the country adopt the vocal, articulatory, and pronunciation patterns of their new territory. This is especially noticeable in young children who move elsewhere. Train yourself to be discriminating in the patterns you adopt as a result of the voices around you. Ear training is another place where tape recorders and videotape recorders are beneficial. Listen and learn! Listen to the voices of professional speakers and other performers. Listen to your own voice. Compare and contrast. Before you can improve your own voice, you must be aware of those aspects which call for improvement. Before correcting a voice or articulation problem, you must first be able to *hear* the difference between the undesired and the desired pattern or sound. When you hear your own voice, listen critically and see what can be improved.

Correct breathing habits are also important for building an adequate speaking voice. Exactly what does a speaker need in the way of breath? You need sufficient breath to carry your voice and to allow you some flexibility in phrasing.

If you run out of breath before the end of a thought, or if you must stop to fill up your lungs in the middle of a phrase, you can do serious damage to the idea you are trying to communicate. Suppose that you were telling a friend that you had just seen a mutual acquaintance screaming with laughter. If your breath supply ran out just before the final "with" and your first phrase was just "I heard Sue screaming. . . ," your reputation as an alarmist would increase significantly. The person with a serious inadequacy in breath control is the exception, not the rule. How you breathe is of little consequence as long as it gives you sufficient breath for projection and phrasing and is not obviously exaggerated. A good example of excellent breath control is given by most capable swimmers who breathe regularly and smoothly.

Following are a few simple breathing exercises which may help you gain control over your breath rate and relieve you of concern about running out of breath during a speech.

1. Relax!
2. Breathe normally for a few seconds. Now exhale a full breath through your mouth slowly and smoothly. After the breath is exhausted, don't force another inhalation: wait until the breath comes by itself. Continue this process over and over again. Your breathing will get deeper and fuller, and a more relaxed feeling will also usually follow.
3. Take a deep breath, release it s - l - o - w - l - y; at the same time count to as high a number as you can while maintaining an even volume for each breath.
4. Take a deep breath. Now expend all of your breath on three numbers. Count 1, 2, 3. Maintain an even volume for each number.
5. When walking, breathe deeply, and exhale your breath for as long a count as possible. Use your walking time at home, school, or work to increase both your breath capacity and breath control.

Silence and rest are both mighty warriors on the side of good vocal habits. Overuse and immoderate use are natural enemies of the relaxed and controlled voice. Silence is something positive, something to be consciously sought from time to time. Be silent. Listen. Rest. Think.

Articulation is the formation of the individual sounds that make up a word. Good articulation is a technique of transparent delivery. The word "fish" has four letters. How many sounds are there in the word? Say "fish" slowly; how many separate sounds do you hear? There are four letters of the alphabet, but there are only three sounds: f/i/sh. The first sound is the same as the initial sound in *free,* the second is the same as the initial sound in *it,* and the third is the same as the initial sound in *ship.* If you form each of these three sounds correctly and then join them in the right sequence, you will have correctly articulated the word "fish." If you were to say "I had vish for supper," you would have misarticulated—you have substituted the sound /v/ for the sound /f/. Articulation refers to how an individual forms and joins units of sound.

Correct articulation calls for both precision and flexibility. If you are over-precise, you tend to sound affected and pedantic. If too flexible, you risk lapsing into sloppy and slurring articulatory patterns. In conversation you allow for the fact that words come very closely together and affect one another's articulation and pronunciation. Some of us from the Eastern seaboard find ourselves articulating "Did you eat?" as "Djeet?" When speaking to large audiences, we slow our rate but still we don't want to do away with natural speech rhythms and patterns. The ideal in articulation, as in voice, and as in the other techniques of transparent delivery, is to articulate in a way that does not call attention to itself within the speech pattern as a whole and which allows the audience to concentrate on the ideas of the speech.

There are few, if any, articulatory problems that cannot be corrected if you wish to do so. Problems such as lisping, nasality, slurring, adding unnecessary sounds (for example, adding the first sound in *garage,* /g/, to words such as Long/g/Island or hang/g/er) can be treated by a qualified teacher working with a well-motivated client. If you have specific voice or articulation problems that you would like to work on, consult a list of certified speech pathologists. Such lists are usually available through departments of speech pathology and audiology, or departments of communicative disorders, at local community colleges, colleges, and universities. Many physicians also have information available concerning speech pathologists who have been certified by the American Speech, Language, Hearing Association. The *certified* speech pathologist, or your physician, is the proper person to consult. As elsewhere there are "quacks" in the field of speech correction. A poorly trained person can do far more harm than good and also cost more in time, energy, and money than the most expensive professional. Don't take chances.

Except for simple substitutions we advise that you undertake correction only under the direction of a qualified person. When working with simple substitution errors, the process of correcting an articulatory error usually includes these four steps:

1. You must hear well.
2. You must be able to hear yourself.
3. You must be able to distinguish between the sound you make and the desired sound, and you must be able to form the desired sound.
4. You must practice the new sound both by itself and as an element of connected discourse.

Pronunciation as a technique of transparent delivery has four aspects: (1) the correct location of accent or syllabic stress, (2) the proper articulation of sounds, (3) the articulation of only the required sounds, and (4) the correct joining of sounds.

The general rule for correct pronunciation is *usage is the norm of speech*. Since the time of the ancient Greeks, correctness in pronunciation has been determined by common usage. The best guides for correct pronunciation are to be found all around you in the pronunciation of educated people. Remember that people may be educated without ever having gone to school. Dictionaries, so often looked upon as infallible and final arbiters of pronunciation and usage, are compiled by a polling of the pronunciation and usage used by a percentage of the educated

pro•nun•ci•a•tion /prə-nən(t)-sē-ˈā-shən/ *n* [ME *pronunciacion,* fr.
MF *prononciation,* fr. L *pronuntiation-, pronuntiatio,* fr. *pronun-
tiatus,* pp. of *pronuntiare*] : the act or manner of pronouncing
something — **pro•nun•ci•a•tion•al** /-shnəl,-shən-l/ *adj*

Figure 7.1 Sample from a Dictionary Showing Diacritical Markings

people in each community. (See Figure 7.1.) This material is then collated and
the pronunciation and usage most frequently used by the people consulted is listed
as the preferred choice. Other frequent usages are also listed. As our American
society grows more and more mobile it is difficult for a dictionary to keep up.
Use a dictionary by all means, but use it with discretion. A dictionary is not a rule
maker, it is a guide to usage. There are many writers who set themselves up as
the dictators of usage. Some such columnists suggest that their's is the only correct
usage or pronunciation. Ridiculous. Many times such writers are simply self-vic-
timized by their own confusion of oral with written traditions and then they foist
their opinions off on their readers.

If in doubt, check it out! Look in a current dictionary (old ones give old
usages and pronunciations, some of which have been dropped) to find the preferred pronunciation of a word. Make sure you understand the diacritical marks
and conventions which the dictionary publisher uses to indicate pronunciation
stress and sound. All major dictionaries include a pronunciation and stress guide
in the pages prior to the word listings. Consult those pages if you are unsure.

The best way to pronounce words correctly is through using them, through
practice. Many people judge us by our pronunciation habits. Check the pronunciation and meaning of a new word as soon as possible after you find yourself
using it. Don't get fancy with your pronunciation, remember that it, like voice
and articulation, serves us best when it is unnoticeable, when it is transparent,
when it lets our ideas shine forth.

The *rate,* pacing, or timing of your presentation is the final transparent
delivery technique we will be discussing. How fast should you speak when delivering a public speech? Fast enough so that every word can be heard, so that the
ideas are easily grasped by the listeners, but not so fast that the audience has to
strain to keep up with you. Too slow a delivery rate is absolutely anesthetizing.
A chairman of the board of a large corporation came to one of us for help. This
gentleman spoke so slowly (slower than 100 words per minute) that it took all of
one's concentration just to keep one's eyes open. After one of his speeches, only
one man applauded and he was slapping his head to stay awake. Once the slow
speaker was made aware (through use of a videotape recorder) of his anguishing
rate of delivery, it was a fairly easy matter to bring him up to a more acceptable
presentation rate. We have found more problems with overly slow delivery than
with delivery that is too fast. In fact it has been our experience that most professional platform speakers use a faster rate of delivery than that recommended in
academic speech texts. Many current public speaking texts recommended a delivery
rate of somewhere between 120 and 150 wpm (words per minute). A few texts
suggest rates around 180 wpm. According to research literature conversational
speaking rates hover around 150 wpm (Kelly and Steer, 1949). In a contest setting

on March 16, 1978, Patricia Keeling-Andrich delivered 403 words from W. S. Gilbert's "The Nightmare" in 60 seconds at Chabot College in Hayward, California. Since research literature suggests a drop-off in auditory resolution at somewhere around 280 wpm, a speed of 403 wpm would be anything but transparent (Beatty et al., 1979). On the basis of a rather thorough review of the literature on this topic we suggest a delivery rate somewhere between 140 and 210 wpm depending on your fastest rate of clear articulation and pronunciation. We would also remind you that situational variables may call for a rather large alteration in speed and pacing. An elderly audience, a large audience in a hall with poor acoustics, an audience with a high proportion of hard-of-hearing people, an audience whose native language is other than that of the speaker, these and many similar situations would demand a slower and more deliberate rate of presentation. Variation, in keeping with the spirit of the rule of 70/30, is important in rate.

Time your own rate of spoken delivery. Take a poem, or a piece of prose, mark the manuscript or page with a / after every 100 words. Read the material aloud with a moderately loud voice and at what you consider to be a pace normal for you. Using a stopwatch (or even better a friend as a listener and helper), read aloud for a minute and mark the place you stop. Now take a count of approximately how many words you spoke in the minute. Material read from manuscript goes a bit faster than normal public speaking material since you don't usually use the same pauses, or make the same kind of adaptations to your audience. Judging the best rate for your speech is another instance where a "sound mirror," a tape recorder or VTR, will be of inestimable help to you. Here is a good time to use contrast. Go as fast as you can. Go as slow as you can. Tape both speeds and then critically listen to the results. Your delivery, or presentational, speed should be kept at the service of your specific purpose and of the ideas you are presenting.

Now you need to synthesize all these techniques into a truly transparent delivery. Your audience contact, clothing, posture, gestures, movement, voice, articulation, pronunciation, and delivery rate should all serve your thoughts. In the beginning this seems like a great many things to attend to all at the same time but through preparation, rehearsal, and repeated public speaking experience, all these diverse techniques of transparent delivery will eventually be coordinated and melded into a single presentational style. In normal conversation you already automatically and without conscious effort coordinate all these elements and use them to help you get your ideas across to others.

☐ Audience Response

You can't argue with audience response to your speech. You may feel that their response was great, or their response was inadequate. It is *their* response. You can only accept their response and use it as a means of judging how you would give the speech the next time.

If there is time for questions and answers, stay in your position in front of the audience and acknowledge the person raising the question. Look at the person asking the question *while the question is being asked*. As soon as the question has been completed, look away to the rest of the audience (otherwise the questioner may go on forever). Make sure you understand the question. Repeat it so that the other audience members will know what it is you are answering, and then:

If you have a good answer to the question, give it.
If you don't have the answer but know where it can be found, tell the audience.
If you don't have the answer and don't know where to get it, admit it.

Don't overanswer the question. This is a serious temptation. Just try to speak as directly and transparently as possible to the question posed and then move on to another question. Have in mind from the start how long you will be able to take questions and then signal the end of the question and answer period by stating "I have time for only one more question," and then take that final question.

It is sometimes a good idea to have a couple of pertinent questions seeded in the audience so that some points you would like to make in a Q & A get a chance to be made.

The question and answer session at the end of a speech is a place to make one last effort to achieve your specific purpose and to get your ideas across to your audience.

In our discussion of humor in Chapter Five we warned you against using material concerning which you have any doubt at all. We would like to extend that warning here by stating that in the area of doubtful humor you cannot completely trust audience response. Audiences are human, and humans will laugh at things which upon more reflection they find offensive. Your audience might laugh at an off-color joke; you may take their laughter as a sign of approval and of encouragement and go on to tell more such stories. Then, sometime after the speech you may be told that the stories were inappropriate and should not have been used. "But," you say to your informant, "the audience laughed at them, they obviously enjoyed them." Perhaps the audience, or many members of it, *did* laugh at the time—that doesn't mean that after the speech they won't comment on the offensiveness of the jokes or stories and allow their disapproval to generalize to the entire speech. Another point concerning offensive speech material is that you may find yourself speaking in a situation where the audience, because of job requirements or similar demands, was compelled to attend your speech. No one should be forced to expose themselves to material they find offensive, especially material supposedly funny. Learning where the line between offensiveness and funniness lies takes time and experience. If in doubt, don't! Be sensitive to audience response, but try not to overinterpret their response.

You should acknowledge your audience response. Generally, in fact almost 100 percent of the time, the audience will applaud your contribution. While still standing before them, look at them, smile, and show that you appreciate their response. If, after the speech, members of the audience compliment you, accept those compliments with grace. You may say to the person complimenting you, "Thank you so very much," or "I really appreciate your kindness," or "You were an excellent audience." Whatever you say, don't be churlish, be gracious.

Although you now may be giving your speeches before a class, you, in the not too distant future, will be giving speeches before different kinds of audiences. Although audiences almost universally share a desire to have the speaker succeed, audiences still differ. In earlier chapters we discussed audience analysis. At this point we want to mention that the same audience takes on different characteristics at different times. You should be aware that audience expectations are affected by the time of day of the presentation, the day of the week of the presentation, the size of the audience, and the position on a program where the presentation appears. If you are the last speaker on the fifth day of a week's workshop and the audience members are just waiting for the end of your presentation to take off for home, you have a different challenge than if you had been the first speaker on the first day of that week's program. If your audience has heard six speakers, beginning at 9:00 a.m. and it is now 5:45 p.m. and you are the final speaker for the day—you better be stimulating. Although the techniques for handling some of these challenges are more advanced than those being covered in this primer we just wanted to alert you to the need to take day of week, time of day, and program placement into consideration during your delivery.

☐ Delivery Checklist

1. Before arriving at the place of presentation, use a mirror to make a final check of your appearance and clothing.
2. Check to make sure you have all your materials, your speaker's notes, and any audiovisual aids with you.
3. While waiting to be introduced, practice relaxation techniques. Take full, slow breaths and exhale slowly. If you can yawn without being seen, do so to relax your throat.
4. Mentally root for your audience. Remind yourself that you want to give them something worthwhile and that you want everyone to enjoy the public speaking experience. Including you!
5. When called upon, or introduced: Stand. Head up. Smile. Walk briskly to the platform.
6. If the master of ceremonies, toastmaster, or host is still at the lectern, smile and shake hands.
7. Stand directly behind the lectern.
8. Put your notes on the lectern.
9. If you are using a microphone, take time to adjust the mike correctly.
10. Leaving your hands hanging at your side, or resting them on the front edge of the lectern, stand quietly, look directly at your audience (not at your notes), and let your audience quiet down.

11. If you received a nice introduction, acknowledge the introduction. Don't go through a ritual of acknowledging all of your hosts or attending dignitaries.

12. Look at your audience, establish eye contact, if appropriate look pleasant, start the introduction of the speech.

13. Using all the techniques of transparent delivery, make your speech presentation. Enjoy it. Be sensitive to audience feedback. If you feel comfortable enough and if the microphone arrangement allows it, move away from the lectern from time to time.

14. Watch your time.

15. At the proper time start your conclusion. Maintain audience contact. Don't walk away while giving your conclusion. Stay in place. Conclude.

16. Don't say "thank you." An automatic "thank you" at the end of the speech suggests an inadequately prepared or rehearsed conclusion. Your speech's conclusion should be so structured and delivered that the audience knows by your content and your intonation that you are finished without your artificially helping them along with "thank you."

17. Acknowledge the audience response.

18. If there is to be a Q & A period, conduct it. Watch your time.

19. After you give your final answer, thank your audience—a simple "thank you" is sufficient.

20. Gather up your notes and walk back to your seat. Sit quietly, breath deeply, try to begin unwinding, "coming down" from the exhilaration of the speaking situation.

After the speech is over, reflect on the whole experience. How do you think it went? What would you change if you had it to do over? What changes in preparation for your next speech will you make as a result of this one? Add a page of notes to the file for this speech in which you *very briefly* give your own reaction to the presentation along with any comments on what you did that was different from what you had rehearsed and what you would do differently if you were to give the speech again.

☐ Summary

Whereas your preparatory outline contains almost everything of record, you should only put into your speaker's notes those things necessary to make you feel comfortable when giving the speech. It is a wise to prepare some notes concerning yourself for the person charged with introducing you. The key term and concept in delivering your speech is *transparent delivery*. Transparent delivery is delivery that doesn't call attention to itself in any way but that allows the audience to comprehend the idea which informs your speech.

Audience contact has three parts: physical audience contact, mental audience contact, and emotional audience contact.

Dress so that you feel good about how you look. Your clothing, posture, gestures, movement, voice, articulation, pronunciation, and rate are all techniques of transparent delivery. You needn't have a "showbiz" voice, just an adequate voice. An adequate voice is one that is both efficient and pleasing. In considering pronunciation remember that usage is the norm of correct pronunciation.

After the speech is over be prepared to answer questions, but don't over-answer questions. If you don't know the answer to a question, say so and offer to find it out for the questioner. If complimented, accept the compliment graciously. After your speech go over it in your own mind seeking for ways to improve it.

Remember that all delivery is aimed not at performance or exhibition but at helping you achieve your specific purpose. Your delivery should be transparent.

Exercises ■ ⬚⬚⬚⬚⬚⬚⬚⬚⬚⬚⬚⬚⬚⬚⬚⬚⬚⬚⬚⬚⬚⬚⬚⬚⬚⬚⬚⬚⬚⬚⬚

1 Prepare an introduction of yourself as a speaker.

2 In discussing the problems of introductions of speakers, we mentioned contingencies that a speaker might have to face on the spur of the moment. Professor John Alfred Jones has developed an extensive list of such contingencies and advises speakers that they should consider how they will handle some of these contingencies *before* they arise. Here is a sample of some contingency situations from those suggested by Professor Jones. How would you handle them if they happened to you?

a What if you arrive to deliver your speech and are asked to speak for an hour instead of 30 minutes because a second speaker has canceled?

b What if there are other programs in rooms on each side of the one in which you are speaking and the voices of other speakers carry into your room through the walls?

c What if you take out your speaking notes but, just as you are introduced to the audience, discover some of your notes are missing?

d What if several people in your audience get up and walk out while you are speaking?

e What if the preceding speaker covers all your material?

f What if you are heckled?

g What if cues from your audience indicate you have already persuaded them, though you have completed only half the speech?

3 Prepare a 5-minute speech showing how research on eye contact may be applied to public speaking.

4 Obtain a recording of a speaker you admire and try to imitate him or her. Record your imitation. Now try some relaxation exercises and do the imitation again. Record the second try. Listen to your two imitation efforts. The combination of relaxation and ear training is sometimes able to work wonders in vocal control.

5 Keep a notebook of your observations on how others, in conversation as well

as in platform speaking, use eyes, posture, hands, gesture, movement, and rate to get their ideas across.

6 Here are a few tongue twisters for exercising articulation.
a He saved six long, slim, sleek, slender saplings.
b Ten drops of black bug's blood in a bucket.
c The seething sea ceaseth and so sufficeth us.

7 Develop a feel for movement and gesture by pantomiming everyday activities.
a Make a peanut butter and jelly sandwich.
b Mix a drink.
c Pour two cups of coffee. Add milk and sugar to one.

Bibliographic References ■

Anderson, Virgil: *Training the Speaking Voice,* Oxford University Press, New York, 1942. An excellent source book for information and exercises on voice and articulation.

Beatty, M., R. R. Behnke, and F. H. Goodyear: "Effects of Speeded Speech Presentation on Confidence: Weighted and Traditional Comprehension Scores," in *Communication Monographs,* vol. 46, no. 2, June 1979, pp. 147–151. A nice study of the effect of rate.

Braden, Waldo W., and M. L. Gehring: *Speech Practices.* Harper and Brothers, New York, 1958. An older, but excellent, text on public speaking.

Jones, John Alfred: "Preparing Contingency Plans for Public Speaking Situations, *Communication Education,* vol. 30, no. 4, October 1981, pp. 423–425.

Kelly, J. C., and M. D. Steer: "Revised Concept of Rate," *Journal of Speech and Hearing Disorders,* no. 14, 1949, pp. 222–226. Reviews the literature and suggests average rate.

Knapp, Mark L.: *Nonverbal Communication in Human Interaction,* 2nd ed., Holt, Rinehart and Winston, New York, 1978. A readable and extremely well researched treatment which affords the interested student abundant information.

Molloy, John T.: *Dress for Success,* Warner Books, New York, 1976. Also by the same author. *The Woman's Dress for Success Book.* Warner Books, New York, 1978.

Winans, James A.: *Speechmaking,* Appleton-Century, New York, 1938. A classic and ever helpful textbook on public speaking.

Zannes, Estelle, and G. Goldhaber: *Stand Up, Speak Up,* 2nd ed., Addison-Wesley, Reading, Mass., 1983. A contemporary public speaking text with many helpful ideas.

Recommended Reading ■

Fairbanks, Grant: *Voice and Articulation Drillbook,* 2nd ed., Harper and Brothers, New York, 1940. Great source of information and exercises on its subject. Offers many helpful ideas on rate of delivery.

Argumentation and Persuasion

Chapter Eight

"All that is done on compulsion is bitterness to the soul."
Fragment of Euenus of Paros as quoted by Aristotle

Humans resent being compelled to do anything. On the other hand humans can be persuaded to do almost anything. In Chapter One, "Public Speaking and Personal Power," we discussed the relationship of human communication and power. If you recall, we defined power as the ability to influence the behavior of others. We exert power over animals and over nature by the use of force, manipulation, and even by our willing acceptance of those aspects of nature we cannot alter. Animals exert power over other animals by the use of brute force. There is, however, the uniquely human form of power that derives from the human capacity for spoken language. This uniquely human power is exercised over our own selves (we seem to be able to talk ourselves into, or "rationalize," doing anything we really want to do) and, through speech communication, over other human beings. Conceptual ideas are both generated and communicated through uniquely human spoken language and its derivatives of reading and writing. Thought, conceptual thought, is the uniquely human instrument of power.

When an individual has a conceptual thought (an abstract thought such as "justice," or "love," rather than a perceptual thought of something concrete such as "a telephone pole," or "a cloud") and wishes to make that conceptual thought understandable and acceptable to other human beings, he or she uses spoken language to do so. When behaving humanly and humanely, our effort to gain the acceptance of others for our own thoughts avoids force or deceit.

In the process of forming, externalizing, and sharing our thoughts we make use of informing (by means of decentering and association), argumentation, and persuasion.

☐ Informative Speaking

Up to this point we have assumed that the most frequently used purpose for your speaking has been to inform. The speech to inform (as mentioned in Chapter Two) has as its goal the audience's enlightenment as to who, what, where, when, how, and/or why. When we inform we reduce our listener's uncertainty concerning who, what, where, when, how, and/or why. Obviously, we cannot convince or

Occasions for Informative Speaking Surround Us (Mimi Forsyth, Monkmeyer Press Photo Service)

persuade our listener of something they know nothing about. There is little point in trying to persuade someone to regularly change the oil in their car if the person doesn't even know what a car is. Prior to convincing or persuading, we must be sure that our audience knows what subject is being discussed. Bringing about basic knowledge of the subject being discussed is the goal of informing and of informative speaking.

In Chapter Two we discussed at length the concept of decentering. Because we presume that you were not familiar with the concept prior to this text's discussion of it, we tried to use concepts you were already familiar with in order to help you understand the concept of decentering. In other words, we associated the new concept with concepts you already knew in order to help you understand "what" decentering means; "why" it is an important and useful concept, and "when and how" to use decentering.

When you try to inform you must first take the conceptual viewpoint of your listener (decenter) and then, based upon what the listener already knows, associate your new information with material with which the listener is already familiar. Suppose you want to talk about the size of the British Isles (England, Ireland, Scotland, and Wales). You could point out that the Isles include approximately 95,000 square miles, but you could really drive home your point by stating that the entire British Isles contain approximately the same amount of ground space as the state of Wyoming. In another instance you could help an audience understand the religion of Islam by comparing that religion with Christianity and by paralleling the teachings of the Koran with the teachings of the Bible. In both these instances you have made use of decentering and then of association to inform someone of something with which they were unfamiliar and thus uncertain. You have reduced your audience's uncertainty—you have informed.

In the process of informing you can use examples, humor, facts, anecdotes, etc., to link your audience's knowledge with the new material you are trying to bring to their attention. In informing you may also find it helpful to consider using speech aids in building associational links (in the speech on the British Isles you could have two maps drawn to the same scale, one of the British Isles and one of Wyoming). Whatever material you present it is helpful to keep in mind the rule of 30/70 discussed on page 114: you tell someone something new in terms of something they already know. You don't tell too much all at once and you do not bore them by telling them something they already know; rather, you intermingle new material with previously known material. Basic information is a necessary requirement before convincing or persuading.

Decentering and the subsequent efforts after association based upon our decentering form the basis for both successful argumentation and successful persuasion. In a study of successful salesmen, who are indeed persuaders, Donald J. Moine (1982, pp. 50–54) suggests that truly successful sales persuaders take on many of the behavioral attributes of their customers. In a manner of speaking, the salesman "puts on" the characteristics of the customer. Decentering and association allows the speaker to "put on" the characteristics of the audience.

In Chapter Two, "Remote Preparation," you were alerted to the tremendously important role that a strong self-concept and positive self-esteem play in successful public speaking. Successful decentering never includes an abandonment of self-concept or self-esteem since such an abandonment would mean the loss of your own point of view and would thus negate the necessity for sharing that point of view through a public speech. We must have gone through the egocentric stage to reach the decentering stage. The egocentric stage never completely vanishes. Whenever we utilize decentering to speak to others, we always have in the back of our consciousness a tendency to speak to others in the manner which is most satisfying to ourselves. We generally like and approve of our own point of view and find that point of view quite acceptable and satisfactory. As a result, even while we think we are successfully decentering, we are always being attracted to an expression of our thought or thoughts that is compatible with our own point of view (Flavell, 1968). This attraction may be called an egocentric seduction. We are continually being seduced by our own primal and latent egocentricity. We like to hear what we already believe put into words and expressed as we would already express it. Decentering calls for an awareness of this ever-present egocentric seduction and an active effort to continually suppress it. In public speaking this continuing active effort impels the public speaker to seek out and utilize associations which are fundamentally common to both speaker and receiver. The appropriate use of association in public speaking is an observable measure of successful decentering.

Successful decentering and the subsequent use of appropriate association are devices that can assist us in persuading others to accept our own point of view, our specific purpose. When speaking of the general purposes of public speaking (page 42), we talked of the speech to convince (which has as its goal the audience's acceptance of the speaker's argument) and of the speech to persuade (which has as its goal the audience's active support and pursuit of the speaker's recommendations). The test of conviction is "do I believe?" The test of persuasion is "will I act upon my belief?" Conviction and persuasion are two parts of a single effort in almost every practical instance. The separation of conviction and persuasion is useful for concentrating our efforts on the different aspects of gaining an audience's acceptance of our specific purpose, but in an actual public speaking setting both conviction and persuasion are usually two parts of a single effort.

When we are persuaded to do something, our commitment is composed of both reason and emotion. In differing situations the balance of reason and emotion that leads to our commitment differs. We may do something because we just plain "want" to do it, because we love someone who has asked us to do it even though we are not certain of the reason underlying the act. There is a saying that it is a poor head that cannot find a reason for what the heart wants to do. On other occasions we take action because we are convinced of the rationality underlying the act even though emotionally we are less than happy about it. Studying long hours is often a case in point.

Argumentation centers upon the reason, the rationality, underlying a position, and has been defined as "The study of logical principles which underlie the examination and presentation of persuasive claims" (Ziegelmueller and Dause, 1975, p. 4). Argument usually precedes and undergirds persuasion. Argument, when considered abstractly, leads to belief but may not result in any observable action. Persuasion is bringing the audience to the active support of the speaker's specific purpose.

It might be noted that in a very real sense almost all human communication is to a degree persuasive. When communicating we present someone else with our own point of view. We utilize decentering, and by means of association we so present our own point of view that we can hope for the receiver's acceptance of our point of view. When we infuse our presentation of our ideas with logic and reason, we use argumentation. When we include the emotions in our presentation, along with logic and reason, we are using persuasion. We generally use both logic and emotion in our persuasive efforts.

The material in this chapter is presented with utility to the speaker in mind. The goal is to help the beginning public speaker consider and implement the goals of argumentation and persuasion. References are included at the end of the chapter for those who would like to delve more deeply into these complex and tantalizing topics.

Even though, in action, argumentation and persuasion are almost inseparable, we will treat them individually for clarity of examination.

□ Argumentation

Argumentation is a means by which reason is used to overcome resistance to sharing beliefs. Resistance to sharing belief has many sources. The major one is a difference of points of view between speaker and receiver. If we share the same point of view, if we have the same world view, then we often share the same beliefs. When arguing we are bent upon uncovering differences of world view between ourselves and others and then using reason to construct or build a similarity or commonality of world view between ourselves and others. We use decentering to uncover the differences and we use reason embedded in association to induce a commonality. A really effective argument utilizes the concept of transparent delivery. Even though arguments in writing are not the same in all respects as arguments in speaking, there is enough similarity for the following quote to illustrate some of the traits of what is sought after in effective, transparent, argumentation.

> Since a successful proof or argument must utilize premises the listener accepts, in what way does it proceed against the person's will? In arguing for a conclusion, are you not just showing him what he already implicitly accepts? While autonomy is not violated by argument as it would be by (involuntary) brain surgery that instilled belief, still, to argue for a conclusion is not merely to point out the consequences of statements which it turns out the person believes; it is to search and cast about for suitable premises, for statements the person does accept that will lead him to the desired conclusion. Recognizing the deductive connection, the person may either accept the conclusion or reject one of the statements he previously accepted, now that he sees where it leads. So the arguer will seek premises the person will not abandon. His goal is not simply to point out connections among statements but to compel belief in a particular one.
>
> I find I usually read works of philosophy with all defenses up, with a view to finding out where the author has gone wrong. Occasionally, after a short amount of reading, I find myself switched to a different mode; I become open to what the author has to teach. No doubt the voice of the author plays a role, perhaps also his not being coercive. An additional factor affects my stance. Sometimes a writer will begin with a thought similar to one I have had and been pleased with, except that his is more profound or subtle. Or after reading the first few sentences I may have thoughts or objections which the author then will go on to state or meet more acutely. Here, clearly, is someone from whom I can learn.
>
> I am willing to accept thoughts I read when I have had similar ones myself; I am more willing to accept my own thoughts than those I read. . . .
>
> At no point is the person forced to accept anything. He moves along gently, exploring his own and the author's thoughts. He explores together with the author, moving only where he is ready to; then he stops. Perhaps, at a later time mulling it over or in a second reading, he will move further.
>
> With this manner of writing, an author might circle back more than once to the same topic. Not everything can be said at once or twice; a reader may not be ready yet to think it all himself. (Nozick, 1981, pp. 6–7)

This quote from Professor Nozick testifies to the role of decentering and association when he urges thes election of "premisses" the listener already accepts; he testifies to the presence of the egocentric seduction in his comments on the acceptability of one's own thoughts; and throughout he testifies indirectly to the power of transparent argumentation. The quotation also indicates some of the

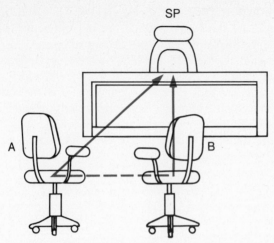

Figure 8.1 Relationship of Specific Purpose to Audience Position Prior to and Following Your Speech: A, Audience's Current Attitudes; SP, Speaker's Specific Purpose; B, Audience Attitudes Necessary for Full Support of Your Specific Purpose. Proof, Evidence, Support, and Delivery Are All Needed in Order to Close the Distance between A and B and Achieve Your Specific Purpose.

ways in which written argumentation differs from spoken argumentation. A listener, unlike a reader, cannot go back and reread the speaker's arguments; a speaker, unlike a writer, cannot allow for time for silent reflection on the part of the listener during a presentation. The speaker must make the best argument possible within very limited time constraints.

As a public speaker you must select your specific purpose and then you must array the proof that will move the listeners to support of your specific purpose as illustrated in Figure 8.1.

Through decentering you assess the audience's position vis-à-vis your specific purpose. There may be aspects of support for your specific purpose which the audience already accepts, aspects which need not be further supported. For example, if you were speaking with the specific purpose of getting your audience to conceptually accept the need for dieting and you argued that dieting is conducive to good health, you would not ordinarily have to argue the desirability of good health. In our culture good health is a generally accepted value. Decentering might however indicate that this particular audience is suspicious of the actual connection between dieting and health; if so it would be the correlating of the two which would call for the massing of logical and reasonable support. Your argument then may allude to the desirability of good health without needing to prove it; rather you will recall to the audience this generally accepted desirability and proceed to build upon it. In your decentering and audience analysis try to locate the aspects of the specific purpose which the audience already accepts. You can use these as part of your association armory in mounting an argumentative campaign to bring about a commonality of world view concerning those aspects of the specific purpose which the audience does not yet accept and support.

Throughout this primer we have argued for the primary purpose of human communication being the sharing of thought so as to improve the human condition in general. We have also argued that spoken language both generates thought and is then used as an instrument for sharing thought with others. Argumentation, as a form of spoken language as well as being a tool of persuasion, shares this quality of what Robert Trapp calls "knowledge generation" (1981, pp. 111–117).

In the earlier quotation from Nozick you will note an emphasis on the reader circling a new idea, coming back to it from time to time, getting familiar with the new idea and its consequences. This strategy is the same one as described in the helical model of human communication mentioned in Chapter One. We circle back upon a new concept while at the same time integrating some of its novel aspects into our already accepted pattern of ideas. Seldom do we totally accept, all at once, a radically new idea. We try to get comfortable with the new idea, to fit it into our customary manner of thinking, to test it against ideas we already believe in and have confidence in.

It is incorrect to suggest that people resist change. We don't resist change, in fact we seek out novelty. *But we do resist too much change coming too fast.* This is an instance of where the earlier mentioned rule of 30/70 may be put into public speaking practice. We should argue so as to make our argument as consistent as possible with already accepted beliefs. Introduce novel aspects of your argument in bits and pieces, avoid overwhelming your audience's capacity for change. This is another point where the public speaker must be alert to audience feedback. Watch the faces of your audience. Are they expressing doubt or incredulity? If so circle back, probe for the exact place where they are finding your argument difficult to accept and then provide additional support until you think that the majority of your audience is ready to move on to the next point of the argument on behalf of your specific purpose. At the same time beware of belaboring a point the audience already accepts. Try to move *with* your audience, neither ahead of them nor lagging behind them. As the old saying goes, "make haste slowly!"

A position similar to the rule of 30/70, but more heavily supported by research, is set forth by Sherif et al. (1965) in their discussion of latitudes of acceptance and rejection:

> An audience's *latitude of acceptance* is the position on an issue or toward an idea or an object that is most acceptable to the audience, plus other acceptable positions.
>
> An audience's *latitude of rejection* is the most objectionable position on the same issue, idea, or object, plus other objectionable positions.
>
> An audience will also have a *latitude of noncommitment* which encompasses those positions not categorized by the audience as either acceptable or objectionable to some degree.

Through decentering and other forms of audience analysis try to assess the attitudinal profile of your audience concerning your specific purpose. Assume you are addressing a meeting of professional librarians. Your specific purpose is to advocate relaxation of copyright laws. Here is a list of possible positions that members of the audience could take as regards the topic of relaxation of copyright laws.

A. Copyright laws should be as strict as possible and violations should be considered felonies, the violators avidly prosecuted and given substantial jail sentences.
B. Copyright laws should be substantially strengthened.
C. Current copyright laws are acceptable and should be obeyed.
D. There is a need for copyright, and copyright violations should be discouraged but not punished by law.
E. I have no strong feelings about copyright laws and believe that the decision to respect the rights of others concerning published materials should be a matter of individual conscience.
F. General access and use of all published materials, without compensation to the original author, may be in the best interests of the advancement of knowledge.
G. All current copyright laws should be revoked and no others instituted.
H. Copyright laws deter the advancement of human knowledge. Everyone should be encouraged by the government to make free and unacknowledged use of all published materials whether or not for profit.

Through decentering and audience analysis you anticipate an attitudinal profile as shown in Figure 8.2.

More than half of your audience accept positions B and C as acceptable positions on the topic of relaxation of copyright laws. Thus the audience's *latitude of acceptance* on the topic includes positions B and C. Similarly, more than half the audience consider positions F, G, and H as unacceptable or objectionable attitudes about relaxation of copyright laws. Thus the audience's *latitude of rejection* on the topic includes positions F, G, and H. Most of the audience neither accepts nor rejects positions A, D, and E. For this audience positions A, D, and E represent their *latitude of noncommitment* on the topic of relaxation of the copyright laws.

Given such a distribution of attitudes on the part of your audience you would be ill advised to argue for acceptance of any of the points falling directly under their latitude of rejection. On the other hand you may well be able to present arguments that would move them toward the points within their latitude of noncommittal. If most of your audience subscribes to positions B and C and through your presentation you are able to move them to support position E, you may consider that you have made significant argumentative progress. Position E then joins B and C in your audience's latitude of acceptance.

Most arguers and most persuaders try to do too much too rapidly. You can always make argumentative headway if you are willing to either take your time or to settle for what might seem to be relatively small, but still significant, changes in the audience's beliefs as they relate to your specific purpose.

In discussing argumentation in public speaking we have repeatedly alluded to the task of providing support for your specific purpose where such support is called for by audience attitudes. What kinds of support are suitable? The answer depends upon how successful you have been in doing your research on the topic, as indicated in Chapter Four on research, and how adequate an insight you have

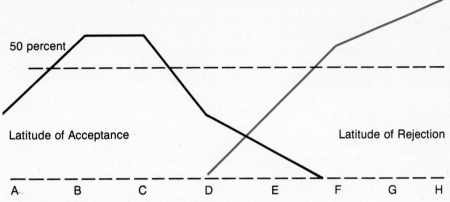

50 percent

Latitude of Acceptance   Latitude of Rejection

A   B   C   D   E   F   G   H

Figure 8.2 Hypothetical Attitudinal Profile of an Audience

developed into the audience's predispositions concerning your specific purpose. Remember not to waste valuable time proving points the audience already seems to accept. You only have so much time available to make a convincing argument. What kind of support do you think will be most acceptable to your audience? Here are some types of support that are often used in argumentative and persuasive efforts.

- **Facts.** Statements are usually considered factual if they can be verified by written or oral testimony as having an objective reality. For something to be accepted as a fact, there usually needs to be a consensus concerning its existence and/or qualities.

☐☐☐☐ *Example*

Last year the copyright office records showed that copyright infringements rose by 25 percent over the previous year. The evidence for this is indicated in the distributed photocopies of the appropriate pages from the copyright office ledgers for the 2 years in question.

- **Testimony.** Statements and quotations from accepted authorities or from sources holding high credibility for your audience are forms of testimony. Human beings have always been influenced by the utterances of those whom they trust and respect. Even though the individual may not be a well-recognized authority on the subject in dispute, if the audience has a great deal of trust in that person, his or her statements and testimony may be all the support that is needed.

☐☐☐☐ *Example*

Suppose you are addressing an audience on the topic of plagiarism, of using other peoples' materials in your work without acknowledging that the material originated from a source other than yourself. You find out that all the members of your audience belong to the same church. You are able to find testimony concerning the evils of plagiarism in the published words of the founder of the church. Using such testimony in your speech could be viewed by the audience as very impressive support for your position against plagiarism. The testimony you choose to use should bear upon the point needing support and should not be contradicted by any later testimony from the same source.

- **Inference.**   When you reason from an already accepted position to another position that seems to follow from the already accepted position, you are using inference. Inferential reasoning is often successfully used in the process of argumentation.

☐ ☐ ☐ ☐ *Example*

Formal syllogistic reasoning may be considered inferential reasoning.
       All men are mortal.
       Aristotle is a man.
Therefore, Aristotle is mortal.

There are many technical aspects and rules governing the use of formal syllogistic reasoning. Consult the recommended reading list at the end of this chapter for some references on this form of support.

Other forms of inferential reasoning, less sophisticated forms, are used by all of us in our making of day to day arguments. When we say "If drunk drivers aren't more severely punished, there will be carnage on our highways," we are making use of inference. If the inferences you use are well reasoned, they can be a formidable source of support for your specific purpose.

- **Analogy.**   When we reason that A is to B as X is to Y, we are using analogical reasoning. Analogical reasoning is a form of inferential reasoning.

☐ ☐ ☐ ☐ *Example*

When we say that the human brain is, in some respects, like a telephone switchboard, or like a computer, we are using an analogy. Most models are analogical in nature. A model car is like the real car of which it is a model in some respects, but not in others. When model airplanes are tested in wind tunnels, those doing the testing will use analogical reasoning, based upon the behavior of the models, which they will then apply to the design of full-size airplanes. Models of human communication, as briefly discussed in Chapter

One, are like actual human communication in some respects but not in all respects. When we argue that the point we are making is like, or similar to, something the audience already supports and that the similarities will generalize to the production of desirable effects, we are usually using a form of analogical reasoning. Earlier in this primer when we were discussing stage fright we alluded to the problems of stage fright as being similar to learning any new and fairly complicated skill, like skiing. In a way we were making an analogy between stage fright and skiing; we might even have said, "Stage fright is like skiing," and then gone on to develop the analogy further. In a speech we could say, analogically, that a college freshman is like a rat in a maze, or that the college course catalog is like a cafeteria menu. Based upon our analogies we could then go on to make certain inferences about how to successfully pass through the maze, or as to how wisely make the right choices from the college course "menu." As you can see, analogical reasoning can assist nicely in making a point to support your specific purpose.

- **Statistics.**   Statistics "deals with the collection, classification, description, and interpretation of data obtained by the conduct of surveys and experiments. It's essential purpose is to describe and draw inferences about the numerical properties of populations" (Ferguson, 1976, p. 61).

☐ ☐ ☐ ☐ *Examples*

When we hear a newscaster predict that one out of every eight drivers on the highway over the Labor Day weekend will be involved in an accident, he is making use of statistical inference. When we said in an earlier chapter that the average rate of delivery in spoken English is about 150 words per minute we were using an example of descriptive statistics. In Chapter Four, "Research," pages 90–91, we offer some advice on using statistics as evidence. Statistics when properly used, can provide an effective, shorthand means of summing data and of providing support for your specific purpose.

- **Example.**   When we provide an instance which illustrates a rule or a statement, we are using an example. The examples given above of facts, testimony, inferences, analogies, and statistics demonstrate the use of examples.

Textbooks dealing specifically with argumentation and reasoning develop the use of proof in more detail than is done in this text. Some of these sources are provided in the recommended readings at the end of this chapter for those who wish more detailed treatment of forms of argumentation and support. What we chose to include here are those forms of support that we, as practicing professional public speakers, generally have found most effective.

Fallacies (Faulty Reasoning)

Reasoning is a peculiarly human activity, and like all human activities it can be done well or poorly. As a speaker, and as a receiver, it is helpful to consider some examples of faulty reasoning. By considering these examples of faulty reasoning, we should be better able to recognize them when they occur in the public speaking of others and to avoid their use in our own public speaking efforts. A good number of the classifications of faulty reasoning come from the study of formal logic and were originally given Latin names. Where appropriate we will mention the Latin names as well as the names in English so that you may recognize the examples in other sources when they are labeled solely by their Latin names.

- **After this, therefore because of this** (Lat. *Post hoc, ergo propter hoc*).   When you argue that you had a good day because at the beginning of the day you rubbed your lucky rabbit's foot, you are arguing that the day's good fortune occurred because of rubbing the rabbit's foot. This is an example of "after this, therefore because of this."
- **Hasty generalization.**   When you argue that since poor communication causes many interpersonal problems, that all interpersonal problems result from poor communication, you are guilty of "hasty generalization." Often speakers argue from limited experimental findings to the general applicability of the findings. This too is an example of hasty generalization.
- **Circular reasoning.**   When you argue that people are funny because they are so humorous, you arguing circularly. You are taking your first statement and reasserting it in other words. No real proof is being offered.
- **It doesn't follow** (Lat. *Non sequitur*).   When you say that rampant inflation will be caused by an excessive diet of strawberries, you are drawing a conclusion that simply doesn't follow from the first part of the statement.
- **Attacking the person** (Lat. *Ad hominem*).   When, instead of taking issue with someone's argument, you attack the character or personality of the person, you are guilty of the reasoning fallacy "ad hominem." This fallacy occurs quite frequently in day-to-day arguments when, for instance, you say "I don't care what reasons she has, she has that little squeaky, annoying voice that proves she's dim-witted." Ridicule is a form of attacking the person.
- **Appeal to threat or force** (Lat. *Ad baculum*).   A "baculum" in Latin is a club or a strong stick. When you stray away from the use of reason and logic in your argument and tell your listeners that if they don't support your specific purpose you are going to see that they are severely punished ("You better agree with me or I'll pound you into the ground"), you are guilty of the fallacy labeled as an appeal to threat or force.
- **Bombast.**   When, by using a very loud voice and big words (like a cartoon characterization of a politician), you try to impress your listeners that they should accept your arguments simply because the arguments are flowing from such an impressive person, you are using bombast.
- **Bandwagon** (Lat. *Ad populum*).   When you argue that your listeners should support your point of view simply because so many other people support that

point of view ("Drink Zippy, everybody is doing it!") and regardless of any logical reasons, then you are guilty of using the bandwagon technique. *Argumentum ad populum* literally refers to an "appeal to the people." The underlying idea is that instead of making a rational argument, the speaker simply appeals to the people for their support. Bandwagon seems to be an extension and specification of this old technique.

Again, as with treatments of logical proof, there are many more particularized treatments of fallacious reasoning. Since most of these proofs and fallacies flow from spoken language, their study may prove especially interesting to the student of public speaking. As contemporary scholars of argumentation have repeatedly pointed out, human argument should be a person-centered activity not a sterile exercise in formal logic. (See Rieke and Sillars, 1975; Ehninger and Brockriede, 1978; Trapp, 1981.)

As a person-centered activity we should be aware, in our use of argument, of some additional considerations. Here are two questions that over the years have intrigued those interested in the presentation of forceful arguments, questions that still occur to a present-day public speaker.

Should You Use Humor in Making an Argument

It depends. If it is a very serious matter, it is dangerous to treat the matter in what may be considered by the audience to be too lighthearted a manner. Aristotle recommended that a public speaker avoid speaking casually about weighty subjects or solemnly and pompously about trivial subjects (Aristotle, 1954, p. 178). There were those politicians who didn't wish to invite President Abraham Lincoln to the dedication of the Gettysburg cemetery because they were afraid he would treat the occasion in too light a manner. At the same time practical experience suggests that the public speaker avoid taking himself or herself *too* seriously and thus fall prey to the sickness of pomposity.

When Making an Argument, Is It Better to Meet the Audience's Objections Head on or to Treat the Subject with Some Ambiguity?

Earlier, in Chapter Six, "Rehearsal," we discussed the differences between external spoken language and inner spoken language and urged you, based upon these differences, always to rehearse aloud. One of the consequences of inner spoken language is an increase in ambiguity. When talking to ourselves, we allow for more latitude since we have a correcting and explanatory mechanism always present and available. When moving our thoughts from inner spoken language to external spoken language, we engage in an exercise in progressive disambiguation, or, if you like, an exercise in which we decrease subjectivity and increase objectivity. The reason why we are mentioning this at this time is that we want to make the point that some degree of ambiguity is absolutely natural in the use of spoken language.

As with the rule of 30/70, people can stand *some* ambiguity as long as there is not *too much* ambiguity. In fact, if you are addressing an audience which you know, through audience analysis, is in basic disagreement with your specific purpose, you might consider avoiding a head-on clash at the beginning of the speech and treating the objections and your reaction to them with some ambiguity so as to help keep the audience's collective mind open to your arguments as you develop those arguments. The risk in coming right out at the beginning of your speech and saying "I know you disagree with me but I am going to show you where you are wrong and I am right" is that the audience may "shut down," right there and then, and all your subsequent words will fall on deaf ears. Our suggestion then is to understand that there will always be some degree of ambiguity in human utterances and to use that ambiguity strategically so as to assure yourself a fair hearing. Beware of excessive hedging or evasion, however, as this will quickly cause an audience to become disenchanted with a speaker (Watson, 1978).

Our experience with audiences suggests that most audiences are fair and are willing to give a speaker a fair hearing. In general, if you as a speaker do a good job in marshalling the evidence, arranging it with an ear to good argument, and present it transparently, you will at the very least be given an open hearing by your audience. Depending upon the cogency of your thoughts and reasoning and the skill of your speaking, you may even succeed in moving an audience to support your specific purpose.

In this section on argumentation we have concentrated on those skills of logic and reason that we believe you may find helpful in convincing an audience. Remember that argumentation and persuasion are most often two aspects of the same effort. Now let's consider how these argumentative skills may fit into a persuasive situation.

Persuasion

Persuasion uses argumentation, emotion, nonvocal support, and all other ethically available means to move the audience to the active support of the speaker's specific purpose.

In an interesting and entertaining book entitled *The Ugly American,* the authors consider the problems of persuading the inhabitants of an Asian country of the good will and good intentions of American diplomacy. In the passage below we are told what a representative American felt underlies successful persuasion.

> "What we discovered," he wrote, "Is that men are persuaded of things by the same process, whether the persuading is done by the Catholic Church, Lutherans, Communists, or democrats. A movement cannot be judged by its methods of persuasion for, short of violence, most successful movements use the same methods. What we discovered in our long discussions in the jungle were these things:

1. We had to make ourselves experts in persuasion.
2. We had to persuade in terms of events which are known to Burmans.
3. We had to persuade in words which would be understood by everyone.
4. Complex ideas had to be put dramatically and powerfully.
5. The persuasion had to be done at a time when the audience would be receptive. And it had to be done on all levels. (Lederer and Burdick, 1958, pp. 59–60)

Here we have a specified persuasive occasion, a very practical one indeed. We find it fascinating to look at the persuasive steps outlined above and to find in them application of many if not most of the principles we advocated in this primer and which have been advocated by many since Aristotle.

In step 1 we see the need for decentering and audience analysis. In step 2 we see the need for the use of association. In step 3 we see the need for adequate preparation and attention to the principles of delivery. In step 4 we see the need stressed again for good decentering and for showing the receivers how the persuasive efforts would meet *their* needs. This step also emphasizes that the persuasive effort cannot focus on just a single aspect of the problem to the exclusion of other important considerations.

When Aristotle discusses the use of spoken language to persuade, he emphasizes that the speaker needs to make every effort to put the audience into the proper frame of mind to accept the persuasive effort. You, as a public speaker, must show the audience how your speech, your argument, meets their needs and their concerns. Aristotle also stresses the need for the speaker to make use of proof, both logical and otherwise, in the persuasive speech. Aristotle says that the speaker, to be a successful persuader, must be able to reason logically, understand human character, and also understand human emotions (Aristotle, 1954, p. 24).

In addition to the above considerations Aristotle gives special emphasis and stress to the character of the speaker as the speaker's character is perceived and accepted by his or her audience. As Aristotle points out, "We believe good men more fully and readily than others. This is true generally whatever the question is, and absolutely true where exact certainty is impossible and opinions are divided." He goes on to say that the speaker's character, or *ethos,* "may almost be called the most effective means of persuasion he possesses" (Aristotle, 1954, p. 24). In his further discussion of ethos, Aristotle suggests that the speaker should be characterized by good sense, good moral character, and good will. Ever since the time of Aristotle students of persuasion have studied and pondered his comments on ethos. There have been historical studies of ethos, critical studies of ethos, and empirical studies of ethos. Whatever else has been found as a result of these studies, all of them generally support the overall observation that the speaker's character is an essential, if not the dominant, element of successful persuasion. This view of the importance of ethos has been supported by our own practical observations in public speaking situations. If you wish to persuade an audience, you must take care to establish your own ethos, your own credibility. A part of the establishment of your ethos may be done by means of the introduction given you at the beginning of your speech. You, yourself, must handle the creation and maintenance of your ethos during the actual speech.

In over 300 presentations before audiences other than students of public speaking, we have asked the audience what *behaviors* of the speaker they take into consideration in making their decision as to whether or not they believe the speaker to be a credible source. This survey is part of a very practical effort to find out what audiences take into consideration in assessing the ethos or source credibility of a speaker. We asked the members of the audience not to take into consideration the introduction of the speaker or what they believed to be the past experience of the speaker and to restrict their answers to those behaviors exhibited by the speaker in the actual presentation they had heard. Here are our results.

1. **Appearance.**   The first thing, in order of time, that created an audience confidence in the credibility of the speaker was how the speaker looked. Grooming and clothing. The more the speaker appeared to meet the cultural norms of cleanliness and good grooming and also the specific audience norms of clothing, the more the audience was willing to listen openly to the speaker.
2. **Eye contact.**   The audiences addressed were predominantly composed of middle-class North Americans. This is an important consideration since eye contact seems to have some cultural and subcultural dimensions. For the audiences polled, eye contact, looking the audience in the eye, suggested straightforwardness and the lack of duplicity. Eye contact was the second, in terms of time, decision point concerning speaker credibility.
3. **Control of self.**   This audience judgment expressed their belief that a speaker who exhibits undue or excessive nervousness or lack of self-control suggests a lack of adequate preparation and, whatever else, got in the way of the audience's giving attention to what the speaker had to say.
4. **Control of subject.**   Having gotten over the judgmental hurdles of appearance, eye contact, and self-control, the audiences now seemed to make judgments as to how much the speaker seemed to really know about the topic being presented. The audiences took into consideration such things as excessive note dependency, the ability to adapt the subject to the audience, the ability to answer latent audience objections, the ability to give examples, the speaker's saying things that supported earlier comments (not being inconsistent), and the speaker's utterances not contradicting the audience's previously confirmed experiences.
5. **Decentering.**   This final judgment was never expressed in the word "decentering" but included the speaker's ability to look at things from the audience's viewpoint and to take into consideration the audience's world view.

This series of five source credibility judgments seems to move from the less to the more difficult in terms of speaker behavior. Appearance is actually quite easy to control, eye contact is somewhat more difficult and benefits from experience and the assistance of a good critic, self-control has been extensively discussed, control of subject calls for both preparation and experience, and decentering is something calling for constant attention and work. The findings given above are not the result of a rigorously controlled experimental procedure, and the student of public speaking is cautioned against accepting them as fact. But we do not find them contradicted by research findings. They are simply practical observations drawn from real audiences. However, as public speakers, we have found them to be both consistent and usable in our efforts to be *effective* public speakers, and we feel confident in passing them on to you in this practical primer.

Even when a speaker puts into practice all the suggestions already given here and in other informational sources, there are still going to be times when the speaker finds a particular audience more than usually resistive to persuasion. When audiences resist persuasive attempts, they may do so for a number of reasons.

They may simply be resisting too much change, too soon—not simply resisting any change at all. Let's repeat once again that the rule of 30/70, of making haste slowly, applies especially in persuasive speaking. Don't try and do too much too soon. Do what the situation allows and seek only that amount of change you are capable of bringing about in a single speech within specific time limits.

Audiences may resist persuasion because of ego involvement. Perhaps they are so threatened by the suggested change that they reject it. In such a case the speaker must be certain to build into the speech proof that the suggested changes will work to the benefit of the audience rather than against their own best interests.

Audiences may resist the persuasive attempt because of their prior commitments. In such a case the speaker must endeavor to show in the speech how the suggested changes will better serve the audience interests than the prior commitments would.

Audiences may resist the persuasive effort because of their own public commitments. This resistance has elements both of ego involvement and of prior commitment, and the speaker must successfully meet those two elements of resistance as well as show in the speech how the audience can subscribe to the suggested changes without totally losing their own credibility with whatever constituency to which they feel responsible.

A number of times in our discussion of argumentation and of persuasion we have alluded to the fact that persuasive speaking, besides using logic, makes use of emotion as well. We need, as Winans would remind us, not only to find the common ground of reason but to find the common ground of emotion. In Chapter Seven, when discussing the contact quotient, we noted that of the three stages of audience contact (physical, mental, and emotional) the third stage, emotional audience contact, was often the most difficult to establish and maintain. Human beings are creatures of emotion and of thought. From the moment of conception our lives are suffused with emotion. How we view the role of emotions in our own behavior, how we judge the appropriateness of emotion in the behavior of others, what we think about the part emotion should play in public decisions, each of these considerations is highly individual although how an individual handles emotion is usually greatly affected by the culture into which the person was born and the culture in which the person grew up. The point is that a public speaker must be aware of the part played by emotions in our day-to-day affairs and take those emotions into consideration when preparing and presenting a persuasive speech. If you are speaking to an audience most of whom are parents, you can be fairly confident of some emotional similarities among the audience members on the topic of child abuse or child molestation. Most parents form emotional bonds with their own children and these emotional bonds generalize to other children as well. People have emotional reactions to almost all words, emotional reactions tinted by the setting in which the person first heard a word uttered, the person uttering the word, and the subsequent emotional climate surrounding later uses of that word. Most of us have some words which we simply don't "like," yet we may be hard pressed to remember the source of our emotional distaste. Following are some comments on four observations on human emotions made by Robert T. Oliver (1957, p. 253).

1. *"Emotions come suddenly, but die away slowly."* You as a speaker may, through an unconscious gesture or word, arouse strong emotions in members of your audience, emotions that spring into being unsought but nonetheless present. On the other hand, you may be facing the presence of emotions that you had nothing to do with bringing into being, emotions which are persisting as a mood, emotions that the audience members bring with them to the speech as a result of some experience earlier in the day. Most of us have experienced the persistence of a mood long beyond the removal of the original cause for the emotion. A public speaker should be sensitive to the emotional tone of the audience.

2. *"Once an emotion has been aroused it tends to fasten itself upon contiguous objects."* When you are really angry you have a tendency to strike out at the nearest object, even when that object or person may have had nothing whatsoever to do with causing your anger. If your audience is angry when you start speaking to them, they may transfer their anger to you. It is observed that police hate to answer disturbance calls that involve family disputes because so often the police officer, intervening in the interest of personal and public safety, finds both antagonists suddenly united against him, the police officer. The angry participants in the family quarrel suddenly turn their anger upon the outsider. In a case where the audience is emotionally angry due to some cause outside of the speaker, the speaker must decide whether that anger can be defused, or turned to the goals of the speaker, or whether the speaker would be better off not speaking to the audience at that particular time.

3. *"Every emotion tends to express itself in action."* It is in the nature of an emotion that it arouses the physical and physiological system of the person experiencing it. When we are emotionally aroused, whatever the focus of the emotion, we tend to want to *do* something. We want to run, to fight, to laugh, to cry, to swear, to lash out, to hug, to *do something*. If a speaker gets an audience emotionally aroused and involved, it is important that the speaker give the audience something to do, something toward which they can direct the action stimulated by the aroused emotion. It is also important for the speaker that she recognize when audience emotions are at their peak because that is the time to stop and to allow the audience to take action upon the speaker's specific purpose. If a speaker by continuing to speak at length, forces an audience to hold its emotional support in check, the risk of those emotions dissipating and disappearing is significant.

4. *"Emotional reactions tend to be similar among all individuals who share com-*

mon experiences in a given situation." It is somewhat of a mystery as to how we can be so similar to one another and yet so different from one another, all at the same time. But it is a fact. Human beings can be depended upon to have many of the same likes and many of the same dislikes, especially if they have been exposed to common experiences in a common culture. Spoken language and culture are so closely intertwined with emotion that a speaker presenting a speech before an audience of a different culture, a culture whose language the speaker is unfamiliar with, is advised to do some extensive research concerning the new culture's emotional structure before making any assumptions of cultural similarity with the speaker's own culture. However, if speaker and audience are all members of the same culture, unless you are unusual, you may depend upon members of your audience having much the same emotional reaction to something, a joke, an anecdote, an example, as you would have. This identification of emotions appropriate to the content of a speech is part of the desired results of adequate remote and immediate preparation, of decentering and then of association. You should also remember that although emotional reactions may be quite generally shared within an audience that there is a strong presumption that there will be some individuals who hold themselves apart from the common emotions and may indeed experience quite different emotional reactions.

No one wants to feel that he or she is being manipulated. When an audience detects insincerity and manipulativeness on the part of a persuasive speaker, all is generally lost. The persuasion, like the argumentation, must be delivered transparently. In persuasive speaking, as in all other forms of public speaking with the possible exception of a speech demonstrating speech performance techniques, transparent delivery is the goal and the norm.

Although there is nothing wrong with making use of emotions in persuasion, let us remind you once again that heightened emotion, passion, suppresses decentering and augments feelings of egocentricity and egocentricity's voluntary expression—selfishness. This is true both for the speaker and for the audience member. Emotions are powerful and when uncontrolled may be quite dangerous. Neither an impassioned individual nor an impassioned crowd is noted for thoughtfulness and rationality.

And thoughtfulness and rationality are what it is ultimately all about. If we *do* choose to use emotion as a means of persuasion, we should be doing so with the goal of helping the audience accept a specific purpose which thoughtfulness and rationality testify to being a preferable course of action for enhancing the human condition.

History testifies to the power of a persuasive speaker. Some speakers have persuaded for the good of humanity (Jesus, Lao Tzu, Confucius, Lincoln) and some speakers have persuaded their followers to perform actions hurtful to humanity (Nero, Hitler). The spoken word, as stated in Chapter One, is the unique source of *human* power. When the spoken word is used persuasively, it is extraordinarily powerful and should be used knowledgeably and ethically. Ethics are important in all uses of spoken language, and are especially important in persuasive speaking. Never should we use our talents as persuasive speakers to move an audience to action not in the audience's own best interest and in the ultimate best interests of humanity in general. Ethics should always influence the speaker's all important ethos.

□ Summary

Argumentation focuses on the use of reason as a means of proof to move an audience from their beliefs at the start of a speech to cognitive support of the speaker's specific purpose by the end of the presentation. Persuasion makes use of argumentation and all other ethical forms of proof to move the audience to take action based upon their cognitive support of the speaker's specific purpose. Although, for the sake of examination and explanation, argumentation and persuasion are treated as if they were two distinct forms of speaking, in reality the two are almost always found together and are usually two parts of a single public speaking effort with argumentation centering upon reason and persuasion centering upon action.

Decentering and the subsequent planning and use of appropriate association are central to successful argumentation and persuasion. Association provides an observable measure of successful decentering. In all public speaking, but especially in argumentation and persuasion, it is important for the speaker to be conscious of and resistive of the egocentric seduction which keeps recalling the speaker to his or her own way of thinking and of speaking.

You must select your specific purpose and then array your support for and proof of your specific purpose so as to move your listeners to endorse and support your specific purpose. Moving the audience to support your specific purpose calls for audience analysis, decentering, and then the planned implementation of association. Don't try to do too much too soon. Remember that an audience is not resistive to change in and of itself but to too much change, too fast. Make use of the rule of 30/70 and the concept of latitudes of acceptance, rejection, and noncommitment. Make constant use of feedback so as to move with your audience rather than ahead of them or behind them in their need for supporting arguments.

Some commonly and effectively used means of reasoning support include the use of facts, inference, testimony, analogy, statistics, and examples. Argumentation, in actual speaking use, should avoid becoming a sterile exercise in the use of logic just for the sake of logic. When arguing you are dealing with real people, and you should make every effort to keep your argument person-centered.

Some fairly common examples of faulty or fallacious reasoning include "after this therefore because of this," "hasty generalization," "circular reasoning," "it doesn't follow," "attacking the person," "appeal to threat or force," "bombast," and "bandwagon." Although fallacies are not always the result of planned manipulation on the part of a sender, they still can have serious and deleterious effects and should be guarded against when acting as either sender or receiver of spoken language.

Persuasion is the ethical use of emotion, nonvocal support, and all other available means to move an audience to the active support of the speaker's specific purpose. In the process of persuasion, ethos, or source credibility, is an all-important component. Some speaker behaviors we have found to affect an audience's judgment of speaker credibility are, in order of audience judgment: appearance, eye contact, control of self, control of subject, and decentering.

It seems that audiences resist persuasive attempts for a wide variety of reasons. A few of the more common reasons for audience resistance to persuasion are natural resistance to too much change, too fast; ego involvement on the part of the audience; an audience's prior commitment to a position other than the position being espoused by the speaker.

Emotions are an important part of humans, and thus emotions must be taken into consideration when preparing and delivering a persuasive speech. The speaker should always remember that heightened emotions suppress decentering.

In terms of presentational techniques, argumentation and persuasion are best achieved through the practice of transparent delivery.

Ethics demand that a speaker never consciously use his or her talents to persuade an audience to do something not in their own best interests nor in the ultimate best interests of humanity in general.

Exercises ■

1 Listen to a speaker who is advocating the "pro" side of a topic. Research, construct, and deliver a 5-minute "con" speech on the same topic.

2 Prepare a 5-minute persuasive speech on the topic of "association as the application of decentering." In your speech make use of an even mixture of acceptable forms of support as well as of fallacious reasoning.

3 Prepare a speech in which you analyze a famous speech in terms of the speech's use of forms of support.

4 Campaign speeches for the position of President of the United States are ordinarily persuasive speeches. Find a recent presidential campaign speech which is available both for listening and for reading. Compare the two forms of the speech in terms of forms of support, both logical and emotional.

5 Listen to or read a recent campaign speech and analyze its persuasive effect in terms of the speaker's apparent use of decentering and association.

6 Find five examples of fallacious reasoning in current advertising. In a 5-minute speech describe the fallacies. Use audiovisual aids in your presentation.

Bibliographic References ■

Aristotle. *The Rhetoric,* W. Rhys Roberts (trans.), The Modern Library, New York, 1954, p. 65.

Ehninger, Douglas, and Wayne Brockriede: *Decision by Debate*. 2nd ed., Harper & Row, New York, 1978.

Ferguson, George A. *Statistical Analysis in Psychology and Education*. 4th ed. McGraw-Hill Book Company, New York, 1976, p. 6.

Flavell, John H., and others: *The Development of Role-Taking and Communication Skills in Children*. John Wiley & Sons, New York, 1968, Chapter One.

Lederer, William J., and Eugene Burdick: *The Ugly American*, W. W. Norton, New York, 1958, pp. 59–60.

Moine, Donald J.: "To Trust, Perchance to Buy," *Psychology Today*, August 1982, pp. 50–54.

Nozick, Robert: *Philosophical Explanations*, Harvard University Press, Cambridge, Mass., 1981, pp. 6–7.

Oliver, Robert T.: *The Psychology of Persuasive Speech*. Longmans Green, New York, 1957, p. 253.

Rieke, Richard D., and Malcolm O. Sillars: *Argumentation and the Decision Making Process*, John Wiley & Sons, New York, 1975.

Sherif, Carolyn, Muzafer Sherif, and Roger Nebergall: *Attitude and Attitude Change: The Social Judgment-Involvement Approach*. W. B. Saunders, Philadelphia, 1965.

Trapp, Robert: "Special Report on Argumentation: Introduction," *Western Journal of Speech Communication*, vol. 45, Spring 1981, pp. 111–117.

Watson, Norman H.: *Deliberate Vagueness as a Rhetorical Strategy: Effects on Source Credibility*, Ph.D. dissertation, University of Denver, August 1978.

Ziegelmueller, George, and Charles Dause: *Argumentation: Inquiry and Advocacy*. Prentice-Hall, Englewood Cliffs, N.J., 1975, p. 4.

Recommended Readings ■

A number of the books and essays included in the bibliographic materials for this chapter provide additional materials for the student of argumentation and persuasion. Here are some other print resources.

Argumentation

Beardsley, Monroe C.: *Thinking Straight*, Prentice-Hall, Englewood Cliffs, N.J., 1966. A readable book on reasoning.

Freely, Austin J. *Argumentation and Debate: Reasoned Decision Making*, 5th ed., Wadsworth, Belmont, Calif., 1981. A well written and clear treatment of logical support and evidence.

Sproule, J. Michael: *Argument: Language and Its Influence*, McGraw-Hill Book Company, New York, 1980.

Toulmin, Stephen, R. Rieke, and A. Janik: *An Introduction to Reasoning*, Macmillan, New York, 1979.

Western Journal of Speech Communication. vol. 45, no. 2, Spring 1981. Special Issue: "Special Report: Studies in Argumentation." A scholarly presentation of some current ideas concerning the study of argumentation.

Persuasion

Brembeck, W. L., W. S. Howell: *Persuasion: A Means of Social Control,* Prentice-Hall, New York, 1952. An older but still nicely presented text. Chapter XI and XII are especially helpful in their consideration of the logical techniques of persuasion.

Cronkhite, Gary: *Persuasion: Speech and Behavioral Change,* Bobbs-Merrill, Indianapolis, 1969. A clear treatment of some current thinking on the psychological aspects of persuasion.

Simons, Herbert W.: *Persuasion: Understanding, Practice, and Analysis.* Addison-Wesley, Reading, Mass., 1976. A helpful discussion and analysis of the differences between values and attitudes as they relate to persuasion.

Situational Speaking

Chapter Nine

"Eternal truths will be neither true nor eternal unless thay have
fresh meaning for every new social situation."
Franklin Delano Roosevelt, September 20, 1940

When preparing a speech the role of the speaker and the composition of the audience may tend to overshadow the importance of the speaking *situation*. However, there are some occasions that almost predetermine the focus of the speech and at times the content of the speech. There are occasions when you will be asked to give a speech when the situation in which you will be speaking plays more than a usual role in determining audience expectations for the speech. There are certain ceremonies which demand certain kinds of utterances. Graduation speeches, speeches of nomination, retirement speeches are among the kinds of speeches where the situation plays an unusually strong part in influencing audience expectations for what will be included in the speech.

You may be a well-known entertainment personality, but if you are invited to give a high school graduation speech, the audience will expect you to address the graduates and the occasion rather than to recount anecdotes of your entertainment career (unless you are skillful enough to bring those anecdotes appropriately to bear upon the graduation situation). There are a very few speakers (like the President of the United States) who because of their unusual prominence may dominate almost any occasion and after a very brief allusion to the situation may then turn the speech to their own ends. For most of us a situation in which the ceremony or the occasion is very important demands that we be careful not to disappoint the audience expectations.

As noted earlier, expectations play a major role in determining the success or failure of a public speaking event. Frustrated expectations may become demands. In any given public speaking situation there are at least two expectational sets present. The speaker has certain expectations and the audience has certain expectations. Through decentering the speaker has tried to assess audience expectations and then through association the speaker tries to adapt the speaker's own expectations to the audience's expectations and experiences. If the audience expects to be amused and the speaker expects to impress the audience with the seriousness of a subject, there is obviously going to be some difficulty in the adjustment of the divergent expectations. We do not mean to suggest that the speaker must always completely defer his or her expectations so as to completely meet the audience's expectations. When there is a divergence between the expectational sets of the audience and of the speaker, the speaker must be aware of this divergence and make a conscious decision as to how to deal with the divergence.

209

There are times when the speaker may be able to slowly alter the audience expectations and reshape audience expectations so that they more closely resemble speaker expectations. In *Julius Caesar* by Shakespeare there is a scene in which Marc Antony is giving a eulogy (a type of situational speech) for the assassinated Caesar and in which Antony starts his speech suggesting that he is going to give a straightforward burial speech but so alters his material as to not only praise Caesar but to cast guilt on those responsible for Caesar's death. It is worthwhile reading this speech ("Friends, Romans, countrymen, lend me your ears; I come to bury Caesar, not to praise him," in *Julius Caesar*, Act III, scene II) as an example of altering expectations. Shakespeare provides us with a number of good examples of a speaker working with rigid audience expectations and shifting their expectations so as to fulfill the speaker's own expectations for the speech. In most cases of situational speeches you will have little trouble in meeting audience expectations.

☐ Frequently Encountered Situational Speeches

We are now going to present the most frequently encountered situational speeches. In each description we will include a discussion of audience expectations, means of meeting those expectations, and other important characteristics of the special situational form.

Introduction

The introducer is expected to get the show on the road. In a speech of introduction an audience expects to receive information as to why this particular speaker is suited to speak to this particular audience on this occasion at this time. You may best meet the audience expectations by adequate preparation. Make sure that you know what the speaker's topic is and what the speaker has accomplished that equips him or her to speak on this topic. Talk to the speaker a couple of days before the occasion, ask about the speaker's background, ask also if there is anything special the speaker would like to have included in the introduction so as to make it easier for the speaker to quickly relate to the audience. Remember that your job is to introduce the speaker, not to introduce the subject of the speech or to cover some of the material that the speaker might cover on the topic. Double-check to make certain that you know how to correctly pronounce the speaker's name. Don't overdo your introduction. The introduction should be as short as is compatible with meeting audience expectations. Be brief!

Welcome

In speeches of welcome the speaker usually is speaking on behalf of the audience. The speaker is expected to extend a welcome to a visitor or a new member of the group and to extend the hospitality of the group. The speaker may also be expected to mention the reason for the person's presence or visit. Again, in meeting the expectations, the speaker must be adequately prepared. This is no time to forget the name of the person being welcomed. You should mention the person's name, where the person comes from, and how long he or she will be visiting (if it is just a visit rather than a permanent position). It may also be appropriate to comment on where the person will be located during the visit. Be complimentary but not sugary. Be brief!

Another form of a welcoming speech is when the speaker is welcoming a group (such as a convention) who may be visiting a school, or a community, or an organization. The speaker acknowledges the importance of the visiting group and then, on behalf of the organization the speaker represents, welcomes the visitors and extends best wishes for the success of their visit.

Farewell

Expectations for a farewell speech depend upon whether you are saying "farewell" for yourself or farewell to someone else. If saying "farewell" for yourself you should express your gratitude for the kindnesses shown you during your stay, give your compliments to the group hosting you, perhaps recall some of the things accomplished during your visit, and mention where you will be going next. This is not the time to praise yourself but to make the audience feel that their decision to invite you was both appreciated and worthwhile. Recall the pleasantness of your stay. Be brief!

If saying farewell to someone else, as in a retirement ceremony, you will again be acting as spokesperson for the audience. You should express the sentiment of the group at the end of the person's stay. You might comment on how the person's visit has made a difference to the audience and to its personal and/or professional goals. You may wish to mention some of the person's specific accomplishments during their stay. You can also mention the ways in which the person's visit or stay will affect the future efforts or feelings of the audience. Compliment the person and wish the person well in future endeavors and life pursuits. Be as brief as is appropriate!

Award/Presentation

If it has not already been done, the audience will expect to learn the reason for the award and the requirements for the award. A *brief* history of the award may be appropriate. It may also be suitable to mention some of the past award recipients if by so doing you elevate the importance of the award. If the award is a physical object you may wish to display it for the audience to see. Mention the accomplishments of the person which qualified him or her for the award. Express the appreciation of the group making the award. Wish the recipient future success. Part of the goal of an award/presentation speech is making the group feel that they made the right decision and that the award honors not only the recipient but the group. Be brief!

Appropriate Presentation and Acceptance Enhances Any Award Ceremony (© Ellen Pines Sheffield 1980, Woodfin Camp & Associates)

Nomination

In a speech of nomination you should set forth the qualifications needed to successfully fill the position for which the person is nominated. Tell how the person fulfills, and possibly exceeds, those qualifications based upon the person's past accomplishments. Foretell the person's success if nominated and how he or she will honor the position. Urge the audience to support the nomination. Once again mention the position and the name of the person you are nominating. Be as specific as possible, and be brief.

Acceptance

In accepting an award or a presentation a person is often expected to respond to the presentation. Thank the presentor and express appreciation to the group making the award. If it is appropriate, recognize others who assisted you in winning the award or qualifying for the presentation. Remember how boring it is to hear overly long or detailed speeches of acceptance (some Academy Award acceptance speeches may help you remember this problem). If you feel comfortable in so doing say something honoring the group. Express your acceptance and your gratitude. Especially in this kind of situational speech make an effort to be brief!

Chairing a Program

The role of chairing a program can carry a number of designations. You may simply be called a chairperson, or you may be called a toastmaster, a host, or a master of ceremonies. Basically the person in any of these roles is expected to start the program on time, to moderate the program, to keep things going, and to end on time. This sounds a lot easier than is sometimes true.

Chairing requires a lot of preparation. You need to know the different aspects of the program in some detail and to have a good grip on the order in which things are supposed to happen. You may need to introduce the speakers or panelists; this calls for advance preparation and being certain that you know how to correctly pronounce their names. You need to use courtesy and firmness in getting the participants on and off the platform on schedule. You need to prearrange signals which indicate how closely the participants are sticking to the prearranged time constraints and you need to gain the participants' cooperation in honoring those signals. You need to tie things together as the program moves along. Sometimes you may have to provide spoken internal summaries so that the audience can see the relationship of the various program elements. At times it will be your responsibility to moderate a question and answer session. At times you will need to conclude the program by thanking the participants and by thanking the audience for their presence and attention. You may need to make an announcement about future programs. You will need to temper firmness with a lightness of treatment that avoids offending. Obviously this is not a role to be lightly undertaken. Do your preparation thoroughly and this task will move fairly smoothly. If possible have a preprogram meeting with all the principal participants. Remember that your role is one of facilitator rather than one of a primary program participant. In moving the program along be firm and be brief.

After-Dinner Speeches

What are generally called after-dinner speeches take on a number of different aspects. There are programs which start with a meal but which, after the meal, include speeches of a general nature. The meal need not be dinner. There are after-breakfast programs (you really have to be an early-morning person to speak at these willingly), there are after-lunch programs, and there are after-dinner programs. Many service clubs such as Rotary, Kiwanis, Lions, Optimists, Soroptimists, Business and Professional Womens Club, and others have lunch and then a regular program. A speech in such a setting meets the criteria of a regular public speech rather than of a situational speech and your speech preparation and delivery should follow the pattern suggested in the earlier chapters of this text. If you are going to give a speech of this nature, you should be aware that time limits for an after-lunch speech are usually very stringent. After-luncheon speeches usually are forced into time constraints by the demands of a regular business day and its attendant schedule. If you go overtime in an after-luncheon speech, you should expect that a substantial number of the audience will have to get up and leave while you are speaking. In after breakfast and after luncheon speeches be exceptionally conscious of the time constraints.

Although many after-meal speakers have a motivational bent, that is, they give speeches that are high on the scale of emotional appeal, such a focus is not always necessary. There is a special challenge in keeping an audience's attention at 7:30 in the morning, or after a good lunch, and emotional appeals often help—but they are far from essential. You *must*, however, work especially hard at decentering and association so as to assure a speech and a presentation that closely approximates the audience expectations. Remember that "approximating audience expectations" does not mean telling the audience only what you think they want to hear. You can meet audience expectations for the general range of topic and forms of support and still present a position that differs substantially from the generally accepted position. There is at least one speaker on the after-breakfast circuit whose speech is entitled "Pumped Up vs. Filled Up" and who talks to the audience about the dangers of accepting motivational speeches which "pump" one up like a balloon and the need for solid information which "fills" one up with the kind of conceptual information that turns into brain muscle. Your first task is to find a good idea and then to present it in your speech.

The second kind of after-dinner speech is the one which follows an evening meal and usually has as its intent the presentation of an entertaining and relaxing speech. These after-dinner speeches usually range in length between 20 and 30 minutes and are heavy on illustration, anecdote, examples, and if you can do it, humor. The topic may be quite serious yet treated relatively lightly. After-dinner speaking of this type usually is the province of more accomplished speakers. These speeches can be a lot of fun for the speaker since the audience is almost invariably good-natured, relaxed, and rooting completely for the speaker's success. You, as speaker, need to relax with this kind of speech. Your relaxation, however, should not extend to the question of preparation. Prepare completely—know your anecdotes by heart, as well as most of your speech, since the relaxed and congenial atmosphere of an after-dinner speech of this type does not generally allow for the extensive use of notes and the possibility of resultant note dependency. Total audience contact is called for in an entertaining after-dinner speech. In this kind of speech you should consider the use of poetry or prose excerpts as material to be included for illustration or example. A speech can be exceedingly entertaining without including a single joke. Sheer intensity of expression, detailed and exciting supporting material, an interesting topic, all can make an after-dinner speech entertaining and successful. There are times that a speaker feels that by stretching the truth she can make a more entertaining speech. Unless the audience recognizes that the speaker is intentionally, for effect, exaggerating, then ethics demand that the speaker avoid this technique.

The third type of after-dinner speech you may be asked to deliver is one which is part of a "roast." A roast is a program which has as its goal the honoring of a person by a series of short speeches given by friends or acquaintances of the person. There has developed a tradition on the part of some to make roast speeches exceedingly caustic. We don't believe that good humor should ever be hurtful and we recommend that if you participate in a roast you should take care to make your comments complimentary, light-hearted, and never so cynical, sarcastic, or critical as to hurt the feelings of the person being roasted. It is acceptable to touch upon some of the person's foibles or weaknesses, if you do so in a kindly manner. Roast speeches also have a tendency to go on and on. In a roast speech, be mercifully brief!

Briefings

A briefing is a special form of a speech which came into popular use during World War II. Briefings were used by military men to describe the sessions in which necessary information was digested and communicated to commanders, staffs, and combat units to aid in planning and executing military operations. The public became familiar with briefings by watching scores of motion pictures in which combat aviators received their last-minute instructions in smoky briefing rooms. Indeed, the tense atmosphere of the briefing, a few hours before takeoff, became a necessary ingredient of war films, and the movie without such a scene was rare.

As Loney (1959, p. 92) points out: Condensed oral reports on plans and operations in military organizations, whether given at company or command level, also came to be known as briefings. Later, the word was borrowed by the business and professional world to indicate analogous informational meetings in their organizations.

The very essence of a "briefing" is to save time. The word is now even used as a verb, "To brief the President." The processes of condensation and selection are time-consuming and energy-expending, but they are the essence of a good briefing.

A briefing is not a summary. If a number of department heads are gathered together and asked to summarize their week's work for the boss, they are each giving a summary. If, on the other hand, a foreman is asked to brief the supervisor on the activities of all his workmen for the past pay period, he must then go through the process of selection and condensation and come up with a short, informative talk—in other words, a briefing.

When participating in a briefing session it is essential to have a complete and exhaustive grasp of the material for which you are responsible. At the conclusion of a briefing the person being briefed may ask questions which will require you to expand upon some of the information you presented in your briefing. Your job is to boil down a great quantity of data into a few statements. The briefing speech should be understandable and as interesting as possible. Clarity is a prime virtue in a briefing speech. Few of us can claim that our briefing tasks are as important as Presidential briefings. Yet, in respect to our own area of responsibility, the briefings we may give have a parallel value.

In preparing for a briefing, be especially attentive to decenter to your audience's conceptual point of view—know how much the person already knows; this will save you time. Read all of the pertinent material and make notes while reading. Use the notes to construct your outline. Plan the integrated use of any audiovisual aids that might add clarity (but not redundancy) to your material. Organization is extremely important because of the condensed nature of the material. Timing is almost always very important and you should use a recording device to help you time your briefing speech to the desired length. If possible have your aids and materials in order and set up in the appointed place prior to the time the briefing is scheduled to begin. Begin on time, maintain an understandable rate of delivery, and stay within the prescribed time limits. Be prepared to answer pertinent questions.

Questions and Answers

If you give a public speech, a briefing, or if you share in a public discussion, you must be ready to answer the questions of your listeners. A listener is responsible for asking a question when there is need for clarification, amplification, or justification.

People ask questions for a variety of reasons. Although most questions are asked with good will, it would be naive to think that seeking information is the only reason or always the main reason for a question. Perhaps the questioner is:

- actually requesting clarification, amplification, or justification of a remark, evidence, or a point of view
- seeking group recognition
- relieving internal tensions
- trying to heckle the speaker
- looking for a way to disrupt the meeting
- trying to delay action on a point up for decision
- trying to keep the audience's attention focused on a particular problem for an extended period
- masking ignorance
- covering up for inattention

It would be helpful if we could always know the questioner's underlying motivation, but this is normally impossible. Good decentering will help. You should be aware of the temper of the audience in reference both to your topic and to yourself. Most questions represent an honest search for understanding and as such they deserve a respectful hearing and a conscientious effort to answer them.

Since not everyone in the audience may have heard the question, it is always advisable, upon the questioner's completion of the statement, for you to restate the question. Restatement of the question serves a triple purpose: (1) It enables the rest of the audience to hear the question; (2) it gives the questioner an opportunity to see whether the speaker heard the question correctly; and (3) it allows you, the speaker, a few extra moments in which to use inner speech to analyze the question and formulate your answer.

If you don't know the answer, *don't hedge*. Admit that you don't know, ask the questioner to leave a name and address, and say that you will send the answer as soon as possible. Most listeners can tell, by the hemming and hawing, when a speaker is hedging—so don't try. Some questions are unanswerable because they aren't questions in the first place. The questioner has taken advantage of the question and answer session to make a short speech of his or her own. If this happens there is little you can do but observe that the point was well taken (if this is true) or to challenge the statement (if this is necessary). It is seldom to the speaker's advantage to get involved in a running debate with a member of the audience.

Some questions are unanswerable simply because it would take too much time to answer them. The speaker should remember that although a question may interest a segment of the audience, it may not hold the interest of all. With this in mind it is seldom advisable to spend too much of the available time on any single question. State that the answer is quite long and that you would be willing to answer it at the end of the period if time allows, or that you would be happy to speak with the questioner personally upon completion of the formal presentation.

If you are confronted by a heckler or an insulting individual, keep your head. Don't overreact, don't get angry. Allow the heckler to state the question. If it doesn't require an answer, ignore it. If it indicates a misunderstanding of your position, set the record straight impersonally and briefly. Audiences are generally on the side of the just—so relax and maintain your patience. If a heckler, or hecklers, seem bent on totally disrupting your speech, appeal to the moderator for help. If none is forthcoming and the hecklers refuse to be silent, there is little more that you can accomplish, so sit down.

A question and answer session is an opportunity for you to make your points once again and to continue to build your credibility as a speaker. Use the question and answer period as one more opportunity to achieve your specific purpose. It sometimes happens that you would like to have certain questions raised in order to reinforce a point made in the speech. Since you cannot really depend upon that specific question occurring spontaneously to a member of the audience it is sometimes worthwhile to have a friend introduce the question during the Q & A. In the Q & A, as everywhere else, practice the technique of transparent delivery. Don't overanswer a question. If you say too much in response you may raise more questions than you answer. Keep the Q & A moving briskly, your answers to the point and as short as possible. In all your answers, try to be courteous, audible, specific, and brief!

Media Interviews

Today there are many instances when you may be interviewed by a representative of the mass media. Representatives of the mass media, newspaper, radio, and

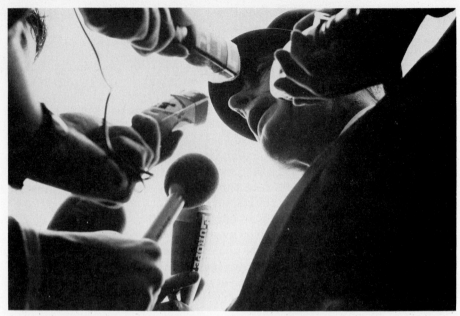

During Media Interviews, Keep Your Answers Short and Specific (© Olivier Rebbot 1978, Woodfin Camp & Associates)

television, may be interested in you, your topic, your position on the topic, or the audience's reaction to your presentation.

If you know you are going to be interviewed try to check out the interviewer's style before your own interview. It is helpful to watch television interview programs to get a feeling for how others handle such situations. You will be able, by watching such shows, or listening to radio interviews, to get a feeling for what seems to constitute effective interview responses. Media interviews demand transparent delivery. Don't try to bluff in a media interview. Remember that time is money on radio or television and make your answers as short and specific as possible. In press interviews time is translated into space. The shorter and more to the point your answer, the greater the likelihood of your interview being placed on the actual program. It seldom pays to say "no comment." A no-comment response is often taken by a listening or viewing audience as tantamount to a guilty plea, or a confession that you have something to hide. Rather than simply saying "no comment," if you don't want to answer a question expand upon why you can't answer the question at this time.

If you are being filmed or taped or appearing on television remember that the television setting condenses space and that small gestures, facial movements, and postural changes are magnified on the screen. Keep your vocal range and gestural range as intimately conversational as possible. Try for understatement in delivery (and in clothing as well). Be as natural as you can.

It is usually inadvisable to try to be humorous in a media interview. Your humor may be mistaken as flippancy or as a sign of triviality and can easily backfire.

Keep your cool! Don't allow yourself to get angry in a media interview. Decentering is suppressed by anger and you may find yourself sounding extremely egocentric and "smart alecky." If you feel yourself getting angry, consciously smother any indications of such anger.

Always remember your own ethical commitment in a media interview. It is all right to make use of the media interview to enhance your person and your cause, but not by unethical means. Be truthful.

Infrequent Situational Speeches

There are some occasions which include speeches and which you may encounter—but not often. For example, there are speeches of *dedication,* such as the dedication of a new building or the launching of a new submarine. In such situations the speaker usually speaks of the need for the building, expresses gratitude to those who made the building possible, and dedicates the building to its use. There are also *anniversary* speeches where the speaker commonly addresses the significance of the anniversary, reviews the evolution or development of the subject, and may suggest hopes and directions for the future. Finally there is the *eulogy* which is a commemorative speech for someone who has died. If invited to give a eulogy, you should review the person's life and accomplishments and thus find ample material upon which to base appropriate remarks. In most cases a eulogy should be fairly short. This is the time to emphasize the good that the person has done and how that good will continue to live with us. A eulogy is the ultimate farewell speech and should leave the audience feeling good about having shared life with the person being eulogized.

Effective situational speeches emerge out of the interaction among an occasion, an audience, and you—the speaker. As indicated in this chapter situational speeches often call for extensive preparation, so don't accept an invitation to present a situational speech unless you are committed to doing the necessary preparation. Effective situational speeches demand the application of all the principles covered earlier in this primer tempered by the demands of the specific occasion. Situational speeches are almost always improved by being brief. The best situational speeches exhibit some style and elegance, are characterized by transparent delivery, and maintain the illusion of spontaneity.

☐ Summary

Situational speeches occur when the occasion of the speech plays an unusually strong role in determining audience expectations. When there is a divergence between the expectational set of the audience and the expectational set of the speaker, the speaker should be aware of this divergence and make a conscious decision as to how to deal with it. For example, imagine you are giving a briefing (an oral report requiring extensive preparation, selection, and condensation) and your boss is the main audience. However, on this occasion your colleagues will also be there and will form a subaudience with expectations different from those of your boss. You must decide in advance how you are going to handle such a situation.

In a question and answer situation, if you don't know the answer to a question—say so! Never overanswer questions! Also remember to keep things moving briskly in a Q & A session.

In media interviews: Prepare, be candid, truthful, and succinct. If on TV practice understatement of voice, gesture, and clothes.

In all situational speaking use transparent delivery and be brief.

Exercises ■

1 Gina Bonvicini has been the outstanding marketing representative for college textbooks in public speaking. She has made 100 percent of her sales quota. In the yearly regional sales meeting of her publishing company the marketing vice-president, Caleb Smith, is presenting Ms. Bonvicini with the award for outstanding sales effort.
   a Person 1: Role play Mr. Smith making the award.
   b Person 2: Role play Ms. Bonvicini accepting the award.

2 The occasion is the graduation ceremony of the district high school. The commencement speaker is the governor of your state. Prepare and deliver an appropriate introduction.

3 It is the end of the course. Prepare and present awards to the following:
   ■ the individual who has made the greatest progress.
   ■ the individual who has given the most successful speech.
   ■ the individual who has made the best use of audiovisual aids.

4 Prepare and deliver a 5-minute briefing on a subject involving statistical data (such as the census report dealing with your community or the results of a public opinion survey). Use audio or visual aids in your presentation. Be prepared to answer questions.

5 You have taken a position as public relations representative for the local United Way program. You must present the United Way staff with information concerning opportunities for coverage in the community's mass communications media. The briefing should be comprehensive and *brief*—no more than 5 minutes.

6 As a representative student you have been asked to give a 5-minute briefing to the local chapter of your school's alumni association on the topic of student opinions concerning the quality of their educational experience at school. How would you gather this information (consult Chapter Four), and how would you go about condensing it for this particular audience?

7 Role play a media interview. One person should be the media interviewer. The second person should be an eyewitness observer of an important historical event

such as the burning of Rome, or the eruption of Mt. Saint Helens, or the bombing of Hiroshima. The observer should have researched the assigned event.

8 Conduct a Q & A session following one of your other speeches.

9 Conduct a media interview following one of your other speeches.

Bibliographic Reference ■

Loney, Glen M.: *Briefing and Conference Techniques,* McGraw-Hill Book Company, New York, 1959. An especially useful resource for information on briefings.

Recommended Readings ■

Morrisey, George L.: *Effective Business and Technical Presentations,* Addison-Wesley, Reading, Mass., 1968. Another good resource on briefings.

Tucker, S. Marion: *Public Speaking for Technical Men.* McGraw-Hill Book Company, New York, 1939. An older reference but well done. Chapter 16 is very helpful in offering advice on handling question and answer sessions.

Appendix to Chapter Nine

Evaluation and Listening

"He wreathed the rod of criticism with roses."
Isaac D'Israeli, *Curiosities of Literature*

☐ What Is Evaluation?

When we consider the merits or demerits of a speech, the speech's significance or worth, we are evaluating or criticizing the speech. Because criticism is commonly, although erroneously, interpreted as negative judgment (e.g. "She's so critical of everything . . . I wish she would develop a more positive attitude toward life"), the term "evaluation" is sometimes preferred. Nothing in the definitions, however, implies that either evaluation or criticism need always be negative. Instead, evaluating and criticizing are recognizing the success or failure of a speech in terms of its specific purpose, and of a speaker in terms of her preparation, organization, delivery, and so forth. Evaluation and criticism suggest ways to improve a speech through addition, deletion, or substitution. For our purposes evaluation and criticism are essentially synonymous and will be used interchangeably.

☐ What Is the Purpose of Evaluation?

The purpose of evaluation and the task of the evaluator are to provide information and alternatives so that the speaker can consider changing his speech or his behavior with the goal of improving his performance. Criticism and learning, according to many, go hand in hand. Cathcart in *Post Communication** states:

> A person who wishes to learn a new task or to improve upon his performance of an old one, will not progress without some criticism. Simply doing something over and over will not necessarily result in improvement, unless the performance is analyzed and compared with a more ideal performance. If one does not know why he is failing to attain the results that he desires, he is not likely to improve. He

*Cathcart, *Post Communication*, Bobbs-Merrill, Indianapolis, 1966, p. 11.

must look at the task he is performing and be able to determine what is happening. Even knowing what is happening will not automatically lead to improvement, unless he has some awareness of the ideal performance. In each of these steps, criticism is involved. It may be self-criticism, or it may be the criticism of an [other]. Without it, no matter the source, there will be little learning.

Evaluation can come from one's self, from others, or from a combination of self and others. Whoever the source, the goals of evaluation are the same: to determine the effects of the speech/speaker on you, to describe those effects to the speaker, and to make suggestions for improvement that the speaker can consider.

As a cautionary note, when evaluating others remember that the suggestions you make may not always be accepted by a speaker. Cathcart speaks of an "ideal performance." If everyone agreed on what constitutes an ideal performance and the means by which one might reach that ideal, evaluative suggestions would immediately be incorporated by a speaker. In reality, everyone has individual skills, abilities, goals, as well as individual notions of what constitutes an "ideal" performance. A speaker should accept and make use of those suggestions that are compatible with her abilities, self-concept, beliefs, specific purpose, and her reasons for speaking.

☐ What Are the Tools of Evaluation?

Perception, comprehension, decentering, knowledge, and judgment are the tools of evaluative criticism. These five tools overlap and intermingle when fashioning an evaluation but for the sake of clarity we will treat them in order.

1. *Perception* is the ability to receive the stimuli carrying the message. You must be able to hear the speaker in order to evaluate the speech. You must be able to see the speaker in order to evaluate the visual components of the speech situation.
2. *Comprehension* is the ability to understand the denotative meaning of the perceived sounds and visual accompaniments. When you know the general meaning of the words being used, and the structure of the syntax in which the words are imbedded, you are comprehending the speech.
3. *Decentering* means taking the conceptual point of view of the person giving the speech so that you can go beyond overall comprehension to the point of appreciating the unique meaning imparted to the words and actions by this particular speaker, at this particular time, in this particular speech situation.

These first three of the five tools of criticism, (1) perception, (2) comprehension, and (3) decentering, are behaviors that are sometimes included under the label *listening*.

☐ Listening

Listening is an overall label for the complex of physiological, neurological, and psychological factors involved in the understanding and retention of verbal materials presented in spoken form. This definition of listening highlights the importance to the evaluation and criticism of a speech of the complex of skills involved in listening. Certainly unless one can perceive the speech, comprehend the speech, and take the speaker's point of view concerning the speech, one cannot realistically evaluate the speech.

Listening may be improved by:

Developing a positive attitude toward listening, understanding that listening is active rather than passive and that you must work at listening.

Building a diagnosis of your own listening habits by completing the listening profile appearing at the end of this appendix. If your self-analysis raises questions, ask your teacher for advice on exercises to improve your listening behavior. Your teacher might give you exercises on one or more of the component skills or on the overall behavioral program called listening.

Decentering. [**GOTO pages 33, 37–40**]

Capitalizing on the differential between speech-speed and thought-speed. [**GOTO Chapter Six, page 143**]

Reducing distractions.

Attending to information acquisition.

Reducing emotional barriers.

Attending to information storage.

Attending to information retrieval.

Watching the speaker. We interpret a lot of what a speaker is saying by reconstructing in our own behavior what we see the speaker doing.

By attending to the "Ten Guides to Effective Listening" set forth by Ralph Nichols and appearing at the end of the appendix.

As mentioned above, without perception, comprehension, and decentering (or "listening"), competent and helpful evaluation is impossible. Human communication involves both sending and receiving, and listening is a convenient label for many of the skills involved in the receiving part of human communication.

4. *Knowledge,* another tool of evaluation, consists of an awareness on your part of the desirable ethical, logical, and presentational attributes of a speech.
   a. The *ethical* attributes lead you to a decision as to whether you believe the ideas in the speech to be right or wrong, good or bad. [**GOTO Chapter Ten**]
   b. The *logical* attributes lead you to a decision as to whether you believe the ideas in the speech to be true or false, fact or fancy, reasonable or unreasonable, supported or unsupported by evidence. [**GOTO Chapter Eight**]

      c. The *presentational* attributes lead you to a decision as to whether you believe that the ideas in the speech were enhanced or impaired by the speaker's delivery, the manner in which the speech was presented. [**GOTO Chapter Seven**]

  5. *Judgment* is deciding for oneself on the success or failure of the speech in terms of the speech's attributes. When giving an evaluation we are telling someone of our personal judgment concerning their effort.

☐ How Does One Give an Evaluation of a Speech?

A. Someone else's speech.

  1. Always try, in the words of St. Paul, to "do the truth in charity." This is what D'Israeli meant by "wreathing the rod of criticism in roses." We want to help the speaker, we want to tell the speaker what was good about the speech as well as in what way the speech might have been improved. Honesty and tact need not be incompatible. We should give our criticism in as nonoffensive a manner as possible. Say "I think the speech would have been better for me had you given more supporting material," rather than "You must be pretty dumb to think someone would believe your speech with that shoddy evidence." Say "It would help if you talked a bit louder," rather than "I couldn't hear your wimpy voice."

  2. Carefully consider the value of giving feedback concerning behavior(s) over which the speaker has no control. For instance, if a person has poor eyesight but cannot wear contact lenses, what help is offered by an evaluator saying she doesn't like the speaker wearing his glasses? Or, if a speaker has a paralyzed arm, how can the speaker be expected to cope with the suggestion "gesture more with both hands"? Remember, one of the purposes of evaluation is to offer suggestions that the speaker can reasonably consider.

  3. While listening to the speech try to construct an outline of what you are hearing. An outline can help an evaluator remember specific and general aspects of the speech, to organize his reaction to those aspects, and to make suggestions for improving certain aspects. [**GOTO Chapter Five**]

  4. The use of structured guidelines is another useful method for organizing your criticisms of someone else's speech. Dividing a speech into content and delivery aspects is one way of providing evaluative structure.

      a. The *content* aspects of a speech might include the speech sections labeled introduction, body, and conclusion; the material included and excluded in those three sections; and the effectiveness of the included material. Another way of evaluating the speech's content is by topically critiquing support materials: apparent use of audience analysis; pattern of organization; language usage; etc. Regardless of method, aspects of content should not be evaluated in a vacuum. Every speaker has a desired audience response in mind and to that end constructs a specific purpose for his speech. In your attempt to evaluate the content aspects of a speech, two questions should be kept in mind:

(1) Can you discern the speech's specific purpose? [**GOTO Chapter Five, pages 112–114**]

(2) Do the contents of the speech contribute to the attainment of the specific purpose?

b. The *delivery* aspect of a speech includes vocal and nonvocal components. The speaker's voice is his primary presentational tool. Vocal components, such as rate, volume, pitch, and fluency, can affect the reception and effectiveness of both speech and speaker. Certainly attention to and evaluation of the vocal components of a speech is important.

c. Nonvocal delivery components include, among others, general appearance, eye contact, gestures, and use of notes. Whereas the vocal components of spoken language carry most of the conceptual meaning of a speech, the nonvocal aspects that accompany spoken language carry much of the speech's emotional message. Because nonvocal behavior is primarily nonvolitional and unintentional, is the task of an evaluator to critique such behavior and bring it to the conscious attention of the speaker.

A Speech Evaluation/Critique Checklist is included at the end of this appendix (see Table 9.1). The checklist is keyed to content and delivery. We do *not* recommend using the checklist while listening to a speech—the list will distract you and detract from the presentation. Our recommendation for you as an evaluator is to outline the speech *during* the presentation and *afterwards* refine your evaluation by checking the outline against the questions on the checklist. Unless your teacher recommends another method of evaluating, the one suggested works well.

Your first task, as an evaluator, is to do all you can to make sure you give the speech as full and fair a hearing as possible. You have to concentrate on the speech as it is being given and not allow other tasks or interruptions to distract you. The best way of forcing complete concentration on the speech is for you to try and construct an outline of the speech as it is being given by the speaker. Use the recommended outline form [**GOTO Chapter Five, page 123**]; as you are attending to the speech try and discern and then fill in the speaker's specific purpose, then outline the speaker's introduction, transitions, body, and conclusion—just the main points and major supporting points, not necessarily examples and asides. You also have to pay attention to the presentational aspects of the speech.

Now, go to the evaluation checklist and assess the success or failure of the speech in terms of the points appearing on the checklist—what you will be doing is cross-checking the list against your outline and your memory of the speech.

The more often you evaluate speeches, the more familiar you will become with the checklist criteria. As you become more and more familiar with the evaluative criteria you will find that as you go through the process of outlining the speech while it is being delivered, you will simultaneously be evaluating the speech.

Finally compose your evaluative remarks so that they will be most helpful to the speaker.

5. Evaluative comments that are most helpful to the speaker are *specific* rather than *general*. Although your general reaction might be appreciated, it is more helpful, from the speaker's point of view, to say "There were times that you used some words that I didn't understand, such as. . . ," rather than "I didn't like your vocabulary." When striving to be specific don't fall into the trap of looking for small problems and then overemphasizing them.

Both *positive* and *negative* evaluative comments can be helpful. But remember that even the most negative of evaluations ("I thought the speech was a total flop!") can be handled constructively so that the speaker's self-concept and self-esteem are left intact: "Although I wasn't convinced by your speech I can see some virtue in your point of view and think I might have found you more convincing had you. . . ."

Regarding *content* and *delivery* criticisms, the most appropriate balance depends upon the speaker's specific purpose and overall presentation. If the content, on the whole, was very good, but the delivery needed work, evaluation will naturally focus more on delivery. If the delivery was OK but the content needed improvement, then the evaluation will be weighted toward content behaviors.

In sum, each speech evaluation contains a balance of specific/general, content/delivery, and positive/negative comments. The most appropriate balance within each of the contrast pairs is determined by the total speech context.

B. Your own speech
    1. Many of the suggestions given for the evaluation of someone else's speech hold when you evaluate your own presentation. You might wonder how you can evaluate your own speech while so much of your energy is directed toward its presentation. Developing the skill of self-listening (monitoring yourself while you speak) is essential. Most of us listen to ourselves in our day-to-day conversations. We catch ourselves mispronouncing a word or neglecting eye contact. Self-awareness should become a conscious and intentional tool of self-evaluation. Additional treatment of the value of self-monitoring may be found in the appendix on the use of the VTR as well as in Chapter Six, "Rehearsal."
    2. Perhaps the most difficult problem in evaluating one's self is objectivity. While every evaluation is partially subjective, it is generally easier to be objective when critiquing others. How can a person be objective about his or her own subjective experience? An audio taping or an audio/video taping can promote more objective self-evaluation. These electronic evaluation aids are discussed in more detail in the VTR appendix.
    3. Whether you evaluate yourself by simultaneous self-monitoring or by using

an electronic device allowing for delayed evaluation, we offer the same guidelines. Examine the content and the delivery of your speech. Critique specific items, but develop an overall impression and general judgment as to your speech's effectiveness. Tell yourself those parts of the presentation that were well done as well as those parts that could be improved.

4. If you have taped your speech, outline the speech as you listen to it. Does your "listener outline" match your "speaker outline?" Occasionally the organization of material in your head or on paper fails to transfer successfully to spoken language. An argument that can easily be developed on paper and easily followed when read may be too involved for an audience to follow when delivered orally. The translation from thought to spoken language may require a speaker to adjust his or her spoken language (e.g., the addition of internal summaries, recapitulations). Self-evaluation during rehearsal can help you remedy apparent problems.

□ Benefits of Evaluation

The foremost benefit of evaluation for a speaker is the opportunity for improvement. Speech evaluation contributes the feedback necessary for the further development of your conceptual abilities and your public speaking skills.

An evaluator also benefits from the experience of speech criticism. Critiquing a speech gives you experience in critical listening, in learning the elements of an effective speech, and in reflecting on your own public speaking skills. In other words, evaluation gives the opportunity to listen and to learn from another's experience. These critical skills are immensely important in a country governed through the informed consent of its citizens. Each of us must take pains to develop our critical abilities since we must make important electoral decisions based upon the public communication of those in office and of candidates for public office. Through evaluation, the evaluator, as well as the speaker, has the opportunity to develop both conceptual abilities and public speaking skills.

□ Listening Profile

Draw your self-diagnostic profile of listening skills by circling the appropriate numbers and then connecting the circles with a straight line.

When listening to a speech do you:

1. try to be in good physical condition, rested, and alert?
2. prepare by being as well-informed on the topic as time allows?
3. recognize and allow for your own prejudices?
4. pay full attention and resist distractions?

    5. compensate for unavoidable distractions?
    6. sit facing the speaker and close enough to hear without straining?
    7. watch for and factor in nonvocal cues?
    8. allow enough time, thus reducing stress?
    9. decenter?
  10. capitalize on the thought-speed, speech-speed differential?
  11. take notes at end of the speech?

Usually	1	2	3	4	5	6	7	8	9	10	11	*Excellent*
Sometimes	1	2	3	4	5	6	7	8	9	10	11	*Could Be Improved*
Seldom	1	2	3	4	5	6	7	8	9	10	11	*Needs Work*

Ten Guides to Effective Listening ■

Ralph G. Nichols

(This is an excerpt from an essay that originally appeared in *The Speech Teacher*, vol. X, no. 2, March 1961, pp. 120–124.)

    1. *Find areas of interest* . . . The key to the whole matter of interest in a topic is *use*. Whenever we wish to listen efficiently, we ought to say to ourselves: "What's he saying that I can use? What worthwhile ideas has he? Is he reporting any workable procedures? Anything that I can cash in on, or with which I can make myself happier?"

    2. *Judge content, not delivery* . . . [Tell yourself] I'm not interested in his personality or delivery. I want to find out what he knows. Does this man know some things that I need to know?

    3. *Hold your fire* . . . We must learn not to get too excited about a speaker's point until we are certain we thoroughly understand it. The secret is contained in the principle that we must always withhold evaluation until our comprehension is complete.

    4. *Listen for ideas.* Good listeners focus on central ideas; they tend to recognize the characteristic language in which central ideas are usually stated, and they are able to discriminate between fact and principle, idea and example, evidence and argument. . . .

    5. *Be flexible.* . . . Note-taking may help or may become a distraction. Few of us have memories good enough to remember even the salient points we hear. If we can obtain brief, meaningful records of them for later review, we definitely improve our ability to learn and to remember.

    6. *Work at listening.* . . . Listening is hard work. It is characterized by faster action, quicker circulation of the blood, a small rise in bodily temperature. The overrelaxed listener is merely appearing to tune in, and then feeling conscience-free to pursue any of a thousand mental tangents.

    7. *Resist distractions.* . . . A good listener instinctively fights distraction. Sometimes the fight is easily won—by closing a door, shutting off the radio, moving closer to the person talking, or asking him to speak louder. If the distraction cannot be met that easily, then it becomes a matter of concentration.

8. *Exercise your mind.* Poor listeners are inexperienced in hearing difficult, expository materials. Good listeners apparently develop an appetite for hearing a variety of presentations difficult enough to challenge their mental capacities. . . .

9. *Keep your mind open.* . . . Effective listeners try to identify and to rationalize the words or phrases most upsetting emotionally. Often the emotional impact of such words can be decreased through a free and open discussion of them with friends or associates.

10. *Capitalize on thought speed.* Most persons talk at a speed of about 125 words per minute. There is good evidence that if thought were measured in words per minute, most of us could think easily at about four times that rate. It is difficult—almost painful—to try to slow down our thinking speed. Thus we normally have about 400 words of thinking time to spare during every minute a person talks to us. . . .

Not capitalizing on thought-speed is our greatest single handicap. The differential between thought-speed and speech-speed breeds false feelings of security and mental tangents. Yet, through listening training, this same differential can be readily converted into our greatest single asset.

TABLE 9.1 Speech Evaluation/Critique Checklist*

Content	Delivery
Introduction ____ Attention getting	**Vocal Components**
____ Develops audience rapport	____ Vocal pitch (high/low/monotone)
____ Introduces/previews/relates to	____ Vocal intensity (volume)
the body of the speech	____ Vocal variety
____ Appropriate length	____ Vocalized pauses (fluency)
	____ Speed or pacing
Body ____ Topic suitability	____ Pronunciation (correct/incorrect)
____ Apparent decentering and	____ Enunciation (clear/slurred)
adaptation to audience	____ Transitions to and from speech aids
____ Organization	____ Transparent vocal delivery
____ Logic	
____ Transitions	**Nonvocal components**
____ Language usage; vulgarity;	____ General appearance
appropriateness to	____ Facial expressions
audience	____ Eye contact
____ Vocabulary; jargon;	____ Gestures
appropriateness to	____ Preparedness
audience	____ Sincerity and/or enthusiasm
Conclusion	____ Credibility
____ Summary; restate; recap	____ Use of notes
____ Sense of completion	____ Use of lectern
____ Specific methods: appeal;	____ Use of speech aids
challenge; declare; quote;	____ Transparent nonvocal delivery
anecdote; illustrate	

How would you state, in your own words, the specific purpose of the speech? Was it accomplished? If so, why? If not, why not?

What is your overall reaction? Why?

Do you have any specific suggestions for improvement? (for both speech and speaker)

*This checklist should be adapted by the evaluator to include appropriate criteria for evaluating "Special Occasion" speeches.

Ethics in Public Speaking

Chapter Ten

"An act has no ethical quality whatever unless it be chosen out of several all equally possible."
William James, *The Principles of Psychology*, 1890

In our time, as in the past, examples of the interaction of public speaking and ethics are plentiful. Adolf Hitler testified in print and in speech that he considered the spoken word his most powerful weapon. Using the spoken word, Hitler rose from obscurity to become the Chancellor of Germany. Using the spoken word, in fact insisting that his personal spoken word be accepted as the law of the land, Hitler talked well over 12 million human beings into their graves. Using the spoken word, Hitler destroyed the interior balance of his own subjects so that those followers turned themselves from normal human beings into malicious and almost bestial predators of their fellow humans. Hitler and his Minister of Propaganda, Dr. Joseph Goebbels, exemplify the power of the spoken word when utilized on behalf of an inhumane ethic. We can also find examples of public speakers who tried through their speaking to implement an ethic of good will, of humaneness, of the universal brotherhood of man. Speakers such as Martin Luther King, Mother Teresa, Gandhi, give testimony to the power of the spoken word when used in support of a humane and beneficent ethic.

☐ Ethics and Ethos

The question of ethics and human behavior is a complex one that could involve hundreds and hundreds of pages. In this text we are considering only a few of the aspects of the interrelationship of ethics and public speaking. *Ethos,* which we considered in Chapter Eight as an important element in argumentation and persuasion, is also related to the concept and treatment of ethics in public speaking. Ethical behavior is often characterized by ethos, by the manifestation of source credibility on the part of the individual. Often a speaker who has ethos is considered to be a speaker with integrity. Integrity, the quality of being a unity, of having it "all together" seems to be a natural rather than an artificial quality of being. Integrity is a quality that issues forth from the person's interior and testifies to the wholeness (or even wholesomeness) of the speaker. It may be assumed that an individual who has integrity will make every effort to avoid behaviors that would shatter that unity of being. Integrity, unity of being, cannot be seen—it is through the person's speech, or spoken language, that we hear testimony to the speaker's interior unity. It is this interior unity, manifested through spoken language, that constitutes one of the most important elements resulting in others saying of the speaker that he or she has "ethos."

Ethos and ethics go together since both are essential qualities of good public speaking. When we say that both are "essential qualities of good public speaking," we are not saying that all effective public speaking is ethical or that all public speakers who are perceived by others as having ethos will indeed behave ethically. What we are saying is that each individual speaker in the quest for excellence should seek to imbue his or her speaking with a commitment to ethical behavior. Each speaker should foster an internal unity or integrity that makes ethical speaking a natural manifestation of an internal state. In a very real sense we are what we do. A commitment to being ethical, a continued effort to be ethical in our human communication behaviors, will finally result in our *being* ethical. The quest for "unity from diversity," or "unity in diversity," is an important human goal that Robert Nozick highlights in his book *Philosophical Explanations* (1981, pp. 417ff).

What exactly constitutes this "ethical behavior" we've been talking about?

The concept of ethics is important to the individual human being and to the human race. Ethics are bound up with the concept of duty; duty to ourselves, duty to other human beings, duty to society. Ethics has been defined as "the department of study concerned with the principles of human duty," and as "the principles of conduct governing a person or group" (*Compact Edition of the Oxford English Dictionary,* 1971, p. 900).

The quotation from William James at this chapter's beginning links ethics and choice. There is no question of individual values or the shared values we call ethics unless the individual has a choice in the matter under consideration. Obviously if we do something because we are forced to do it because of threat or torture, or because of our incapacity to form a right judgment concerning the action, then choice does not enter into the action and the question of ethicality becomes immaterial. We only hold human beings responsible for actions concerning which they have a choice. If an accused person claims that he or she was insane at the time of the supposed crime and if that person is adjudged to have been insane at the time of the crime, we do not consider the person to have had the capacity of making a free choice and we do not hold the person responsible for the action. As William James stated, there is no ethical quality unless there is freedom of choice among a number of possible courses of action. We raise questions of ethics when individuals make a choice from among a number of alternatives. What we are evaluating is the quality of the individual's "intentional" action. However, without the possibility of more than one action, there is no choice and without a choice there can be no intent. If we *must* do something, if we have no choice about doing something, then there is no need for intent to do that thing. Bodily reflexes, such as the gag reflex, or the knee jerk, are neuronically and muscularly programmed and given the appropriate stimulus the performing of the reflex is obligatory and requires neither choice nor the intent that follows from having to make a choice.

So far we've argued that in order for there to be an ethic there must be a choice and that when choice is present, intent then develops. Choice is the plant from which flowers forth intentionality, individual values, and social ethics. Choice is rooted in speech and in spoken language. It is through speech that the human being is able to decenter, to move outside herself or himself, to take the point of view of another, to see that there may indeed be "other" points of view, to shift away from total subjectivity. Speech leads to the development of the symbol, and it is in the symbol that the plant of choice finds its nurturing soil (Dance, 1982; Johnson, 1978; Adler, 1967; Duncan, 1962).

The force of this argument is that human choice, intent, values, and ethics are inextricably bound up with the human capacity for speech and for spoken language. Thus the question of ethics in public speaking becomes of paramount importance.

☐ Some Effects of Ethical Behavior

An individual's behavior, and the ethical quality of that behavior, affects (1) the person herself or himself, (2) other individuals, (3) the society in which the person lives, and (4) humanity in general.

Ourselves

Since spoken language simultaneously shapes an individual's interiority and reveals that interiority to others, individuals have an obligation, an ethical responsibility, to understand themselves and to open themselves to new information for the purposes of fully forming their interior state of being. We can learn much about ourselves simply by listening to our own spoken language. This kind of self-listening provides an intrapersonal sonar often enabling us to "sound" the depths of our own person. To consciously and adamantly close oneself to new information which might alter one's previously arrived at decisions or judgments is to behave unethically toward oneself. It is exactly this kind of unethical human communication behavior that contributes to the maintenance of false stereotypes, prejudices, and bigotry.

Spoken language has the unique power of revealing our inmost selves to others. With this power goes a responsibility to avoid the conscious misrepresentation of our interiority. This doesn't mean that we have to tell everybody everything about ourselves. Prudence and good judgment clearly indicate that there are times and situations in which it is entirely inappropriate to share certain aspects of our interiority with others. The obligation is not to tell everything as much as it is not to tell that which we know to be untruthful. The capacity of the spoken word to reveal our innermost being is a unique capacity, what the ancient Greeks called an "arete," a "unique excellence." To use our capacity of spoken language to consciously mislead, to lie, to be untruthful is to do harm not only to others, to society, to humanity in general, but to do untold harm to our own selves. Such use of spoken language turns it from being our "arete," our "unique excellence," into being our "*hamartia,*" the Greek term for "tragic flaw." Lying, being consciously untruthful, destroys our own inner unity, our own integrity, and our ethos. Thomas Jefferson said this about untruthfulness: "He who permits himself to tell a lie once, finds it much easier to do it a second and a third time, till at length it becomes habitual; he tells lies without attending to it, and truths without the world's believing him. This falsehood of the tongue leads to that of the heart, and in time depraves all its good dispositions" (Byer, 1976, pp. 27–28).

Other Individuals

Important ethical considerations are at stake when, through public speaking, symbols and significant symbols are (1) consciously being manipulated so as to shape another human being, (2) without that other's awareness of the speaker's intent, and (3) with the added intent of so shaping the other that the outcome will not be in the other's best interest. Public speaking, as we have repeatedly stressed, is an extremely powerful human behavior. This powerful behavior should not be used to consciously mislead or to convince people to take actions not in their own best interests. Examples of such behavior are plentiful. Salespersons who persuade customers to overbuy, or to buy products not suitable to the customer's needs (e.g., selling a set of encyclopedias to someone who cannot read) exemplify this behavior. If we, as speakers, feel constrained to speak to others with the goal of persuading them to take action not in their own best interests, then our duty, our ethical obligation, is to make our goal and its possible outcomes known to our audience during our presentation. There are occasions when a speaker might try to persuade someone to do something, the benefits of which might not readily be apparent to the audience member. An example of such an instance would be efforts to persuade someone to join the military (which while personally undesirable may be necessary for the long-term preservation of the individual's freedom). In Chapter Eight on argumentation and persuasion we reminded you that heightened emotion suppresses decentering and may result in heightened self-centeredness and selfishness. Your awareness that emotion may affect judgment lays an ethical responsibility on you as a speaker with regard to your use of emotional appeals in persuasion.

Society

We have an ethical responsibility to use our public speaking power to enhance the appropriate goals of the society in which we live. Most readers of this text live in the United States, a society which demands freedom of information in order that the citizenry may make fully informed decisions concerning the conduct of the country. When a government official is intentionally untruthful in communicating with the people, then that official's public speaking behavior is both personally and socially unethical. In recent history Americans have experienced blatant lying on the part of a President of the United States and the people's reaction was swift and sure. In a society such as ours we must continually be sensitive to the public right and the public need for truthfulness in government communication.

Our ethical responsibility to the society in which we live does not mean that if we live among criminals that we should speak so as to make criminal behavior more successful. The key phrase is "appropriate goals of the society in which we live." Humanity in general has formed itself into many, many separate societies. Criminal conduct, prejudice, bigotry, or any other kind of behavior that goes against our ethical responsibility to humanity in general, whether or not that behavior is sanctioned by our particular society, is unethical. Whatever Hitler or his minions demanded in terms of the extermination of the Jews, all German citizens of well-formed conscience had an human ethical duty to resist. Genocide, whether or not socially supported, is always inhumane.

Humanity

We have an ethical responsibility to use our public speaking power to enhance the development and conduct of humanity in general. We seek autonomy for ourselves and for others, we seek the reduction of dependency, we seek the development of our fullest capabilities, we seek freedom from those things which would circumscribe or curtail the appropriate use of our capabilities. Again "appropriate" is a critical word since it sets our own goals within the overall goals of other human beings. Freedom of self is bounded by the freedom of others. Our rights have meaning only insofar as the rights of others also have meaning.

The Ethical Speaker Encourages Autonomy for Others (© Joel Gordon 1979)

For the public speaker, ethical behavior is that speaking behavior which exhibits intentional choice and is adjusted to the well-being of those affected by the speaking behavior.

☐ Ethical Principles in Public Speaking Practice

Much of what is discussed in this chapter probably seems abstract. You may well wonder what you, as a public speaker, can do to transform ethical principles into personal, practical, public speaking behaviors. Let's admit from the start that not everyone is going to share the identical ethical posture. You are going to have to spend many hours of thought and reflection working through specific ethical problems before you feel comfortable with your personal code of ethics in general and your public speaking ethics in particular. There is general agreement on the ethical aspects of some public speaking practices. The following statements are based upon those areas of general agreement.

1. **Be truthful.**   It is considered unethical to be untruthful. Intentional untruthfulness is a perversion of the human arete of spoken language and damages all concerned.

2. **Prepare adequately.**   It is unethical to abuse an audience's belief and time by subjecting them to a speech which has been inadequately researched. You are ethically obliged to present ideas that you believe in and for which you have support. While you may be asked to engage in a classroom exercise where you speak on behalf of a principle with which you are in complete disagreement, in actual public speaking the audience has the right to believe that *you* believe in what you are saying. Your speech should not include unfounded statements or false accusations. You should be as careful of safeguarding the reputation of others from knowingly false accusations as you are of safeguarding your own reputation by avoiding intentional untruthfulness.

3. **Always give credit where credit is due.**   It is unethical to plagiarize, to pass off the ideas or words of others as if they were your own. Plagiarism is considered a "capital" offense in public speaking. In your preparatory outline you should always make adequate reference to the sources from which you derived any ideas or words not your own. We are not talking about single words, but phrases or sentences which you derive wholly from someone else. We are not talking about ideas commonly available, but about substantive ideas specifically derived from the speech or writing of someone other than yourself. The techniques for citing sources in your outline are the same as those used for references in a research paper. A problem occurs when you want to acknowledge a source while actually delivering the speech. Certainly you don't want to slow down the whole pacing by always citing the entire printed or other source. Many speakers simply note the name of the individual or the title of the general work from which they derived the quotation, or idea, or general argumentative structure. "As Senator Clay once observed. . . ." "The dictionary tells us that. . . ."

"Gibbon, in his *Decline and Fall of the Roman Empire,* draws an interesting parallel. . . " "Published research in the field of spoken language informs us that. . . ."

If you are giving a relatively long speech which contains materials from a number of sources, you may wish to have a handout prepared which lists the sources and which is made available to the audience members. Even in this case you are still obligated, while speaking, to recognize the sources upon which you have drawn. When in doubt it is wiser to err on the side of overacknowledgment of sources than to be thought guilty of plagiarism.

4. **Do all you can to foster autonomy and to actualize potentiality in yourself and in others.** It is unethical to speak so as to intentionally mislead an audience or to give them partial information which may result in their making poorly informed decisions harmful to their life or liberty. Public speaking should be used to enhance individual and social life rather than to manipulate for selfish ends. Deliberate half-truths, deliberate overinterpretation of partial information, deliberate use of statistics to confuse, intimating knowledge which you do not have—all are examples of unethical public speaking behavior.

☐ Summary

Human choice, intentionality, values, and ethics all have their origins in human speech. Human speech carries with it unique powers and consequently unique ethical responsibilities to the speaker, other individuals, society, and the human race. The public speaker has an ethical responsibility to be truthful and to so speak as to enhance the development of autonomy in self and in other individuals and the development of responsible freedom in society.

Exercises ■

1 Prepare and present a 5-minute speech on the subject of lying.

2 Prepare and present a 5-minute speech on the subject of ghostwriting. In preparation read Franklyn Haiman's essay "Ghostwriting and the Cult of Leadership," together with the responses to that article prepared by Ernest G. Bormann and J. Jeffery Auer. The essay and the responses appear in *Communication Education,* vol. 33, no. 4, October 1984, pp. 301–307.

3 Prepare and present a 5-minute speech on the subject of plagiarism in speeches and term papers.

4 Prepare and present a 10-minute speech on the subject of professional ethics in the field of mass communication.

5 Prepare and present a 7-minute speech on the interrelationship of ethics and freedom of speech.

Bibliographic References ■

Adler, Mortimer J.: *The Difference of Man and the Difference it Makes,* Holt, Rinehart and Winston, New York, 1967.

Byer, Robert S.: "An Interview with Thomas Jefferson," *Flying Colors* (Braniff Airline's in-flight magazine), vol. 5, no. 2, April 1976, pp. 27–28.

Dance, Frank E. X.: "A Speech Theory of Human Communication," in *Human Communication Theory: Comparative Essays,* Harper & Row, New York, 1982, pp. 120–146.

Duncan, Hugh D.: *Communication and Social Order,* The Bedminster Press, New York, 1962.

Johnson, J. R.: *The Relationship Between Speech Communication Egocentrism and Reading Achievement,* unpublished doctoral dissertation, University of Denver, 1978.

Nozick, Robert: *Philosophical Explanations,* Harvard University Press, Cambridge, Mass., 1981.

Oxford English Dictionary: Compact Edition, vol. I, A–O, Oxford University Press, New York, 1971.

Recommended Readings ■

Bok, Sissela: *Lying: Moral Choice in Public and Private Life,* Pantheon Books, New York, 1978. A wonderfully readable and important consideration of the part played by lying in our everyday lives.

Dance, Frank E. X.: "Speech Communication: The Revealing Echo," in *Communication: Ethical and Moral Issues,* Lee Thayer (ed.), Gordon and Breach, New York, 1973, pp. 277–285. The essay considers the role played by speech in revealing a person's interior world. The entire book deals with the subject of this chapter.

de Chardin, Teilhard: *The Phenomenon of Man,* Harper and Brothers, New York, 1959. A rather amazing treatment of the emergence of "withinness" in animal forms, including man. De Chardin also touches on the part played by sound in the revelation of "withinness."

Gregg, Richard B.: *Symbolic Inducement and Knowing: A Study in the Foundations of Rhetoric,* University of South Carolina Press, Columbia, S.C., 1984. A rather weighty, but interesting study which includes attention to the role of speech communication in the development of choice and intentionality.

Johannesen, Richard L.: *Ethics in Human Communication,* 2nd ed., Waveland Press, Prospect Heights, Ill., 1984. A recent scholarly survey and consideration of the question.

Nilsen, Thomas R.: *Ethics of Speech Communication,* Bobbs-Merrill, Indianapolis, 1966. An early, but very helpful, discussion of a speaker's ethical concerns.

Ong, Walter J., S. J.: *The Presence of the Word,* Yale University Press, New Haven, Conn., 1967. Takes de Chardin's concept of "withinness" and shows how it translates, through speech, into human "interiority."

Appendix to Chapter Ten
VTR and Public Speaking:
What? Why? How?

"O wad some power the giftie gie us
to see ourself as others see us!"
Robert Burns, *To a Louse*

☐ What Is a VTR?

VTR is the abbreviated form used for the phrase "*v*ideotape *r*ecording." In this phrase *video* refers to the transmission and/or reception of a visual, televised image. When the visual information in a televised image is recorded on a magnetic tape, the product is a *video tape,* or a *videotaped recording*. Since the advent of "talkies" (in contrast to the early, silent movies), most video recordings also include accompanying sound. Because virtually all VTRs include sound, "audio" is implied but generally omitted from the phrase "videotape recording."

A typical VTR setup includes a video recorder, a playback unit, a camera, a microphone, and a television or monitor screen. The first VTRs were stationary primarily because of their size and weight. Early models usually had a large and heavy single unit containing both the recording and playback elements. The camera was cumbersome, and the tape decks were usually reel-to-reel. With the continued move toward miniaturization of electronic components VTRs have become markedly smaller and lighter. Today there are portable units including playback and recording and weighing less than 8 pounds. In the portable units the recording function and the playback function are usually separated, saving the needless weight of toting a playback unit to a recording session. A camera for a portable unit can weigh 4 pounds or less. The magnetic tape is contained in a cartridge similar to but usually larger than an audio cassette. Because of the use of cassette cartridges, newer units are often called VCRs (*video cassette recorders*). The trend toward miniaturization is continuing and the likelihood is high that there will be even smaller systems in the future.

To summarize: a VTR or VCR is an electronic system that records, on magnetic tape, the visual image and accompanying sound of live action. The recording creates a permanent record of the event which can then be replayed (or played back) at a later time.

☐ Why Can VTR Help You as a Public Speaker?

Evaluation is an essential element of public speaking improvement, and videotape recording provides innovative and sophisticated assistance in the evaluation process. The popularity of home VCRs has acquainted many people with the entertainment aspects of recorder/playback units. There is an ever-increasing number of video stores that act as lending libraries, renting videotapes of popular motion pictures to their customers. And, long before home units, VTRs were used extensively in the mass media industry, taping news reports and special productions to be aired at a later time or date. It was not until fairly recently that the tremendous educational potential of videotape recording was recognized.

In the appendix to Chapter Eight, "Evaluation and Listening," we discussed the importance of speech evaluation by one's self and by others. When you evaluate your own presentation by self-monitoring (by simultaneously listening while you speak), the difficulty of concentrating simultaneously on both physical activities can hinder a thorough evaluation.

Besides self-monitoring, another way of evaluating yourself is by taping your speech on an audio tape recorder, an instrument accessible to most students. You can make an audio recording during a rehearsal or during the actual presentation. If you choose to record the actual speech, then the recording can be used for a later evaluation. If time allows, we recommend that you tape-record your speech during rehearsal. Then by evaluating the rehearsal tape prior to the final presentation, you can adjust and improve the speech's content and the vocal/auditory portion of the speech's delivery.

While an audio tape recording of your speech provides acoustic data for evaluation and facilitates a more objective assessment, it falls short of presenting the full impact of a speech. A public speaking experience includes a speech, a speaker, an audience, and their interaction. The force of a speech is carried in the nonvocal as well as the vocal elements. An audio tape cannot provide an adequate record of the nonvocal elements of a public speech. The most complete and most useful feedback is provided by a combination of both audio and video recording. Such a combination is presented in a videotape recording.

Perhaps videotaping equipment is not as readily available to you as is audio taping equipment. Nonetheless, the time spent in seeking out and using videotaping services will be amply repaid in your public speaking improvement. Today, almost all educational institutions have videotaping equipment. Many have special video rooms used only for tapings and playbacks. Though classes and instructors may have priority over individual students in scheduling VTR facilities, there are often time blocks reserved for students. (If such facilities are available, your instructor may be able to assist you with VTR arrangements.) Once you have made taping arrangements, ask the media services staff person if it is possible to keep a tape for the entire term. If not, investigate the cost of purchasing a tape or a cassette for yourself. Taping yourself at different intervals in time during the term will give you a developmental record of your public speaking skills. Use the VTR

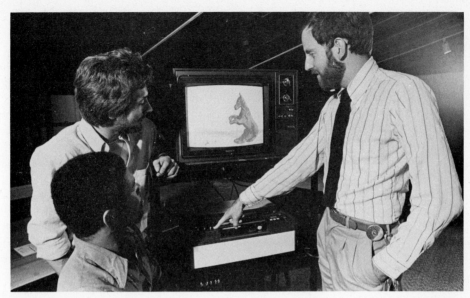

A VTR Gives Us the Chance to See Ourselves as Others See Us (© Tom Turner 1983, Design Conceptions)

as you would use an audio recording, both for rehearsals and for formal presentations.

The greatest advantage of the VTR is the chance it gives us "to see ourself as others see us." You can watch the television monitor and see and hear an image that is essentially the image your audience saw and heard during the formal presentation. You see yourself differently from in a mirror since in a mirror your image is reversed while in a videotape recording your image looks to you as it does to others. The electronic technique of recording a live presentation for later playback enables you to step outside of time and place and to physically and psychologically separate yourself as an evaluator from the taped image of yourself as a speaker. You can separate the moment of recording from the moment of playback, and that physical separation of events facilitates decentering and encourages objectivity. [**GOTO Chapters Two, Four, and the Appendix to Chapter Nine, "Evaluation and Listening."**]

Objectivity on your part will encourage a more honest and helpful self-evaluation of your speech content and delivery. A VTR helps you to see and hear yourself give a speech. You can begin to form an objective image of yourself as a speaker, an image that you can compare with other speakers as well as with your own notion of an ideal speaker. In the Appendix to Chapter Nine, "Evaluation and Listening," we stated that the purpose of evaluation was to offer feedback and suggestions that the speaker could realistically consider. When you develop a self-concept that includes you as a speaker (a positive side-effect of self-evaluation using a VTR), you have a standard against which you weigh, accept, and/or reject the criticisms of others.

☐ How VTR Provides Feedback

It is important to consider and to test the feedback received from others as a tool for self-improvement. It is also important to have an image of yourself as a speaker that you can adjust rather than simply accepting an image thrust upon you by others. The VTR experience of seeing and hearing yourself may provide more internal motivation to change than can be provided by outside sources.

VTR feedback is both auditory and visual. In addition, VTR feedback can be either immediate or delayed. Some speakers prefer to view a playback shortly after their presentation because it is a source of immediate reinforcement (e.g., "Whew, I didn't do as badly as I thought"). Other speakers delay playback, and while their reasons for doing so may vary, the increased interval in time when they finally view and evaluate their performance promotes objectivity.

Depending upon the sophistication of the equipment, the feedback provided the playback viewer may be in black and white, or color; may include options such as slow motion, or stop action; and allows for repeated replays of short segments or of the entire speech. However, even the most basic and simplest VTR system allows the creation of a permanent record of a speech event. This permanent record can be played back again and again, providing a preserved slice of one's public speaking life.

☐ Some Guidelines for Videotaped Presentations

For all the reasons we have discussed in this appendix, videotaping student speeches is a learning tool being increasingly utilized in public speaking classes and workshops. For those of you who have had little or no experience with a VTR session, we offer the following suggestions regarding the speaker and the evaluator.

Speakers

1. Your VTR presentation should be treated, as much as possible, like any other speech. Although there will be some differences created by the situation, your speech preparation, research, organization, and rehearsal need not be treated differently from any of your nonvideotaped speeches.
2. The taping may take place in your classroom or in a special taping room. Wherever, the best arrangement for the room is with the lectern or speaker's stand in the front, facing rows of audience chairs. This arrangement helps simulate an actual public speaking presentation.
3. The location of the camera in the taping room varies: It might be on a tripod in the back, it might be mounted in the corner, or be behind a one-way mirror. Some rooms may even have more than one camera.

   Although it would be foolhardy to expect you to completely forget the camera's presence, it is important that you speak to your audience rather than to the camera. Remember, viewing this VTR speech will give you the chance to be an audience member for your own speech. The idea is to see and hear yourself as others see and hear you. If you give your speech to the camera, you will have no indication of what your eye contact is like during a non-VTR presentation.

4. Avoid rapid and broad movements for two reasons:
   a. Even the best camera operator will have trouble keeping you in focus and may not get a sharp visual image on the recording.
   b. Because of the way space is framed by the camera lens and because of the size of the monitor screen, action and movements on the playback appear exaggerated. The ratio of foreground (the speaker) to background is altered in the transfer of the image to tape.
5. VTRs include sound as well as visual images; therefore a microphone will be somewhere in the taping room. The microphone might be attached to the camera, to the lectern, or suspended on a boom above the speaker. Occasionally a lavaliere microphone (one worn around the neck or clipped to your clothing) is available. A VTR microphone for classroom taping is rarely connected to a loudspeaker. So, although you are speaking into a microphone, usually your voice is being recorded but not amplified.

   Speak to your audience in your normal speaking voice. If an adjustment in playback volume needs to be made, it can be made through the VTR equipment by the operator. When the tape is replayed, you will have the opportunity to hear whether or not your volume is sufficient for the situation and area.
6. If you are a speaker who likes to move away from the lectern, be sure that the microphone moves with you or is sensitive enough to pick you up from anyplace you move.
7. Your clothing for a VTR speech should be chosen with the same considerations as for any other public speech. [**GOTO Chapter Seven, page 166**]
8. Finally, although you may be concerned the first time you are videotaped you will generally discover that your anxiety will decrease as the frequency of tapings increases.

Evaluators

1. Our basic suggestions for evaluating a speech are recommended in VTR playback situations as well. [**GOTO "Evaluation and Listening," Appendix to Chapter Nine**]
2. Research indicates that there is a tendency for VTR evaluators to focus more on delivery factors than on content factors (Bock, et al., 1977; Miles, 1978). The reasons for this behavior are not entirely clear. It is the responsibility of the evaluator to conscientiously attend to content as well as to delivery, even if the tape needs to be replayed several times in order to thoroughly evaluate the speech.
3. Depending upon the type and sensitivity of the microphone used in the recording, you may be aware of background noises in the room. Try to concentrate

your attention on the speaker. If there are some loud noises during the speech, note how the speaker deals with them.

4. Remember the cautions given to the speaker in items 4 and 6 above. When you evaluate a speaker's movements and gestures, remember that they may look more exaggerated on the VTR than they appeared in the formal presentation. If the person is planning a career in television, it will be helpful if you suggest that he tone down his movements. If he will be primarily speaking to live audiences, it might be more helpful to note the appropriateness, redundancy, and overall style of his gestures and movements.

5. If the VTR playback equipment includes stop-action and slow-motion options, and you choose to use these options, try not to lose a feeling for the overall continuity and flow of the speech.

6. Remember that honesty and tact are not incompatible. Speakers seeing themselves on VTR for the first time seem to be quite vulnerable and may be overly protective of their self-image. You, as an informed and sensitive evaluator, can do much to make the VTR event the beneficial teaching experience it is intended to be.

Bibliographic References ■

Bock, D. G., L. Powell, J. Kitchens, and J. W. Flavin: "The Influence of Sex Differences in Speech Evaluation: Situational and Media Effects," *Communication Education,* vol. 26, no. 2, March 1977, pp. 143–153.

Miles, P. L.: "Student Video Self-Critiques," *Communication Education,* vol. 30, no. 3, July 1981, pp. 280–283.

Continued Growth as a Public Speaker

Chapter Eleven

"Not a having and a resting, but a growing and a becoming is the character of perfection as culture conceives it."
Matthew Arnold, *Culture and Anarchy*, 1869

In the earliest pages of this text we mentioned the destination which you the reader and we the authors had in common. That destination was the development of your ability to prepare and deliver an effective, ethical public speech.

We hope that through your own energies, the good services of your instructor, the willingness and support of your audiences, the opportunities for practice, and the materials presented in this book you have either reached the destination or are close to it.

The destination was a destination for a beginning speaker and for a public speaking primer. The destination is only the first stop on a continuing trip. The final destination depends on your own interests, skills, and opportunities. We also talked, early in the book, about the road to public speaking proficiency being one only you, the speaker, could walk. We, the authors, have tried to erect some signposts along the road, signposts which point in the direction of the final destination.

"This way lies good outlining!"
"In this direction you should find the path to effective preparation!"
"Avoid this shortcut since it leads to ineffective delivery!"
"Ethical public speaking practices ahead!"

Those signposts still stand. Those signposts still point in the direction of the final destination. In this last chapter we would like to remind you of some of the signposts encountered throughout the primer and to suggest some ways to continue traveling the road to your final destination with ease and with pleasure.

☐ Signposts

This Way to Decentering Pass!

As discussed earlier the concept of transference of meaning in human communication is a dead end. The manner in which human communication (by spoken language) really works is through association (by means of decentering). Decentering is the royal road to adequate audience analysis. Decentering provides a pass which cuts through difficult terrain and allows the public speaker to zero in on those associations with the audience that will enhance the speaker's chance of fully achieving his or her specific purpose. Since, as we know, effective association depends on decentering, we must always continue developing our decentering abilities. Meeting people, sharing ideas, reading both fiction and nonfiction, attending plays, movies, concerts, talking with children, watching people at work and at play, reflecting on our own motivations and the behaviors that express those motivations, all of these can assist us in fine-tuning our decentering capacity and ability. Conscious and deliberate attention to enhancing decentering will help produce broad and deep decentering behavior. As we become more accomplished speakers, we must continually beware the egocentric seduction, the tendency to see everything from our own personal point of view, and even worse to consider that point of view to be the only correct one. While working on decentering, we must also keep in sight our own personhood, our own being. We can only decenter if we have a center from which to move away. It is important to have a firm idea of exactly who we are as we make efforts to take the point of view of others. Maintain a rich and harmonious center to which to return from your efforts at public speaking association. A good self-concept and responsible self-esteem are prerequisites for effective decentering. Only by knowing who we are and by liking the person we are are we able to know and to like others.

Shortcut to Confidence!

You have been working on constructing a PIER, a structure to support your self-confidence as a public speaker. The four components of PIER can be worked on throughout your public speaking career.

"P" for Preparation

Your preparation skills will, by now, have become more polished. However, *never* think that you can give a good speech with absolutely no preparation. You should keep on working to make effective preparation skills more and more automatic so that you will have to spend less and less time in the mechanical stages of speech preparation. Maintain a research curiosity. Keep on the alert for materials that bear on your interests. Keep a file of those materials. Your speech materials file, if you start it now, will grow so that you will have an advantage whenever you start to prepare for a public speech. Never throw away your outlines; keep them on file because if you have been doing correct preparation you will have been noting sources and materials that you will be able to use in future speeches throughout your career. You will find after speaking a few times that there are certain parts of your outline that seem to work especially well. You will find that you have done enough research and worked over the presentation sufficiently so that most people in the audience have little difficulty in understanding and appreciating your ideas and viewpoint on a particular point. These especially successful parts can be organized and filed into "units" which you can then use in other speeches where the same or a similar concept is under discussion. If you keep track of such "success" units, you will be building a repertoire of materials for future speeches. Continue to polish and refine your technique of phrasing the best possible specific purpose for your speech. A well-phrased specific purpose will assist you greatly in your effort to increase your decentering capacity and will also pay off in making your outlining tasks easier.

"I" for Idea

Mentation, ideas, are the main reason for the existence of spoken language. We use these ideas to develop our own inner being and resources as well as to elevate our interpersonal relationships with other human beings. One of the earmarks of a great speech is when the audience remembers and is thrilled by the ideas while failing to pay any particular attention to the manner in which the ideas were delivered. Such an audience response is the result of masterful delivery control and therefore a transparent delivery style rather than the absence of delivery skills. Continue trying to get your idea-consciousness to supplant any self-consciousness which may be hindering your fullest public speaking effectiveness. As you are building a materials file, also build an ideas file. We speak better about things in which we are interested. Keep a file of concepts and arguments which interest you. These concepts and arguments may well form for you the kernel of some tremendously important and effective public speeches and briefings in the future. Keep working on your spoken language clarity and the conceptual clarity that accompanies it.

"E" for Experience

Whatever progress you have made on the road to better public speaking, much of that progress has been the result of repeated public speaking experience. Experience, especially under the tutelage of a competent instructor, is an invaluable help to the student of public speaking. Experience is not enough by itself. We have all heard the adage "Practice makes perfect." That adage (that is grounded in good theory) is true only if it is good practice. In many cases, rather than practice making perfect, what happens is that practice makes "permanent." Unfortunately if you have been practicing the wrong things, or practicing the right things incorrectly, what is made "permanent" is error. Take advantage of all the feedback that you can get. Do not wait for feedback to come to you—actively seek it out. After you give a speech ask members of the audience what they think you could do to improve your speech for future delivery. If the feedback is positive and reinforcing, enjoy it and store it away for future comfort. If the feedback suggests problems in your public speaking, be thankful for it and use it to get better and better. As soon as possible after you have been given some feedback, write it down in a notebook to which you can refer when you are preparing and rehearsing your next speech. After having given a number of speeches, you should be getting better at building a more accurate rehearsal simulation. Remember to prepare thoroughly and to rehearse *aloud*. Moving your ideas from inner speech to external speech will continue to help you in clarity of thought as well as in clarity of spoken expression.

"R" for Relax

Although still difficult, relaxing should be somewhat easier after your repeated experience in public speaking. However, even after having given over 2500 public speeches, we still need to give conscious attention to relaxation prior to performance. This is true of almost all professional public speakers. Controlled relaxation makes thinking on one's feet easier. Controlled relaxation contributes to transparent delivery. Controlled relaxation improves vocal and bodily tone. Preparation, rehearsal, experience, conscious attention to breathing technique, all should be worked on so as to continue to develop your ability for controlled relaxation.

Transparent Delivery Throughway!

Having completed a number of speaking experiences, you are well aware that some things that look easy are quite difficult. Giving speeches makes you appreciate the talent of an accomplished performer. An actor like Sir Laurence Olivier, a popular singer like Barbra Streisand, an operatic star like Luciano Pavarotti, a comedian like Woody Allen, each of these performers make their performances appear natural. We don't usually remember exactly how Woody Allen told a story that brought us to laughter, or exactly how Laurence Olivier behaved that brought us to tears, it is seldom that the mechanics of their performance calls attention to itself. In great art, artifice is hidden. The saying is "art hides art." Perfecting a truly transparent public speaking delivery is a challenge so great that few speakers ever fully reach the goal. So, here is an area of real effort at continued growth. Again, when soliciting feedback be especially sensitive to comments such as "Your gestures were great!" "Your voice is so resonant that I just like listening to you talk regardless of what you are talking about." "I couldn't hear you." Whether positive or negative, comments on delivery should be assessed for what those comments may be implying about your delivery intruding upon the ideas you are presenting. Keep working on perfecting transparent delivery.

Remember the rule of 30:70? Because of your public speaking experience some of the problems that would have fallen in the area of 30 percent unpredictability at the beginning of your class now seem both predictable and relatively unthreatening. You most likely are able to be heard by the audience. Probably you are more comfortable with using speaker's notes. You have found some techniques that seem to work well for you. Don't rest comfortably now that some of the unpredictability has sifted down into the 70 percent predictable level. Work on meeting new challenges. Try the same speech before a new audience. Try a new speech before an audience that liked your previous speech(es). You must beware of endlessly repeating your past successes. This is a real temptation for all of us. We find something that works and then we work it to death. There was a time when one of us started almost every speech with a quotation. Why? Because a couple of times starting a speech with a quotation worked—so why not keep on doing it? Why not? Because it becomes a bore, that's why! In addition it stifles the growth of the individual as a public speaker. Imagine new approaches to presenting an idea, to developing an argument, to using audiovisual aids, to opening your speech, to concluding, to making transitions. Try these new approaches—not all at once, but bit by bit. Keep extending your conceptual and behavioral repertoire as a public speaker. Remembering that ideas are all important in a public speech, keep working toward developing the illusion of spontaneity in your speaking. Always try for the vivid realization of your ideas at the moment of their utterance. Keep striving for a personal and effective style in your speaking—a style that proclaims the person you really are.

In all your efforts to grow as a public speaker you must keep in mind your ethical responsibilities, and you must allow your ethics to inform your speech preparation and to sound forth in your spoken words.

Besides those signposts which point out the destination direction, we also find signposts that warn us of dangers lying ahead, signposts like:

Sharp curves ahead!
Beware bumps!
Falling rocks!
Dead end!

That certainly seems to be enough warning. Here are a few things that can impede your public speaking growth:

excessive self-satisfaction
stale ideas
no opportunities to speak
always repeating past successes
always speaking before the same audience
only using one mode of presentation
florid and overblown delivery
weak audience contact
poor transitions
overemotionalism

Each of these problem areas present something to think about and to work on as you continue your efforts to improve and grow as a public speaker.

There is absolutely no way to continue to develop and grow in public speaking without giving public speeches. If you don't continually give public speeches, you will find that as a result of disuse your public speaking skills will deteriorate. Your voice loses its edge, your timing goes off, and your ability to think on your feet suffers a decline. You must seek opportunities to speak. You want to speak on topics that interest you before varied audiences. But how can you do this? Where can you find audiences willing to grant you platform time? This isn't as difficult a problem as you may think. Here are just a few suggestions for multiplying your speaking opportunities:

1. Speak out in classes. If you are taking a course in political science and there is an opportunity to participate in the election campaign of a local person—join in.

2. Take other classes in the field of speech communication. There are special courses in persuasion and in argumentation, as well as advanced courses in public speaking. There are courses in other departments which bear directly on some public speaking skills. Courses in linguistics, in cultural anthropology, in psychology, in logic, in literature, in history, and in other disciplines help you in decentering and often bear directly upon skills such as argumentation and persuasion.

3. There are organizations especially oriented toward the development of public speaking ability. One of the best known of such organizations is Toastmasters International (TI). TI has more than 100,000 members. There is a TI local club in almost every community in the United States. TI is open to both men and women and its main goal is the development of the public speaking and leadership skills of its members. In larger cities there are usually numerous TI clubs, some that meet at breakfast, some that meet at lunch, and some that meet at dinner time. You can usually find a club that meets at a location and at a time which meets your personal schedule and desires. Go and visit a TI club, listen to what they have to offer, and then consider whether or not the club will give you the opportunity to give speeches in front of a group of friendly and supportive listeners who share your own goal of personal public speaking improvement. If you cannot immediately locate a local TI club, write to the address of TI International given at the end of this chapter.

4. Every community has service clubs. Clubs that are interested in general citizen development and which usually also have some special aims. Examples of such service clubs include Rotary, Kiwanis, Lions, Soroptimists, and many, many others. Almost all these organizations hold weekly meetings, and almost all these organizations have speakers as part of their weekly programs. In other words these clubs are continually seeking speakers for their meetings. Since most of the service clubs are voluntary, nonprofit organizations they typically do not offer an honorarium to their guest speakers. Call one of the clubs and ask for the name of the club's program chairperson. Call the chairperson and let him or her know of your interest, your area of expertise, and your experience. In many instances you will find yourself on a program in the near future. If you really want to speak in public and you continue to grow at such speaking you will begin to build a reputation that results in increased public speaking opportunities.

5. Watch your local paper for listings of organizations and meetings in your community. Go to hear other speakers in order to learn from their experiences as well as from your own. Again, you may meet the program chairperson who would be interested in you as a possible speaker for a future meeting of the group.

When talking about models of human communication earlier in this primer we mentioned the helical model. The idea behind the helical model is that our human communication skills progress from a beginning point and that they are continually expanding, moving forward, but still coming back in upon, but not touching, their previous levels of development. Your public speaking skills also develop helically. You are constantly moving forward and yet you are constantly coming back to some of your earlier developmental levels.

Be patient! In all human learning there are occasions of rapid development and then plateaus when nothing seems to be happening. We sometimes can get terribly discouraged when we find ourselves on one of these plateaus.

Be patient! Keep on working, keep on speaking, keep on challenging yourself! You will finally move off the plateau and continue your forward and upward development as a public speaker. You become a proficient public speaker through the effort of thought, preparation, research, and practice that goes into speaking in public. Action shapes being. You will become a public speaker by following the suggestions given in this text and given by your teacher and by shaping these suggestions into practical activities through your personal public speaking activities.

In the beginnings of this primer we quoted Herman Hesse's book *The Glass Bead Game* (sometimes called *Magister Ludi*) and gave a description of the glass bead game: "The Glass Bead Game is thus a mode of playing with the total contents of our culture: . . . all the insights, noble thoughts, and works of art that the human race has produced in its creative eras, all that subsequent periods of scholarly study have reduced to concepts and converted into intellectual property— on all this immense body of intellectual values the Glass Bead Game player plays like the organist on the organ" (Hesse, 1969, p. 15).

A nice thought, the sound and complexity of an organ swelling into a full echo of the speaking mind of human beings. Our spoken language is a wedding of both spirit and flesh. Our spoken language enables us individually to make our thoughts and feelings known to our fellow human beings and thus enables human beings to come together into social groupings. Our spoken language and our thoughts are so interrelated as to facilitate one another's growth and development. The glass bead game is a game of both symbolic and nonsymbolic forms of reality, and the public speaker is projecting the glass bead game of the mind to the members of the audience who may thus join in playing the glass bead game for the benefit of humanity.

Public speaking is naturally exhilarating. There is a thrill to thinking your thoughts with others and in helping all come to a better understanding of the mind of humanity in the words of you, the speaker. Public speaking is unique to human beings. Continue to play this glass bead game of the human mind and to enjoy the excitement and challenge of public speaking.

☐ Growth Resources

Courses

Public speaking courses are offered in regular sessions at community colleges, 4-year colleges and universities, as well as through adult education programs sponsored by governmental units and organizations such as free universities.

Clubs

Toastmasters International headquarters' address is 2200 N. Grand Avenue, P.O. Box 10400, Santa Ana, CA 92711. Their phone number is (714)542-6793. TI headquarters can furnish lists of local clubs. Other organizations, such as the Junior Chamber of Commerce, sometimes offer short courses in public speaking or presentational speaking. There are other clubs for public speakers, such as the International Platform Association, and the National Speakers Association, but these clubs are more for the accomplished speaker rather than the beginning speaker.

Newsletters

These newsletters all involve subscription fees but are worth the charges involved. Your authors have personally examined and used each newsletter listed.

The Executive Speaker

The Executive Speaker Co., P.O. Box 2094, Dayton, OH 45429. Published monthly. The publisher culls speeches of corporate and business executives and gives you an idea of what is being said and how by important people in the business world. Some issues focus on a theme, such as transitions or closings.

Orben's Current Comedy

The Comedy Center, 700 Orange Street, Wilmington, DE 19801. Fresh, topical humor. Published twice a month. Bob Orben is a professional comedy writer with a feel for what works in public speeches. Not every one-liner is a block buster but you can almost always find some appropriate material in each issue.

Sharing Ideas among Professional Speakers

Dottie Walters, Publisher, 600 W. Foothill Blvd., Glendora, CA 91740. Published every 2 months. Interesting newsletter filled with tips from professional platform speakers as well as ideas on getting into public speaking as a business.

Bibliographic Reference ■

Hesse, Hermann: *The Glass Bead Game,* Holt, Rinehart and Winston, New York, 1969.

Name Index

Subject Index

ABOUT THE AUTHORS

Frank E.X. Dance is Professor of Speech Communication at the University of Denver. His Ph.D. was earned at Northwestern University and he has taught at a number of schools, including Chicago's Wilson Junior College; the University of Wisconsin-Milwaukee; the University of Kansas; and others. Recently awarded the University of Denver's Master Teacher award, Dr. Dance is a fellow of the International Communication Association (ICA), and is a consultant for a number of major business and professional organizations including IBM. He is an active public speaker and has given over 2500 platform presentations. Author of *Human Communication Theory* (published in 1982 by Harper & Row), *Business and Professional Speech Communication* (with H.P. Zelko), *The Functions of Human Communication* and *Speech Communication* (both with Carl E. Larson), and *The Citizen Speaks* among other books, Dr. Dance has also written many chapters, monographs, and articles for such journals as *Communication Education,* the *Journal of Communication,* and *Adult Education.*

Carol C. Zak-Dance is an Instructor in the University of Denver's Weekend College and New College programs. She earned her Ph.D. at the University of Denver and has served on the speech communication faculties of Arapahoe Community College and Regis College. Dr. Zak-Dance is a member of the editorial board of *Communication Education.* An active platform speaker she regularly plans and conducts presentational and public speaking workshops for IBM and for other state and national organizations. Dr. Zak-Dance maintains her interest in language development and childrens' speech communication.